To Michelle,

Enjoy my very first published book which encourages people to discover their "why" which is a major key in life!

To Your Maximum,

Dr. B

DISCOVER your INNER Strength

CUTTING EDGE GROWTH STRATEGIES FROM THE INDUSTRY'S LEADING EXPERTS

Copyright © 2010

Published in the United States by
Insight Publishing Company
Sevierville, Tennessee
www.insightpublishing.com

All rights reserved. No part of this book may be reproduced in any form or by any means without prior written permission from the publisher except for brief quotations embodied in critical essay, article, or review. These articles and/or reviews must state the correct title and contributing authors of this book by name.

Disclaimer: This book is a compilation of ideas from numerous experts who have each contributed a chapter. As such, the views expressed in each chapter are of those who were interviewed and not necessarily of the interviewer or Insight Publishing.

ISBN 978-1-60013-547-7

10 9 8 7 6 5 4 3 2 1

Table of Contents

A Message from the Publisher

The Interviews

A Remedy for Courage *Kimberly Gayle*	1
A Values-Based Approach *Dr. Stephen Covey*	17
Having What You Want is Easier Than You Think *Jessica A. Haynes*	31
Keeping His Fire Alive Within *Jeanne M. Harper*	59
The Secret to Sustainable Success *Blaine Bartlett*	85
Secrets of Discovering Your Inner Strength: The Seven Paths to Success *Mary Wayne Bush*	105
Attitude Is Everything *Dr. Kenneth Blanchard*	137
Principals of Resilience *Renee Robinson Sievert*	153
Discovering Your Inner Strength for Maximum Success *Dr. Brian Williams*	173
Healed Hands, Healing Hearts … a "Survivors" inside perspective from the Australian Outback *Michael Skupin*	203
Using Strategy to Discover Your Inner Strength *Brian Tracy*	245
Strength Lessons from the Living Room to the Board Room *Dr. Lynn Workman Nodland*	259
Quantum Communications & Learning: Reaching Your Subconscious Mind *Dr. William Kenner*	293

A Message from the Publisher...

I'VE FACED MANY CHALLENGES IN MY LIFE and I know what it means to struggle. I sure wish I'd had this book during those times. We handpicked some of the most successful people we know who have had to learn how to discover their inner strength. The authors I interviewed for this book have the experience and knowledge that will help everyone learn a little more about this vital component for success—inner strength.

This book is custom designed for those who want to increase their skills and knowledge. Self-development is vital to success. One author made this poignant observation: "Self-development tends to fall to the bottom of the priority list for most people and they are not the only ones to suffer for this choice. Their family suffers. Their coworkers suffer. Their employees suffer. All of the crucial relationships in their life suffer because they are not being the absolute best they could truly be."

If you strive for excellence and want valuable information about how some of the most successful people in business today have found their inner strength and achieved success, this book is the resource you need. People who want to hone their skills to cope with life's challenges will learn from what these authors have to say. I know that I did and I believe you will too

—**David E. Wright, President & Founder**
International Speakers Network and Insight Publishing

A Remedy for Courage

An Interview With…
Kimberly Gayle

DAVID WRIGHT (WRIGHT)

Today we're talking with Kimberly D. Gayle. She is an executive and professional life coach for Executive Intervention, LLC, a training and development company that designs and facilitates customized training programs in the areas of change management, employee performance development, and information technology. She creates and designs professional coaching programs in order to serve as post-training support for corporate change initiatives, as well as personal development plans specifically for individuals who want to define and achieve professional and personal goals.

Kimberly, welcome to our project, *Discover Your Inner Strength*.

KIMBERLY GAYLE (GAYLE)

Thanks, David, I'm delighted to speak with you.

WRIGHT

So tell me about what you do and how this topic of discovering your inner strength interests you.

GAYLE

Well, I am the co-founder of Executive Intervention, LLC, a training and development company that designs and facilitates customized training and coaching programs and I find this topic to be intriguing because I assist coaching clients in finding their inner strength in a variety of ways. Many of my clients are either in the "I'm stuck zone" or fighting unforeseen circumstances such as a layoff, career transition, or simply finding purpose and meaning.

Either way, I know, even within my own life, that finding inner strength is more than a notion, especially if you feel your particular situation seems enormous, unsolvable, and in some cases unreachable. I think that at some point we all have struggled with finding ways to get ourselves out of a rut or situation that seems endless. So as an executive and life coach, when working with clients, I thrive on working through these difficult situations by encouraging new possibilities that can create a hopeful outcome suitable to my client's satisfaction. It isn't always easy finding inner strength, especially when you don't have the support you need to overcome obstacles. When faced with obstacles, however, the benefits of coaching are endless, whether it's identifying fears or weaknesses or reaching down deep in order to harness the strength you didn't even know existed.

WRIGHT

How does your organization define coaching?

GAYLE

Coaching, defined by the International Coach Federation, is "partnering with clients in a thought-provoking and creative process that inspires them to maximize their personal and professional potential."

Coaches are committed to the coaching process, while our clients are responsible for the results. It's our responsibility to ask powerful questions, to listen fully, to be supportive, to provide awareness, to identify patterns, to encourage the possibilities, and to press for accountability when accountability is embraced.

Coaching is not psychotherapy in the sense that may focus on an individual's past by way of uncovering painful experiences. It's about designing a future that's much brighter than your current situation, and providing proactive strategies to get there.

There are many of us who "vision cast" daily. What we want, what we desire, our dreams, and our goals are often twirling around in our heads. The coaching process helps us use visualization methods to take those desires and goals from inside our minds and transform them into tangible results.

WRIGHT

So what coaching methodologies do you use?

GAYLE

We progressively use the Co-Active Coaching Model, created by Laurie Whitworth, Karen Kinsey-House, Henry Kinsey-House, and Phillip Sandahl. This model states that coaching is "a powerful alliance designed to forward and enhance the lifelong process of human learning effectiveness and fulfillment."

We assume that the client is naturally creative, resourceful, and whole. We do not try to "fix" the client or create a predetermined solution. We ask the right questions and invite discovery, and because we encourage them to cultivate the answers they have within, they tend to appreciate their own solutions and commit to move forward and take action.

We also encourage fulfillment by living a balanced lifestyle. So we take a thorough inventory of different areas of their lives, including family and friends, career, personal and spiritual growth, health, physical environment, recreation, and finances. We often ask our clients to rate each area by way of being very satisfied to not being satisfied and identify areas they can improve. The danger of living an imbalanced lifestyle is the enormous amount of stress it can cause. When a major crisis occurs like losing a job or divorce, we feel as though life is over for us.

From the perspective of coaching leaders or managers in a corporate or organization setting, our goal is adaptation. Because environments can change and people can too, this approach simply helps leaders learn about themselves, how they interact in their culture, how well they develop people and relationships, and how they can influence others to produce tangible results.

Isn't it amazing that one leader can replace another and make a significant difference in an organization? The previous leader can meet all the qualifications on paper but somehow his or her leadership style doesn't fit the culture of the organization. So we often complete 360-degree feedback evaluations to identify behavior patterns, mental models, and psychological preferences and needs. Once our clients understand how others see their leadership style, we can prepare for change by formulating new mental models that can put them on a new path by inventing new behaviors and identifying and overcoming barriers. We often practice those new behaviors during the coaching process so they can be comfortable enough to execute those new skills they have developed.

WRIGHT

What common challenges do you see with your current clients?

GAYLE

Due to the instability of the job market, David, we are noticing a high level of stress and uncertainty among our clients. Major layoffs and business downsizing are just a few common challenges our clients are facing. Our clients who do have jobs are no longer feeling secure or safe in their working environments, so they partner with us to create an action plan just in case they do. It's one thing to go to work happy, it's another to go to work in fear. They are frustrated and discontent because finding work these days is simply not an easy task.

I'm talking about well-educated and experienced professionals. According to their perception, they did all the right things required of them—they graduated from high school, went to college, and work for a lucrative company. Yet, David, what's even more interesting is the fact that, as a result of this increase in fear and anxiety, I'm also assisting clients with new business start-ups. They are moving toward finding purposeful and meaningful work. They are taking more risks in their own business ventures, as opposed to relying on corporate America for security. No longer are they driven by pensions and loyalty because the security and pensions aren't there anymore—have you looked at your retirement plan lately?

So for our existing small business owners, they too share the burden of economic hardships. They are looking for strategies to keep afloat during this time in order to maintain a stable income. They've taken bold steps, yet they too feel overwhelmed. One of my small business owners asked me the question, "Where's our stimulus package? Has the government forgotten about us?"

With economic conditions the way they are currently, company managers are finding coaching helpful to deal with anxiety, stress, and employee morale and productivity issues. The culture of fear is enormous in the corporate environment but there still remains a high expectation of productivity. What can you do to motivate your employees? How do you remain hopeful with so much uncertainty? How do you remain employable and keep up with the skill sets required to stay competitive?

I guess what I'm saying, David, is I know what it's like to sit on the other side of the table when someone breaks out in tears because they don't know how they're going to make it from day to day because of all the stress life has to offer at this time in our country.

The question now is, "In the midst of all of this turmoil, how can people find their inner strength to tackle these challenges and move beyond their doubts, fears, uncertainties, and, for some of them, their realities?"

WRIGHT

So what coaching programs do you offer that can assist others in finding their inner strength and tackling these challenges during difficult times?

GAYLE

Well, we've seen an increase in our personal development program, where individuals are just taking the time to focus on their own personal growth. They want to gain control of how they live their life and make priorities around their individual, professional, and personal goals. Many times, clients are working on self-confidence issues, getting over a major obstacle, or whatever it is that they consider as a setback. Trust me; it was something that has made the client fed up enough to require assistance in moving forward and hiring a coach. In fact, the 2008 North American Region ICF Global Survey noted that the top three reasons why people hire coaches are 1) self-esteem/self-confidence, 2) work-life balance, and 3) career opportunities. Also, 96 percent say they would repeat coaching, 86 percent reported being very satisfied with coaching, and 23 percent reported receiving coaching for a duration of six to nine months.

Our commitment to our clients as partners is to inspire them to get what they truly really want in life. Reasons why our clients call us include:

- To gain clarity in their purpose
- To get unstuck and find the lucrative career of their dreams
- To develop more of a balanced lifestyle

- To become more of a risk-taker and not be driven by fear

WRIGHT

What progress or changes have you seen being made with your clients?

GAYLE

There are four major changes I often see in my clients:

1. *Mind-set and belief system shift.* I've seen continued growth from the beginning of our sessions to the time they discover they do have courage, strength, and value. It's an amazing experience to see how they determine that there are things they cannot control, like the job market, and there are things they can control, like their attitude and mind-set toward the situation. It takes a continued conscious effort to remain positive while accomplishing goals when there is fear and uncertainty.

2. *Self-confidence.* Usually self-neglect comes from putting others' needs before our own and having regrets in doing so. "Putting me first" is a concept that many people who suffer from low self-confidence find difficult to grasp. I see clients become strong beings, more confident about who they are and what they want once they recognize that the life they're living currently are the dreams and desires of others. But once the opportunity arises and they discover that they do have their own desires, a new person arises within.

3. *Uncovering fears.* People are afraid to fail. They'd much rather stay in a place that makes them unhappy than to explore other options, take risks, and tackle the fear in order to be happy. For example, I've observed that people operate in what I call secret giftedness. For many

of my clients, when I compare what they currently do for a living, and what they desire to do, I'm simply amazed at what they've been hiding. I'm referring to potential authors, interior designers—entrepreneurs who are living in silence because they simply don't believe they can accomplish what they have a passion for.

So when I see my clients tackling the gremlin—that inner voice telling them they cannot achieve—and start making strides and movement toward what brings them a joyful life, I am simply amazed. So it makes it worthwhile to know that the extra support, the listening, and asking the right questions all matter in the coaching process. And last:

4. Taking more risk and having more courage. Coaching can stretch a person's hidden abilities and sometimes the fieldwork that is assigned can challenge them to do things they feel uncomfortable about. If they find it difficult to network, for instance, one assignment may be to attend a social networking event and meet five new people. If they need to have a difficult conversation with a boss or someone in the human resources department at work, they may be assigned to speak with those individuals within a particular time frame.

WRIGHT

So coaching really does help people move forward. You make it sound so easy. Can all people find their inner strength through coaching?

GAYLE

I would say the ones who are really serious about changing their lives can receive success through coaching. It's just like going on a diet. Most people who struggle with their weight have gone through so many diets that they continue to try that one quick-fix exercise or weight program that will help them lose that magic number. If a person doesn't understand that being healthy requires a lifetime commitment and not a quick fix, then chances are he or she will fall short of the goal. You just have to engage yourself with a hunger and a drive to carry out the commitment you set out for yourself. And even if the outcome is not exactly the way you planned it, re-evaluate and redesign the possibilities until something favorable happens.

Wanting to move forward and make changes sometimes are affected by matters of the heart. If it's not in your heart to want to achieve success or to even find your inner strength, it will be difficult to move forward, even through coaching.

WRIGHT

So what recommendations or growth strategies can you give to someone who doesn't have a professional coach or doesn't have support from friends, family, or even from the community?

GAYLE

David, here are strategies I find helpful:

1. People have to recognize that change will be and continue to be a part of our lives whether we like it or not. The emotions of change, whether it's losing a job or moving forward from a bad relationship, will bring feelings of sadness, anger, and frustration. Suffering is never easy, and grieving is a must-do process. Reality will hit us through stress, loneliness, and hopelessness. Dr. Frederick Cousin's Cycle of Change Model says it best: First you experience happiness, being exactly where you want to be, then all of a sudden the cycle of loss occurs and everything in your world begins to fall apart. We must then go through the agony of suffering so that we can truly experience the unwanted

pain in order for hope, that final stage, to occur. It is through hope we then begin to make and notice progress and to feel good about ourselves enough to return to the first stage of happiness.

2. Finding that inner strength and happiness really depends on how I manage through those phases of pain and suffering. I must realize I can redefine or redirect my path through life by pressing through those hard times.

3. Ask yourself the question: "What roadblocks are hindering me from creating the life I want?" Identify those fears, energy drainers, unmet desires, and needs. Take a moment and evaluate where you are.

4. Determine your values. Are you living out your core values? Values help guide, direct, and allow us to make critical decisions. When you align your life around your core values, it will satisfy your need for belonging and yearning for deep and purposeful meaning. Martin Luther King Jr. stated, "If we are to go forward, we must go back and rediscover those precious values that all reality hinges on."

5. Examine your mind-set and belief system. What are your thoughts—thoughts of joy, peace, happiness, or bitterness, anger, or frustration? Do you believe you can move forward? I heard a saying once that says you are what you think. It really is true. Practicing positive thinking, prayer, meditating, and affirmations are all good techniques to get through those difficult times.

6. Purposeful living. Are you living out your purpose? Find that one thing that brings you joy. Although you may have climbed the corporate

ladder and reached all the expectations your family has set for you—making Dad or Mom proud—are you living out what you really truly feel in your heart?

7. Keep it in balance. When we focus solely on one aspect of our lives, such as working all the time with no play, and seeing or spending little or no time in the relationship section, when the job is gone, whom do you call? Who's your support base? Relationships are really important.

8. Gratitude. What are you grateful for? Don't spend a lot of time on what you don't have or what you don't want. Focus on what you do want and be grateful for what you already have. Consider that the gift of life is enough to be grateful for.

9. Give back. When we focus so much on our issues or concerns, it's hard to see how well we have it in comparison to others. Sometimes it takes stepping back and looking at other situations and asking, am I the only one in this situation? You do know that there's rarely an issue out in the world that someone else hasn't experienced already. Take the time and give back in your community. Volunteer—just go out and get involved with an organization that needs your service.

10. Find a support system. You cannot go through something that requires finding your inner strength without getting support from somebody or somewhere, otherwise you will suffer in silence. If you can't rely on family and friends—there is plenty of professional help out there, along with support groups to assist you.

WRIGHT

So how do you view the future of coaching?

GAYLE

The *National Post* report, written by Ray Williams says that coaching is the second fastest growing profession in the world, rivaled only by information technology. Due to the high economic restructuring in the eighties, it has been by far one of the largest growing industries today. In fact, executive coaching has become a significant human resource strategy for emerging executives and leaders. As stress and failures of executives increase and the demands of complex competencies are required, the stakes are high. Coaching is a great option for those leaders to keep up with the emerging pace.

WRIGHT

So what do you want people to know about you personally—about your role as a life coach? In fact, do you have a personal story of your own in which you had to find your inner strength?

GAYLE

What I want people to know about me is that I have a passion for what I do. It was a journey of discovery—a thirst and hunger to find how I can contribute with the use of my gifts and talents that came from deep within. Middle age might have something to do with it too. But I just didn't want to leave this world knowing that I didn't use what the good Lord gave me. I hired a coach to help me through a rough time in my life, and I definitely came out so much stronger, motivated, hopeful, and encouraged. In fact, why become a coach if you've never been coached?

We all can use some support through mentoring or coaching. Even for me as a life coach, my life is not picture perfect. I have experienced many adversities, especially at one point in my earlier years when I was a single parent and found myself unemployed and living with a parent who helped support me. I had already finished college, but I had to come back home for support. When I finally found a banking job and became dissatisfied after receiving a nickel raise from a good performance evaluation, I said to myself that I wanted more for my son and me. It was extremely difficult paying childcare expenses with limited income.

So I took a leap of faith and went back to college to obtain a master's degree. I received an assistantship with the university where I worked, an internship, and went to college full-time. Living on $600 a month and paying $70 a week for childcare, with a $300 car payment, only left me with $20. So I had to survive with the help of student loans to make it daily. I went through college with serious ambition because I knew I had to support my son. He was my source of motivation.

There were times when my son would write in my books or papers and I would get frustrated. I had to juggle spending time with him, working, and staying up late to do papers. But through it all, I made it. I couldn't have done it without my faith in God and the support of my mother. So in tough times I often ask myself, "What is your source of motivation?"

One of my best friends says to me all the time, "When you're at your lowest, the only way you can go is up." So even with my own personal experience, when I listen to my clients I always convey that optimistic point of view to encourage them to move forward. Believe it or not, coaching others is a learning and gratifying experience that continues to motivate me. I'm committed to giving the best customer care I can because when I was sitting in the other seat needing to be coached it was given to me. Coaching truly can be an extraordinary support method to finding your inner strength and a great remedy to finding courage.

WRIGHT

Well, what a great conversation. I'm beginning to understand coaching. I really appreciate the time you've spent with me today to answer all these questions. I have really learned a lot, and I'm sure that the readers will as well.

GAYLE

Thank you, David, for having me.

WRIGHT

Today we've been talking with Kimberly D. Gayle who is an executive and professional life coach. She creates and designs professional coaching programs in order to serve as post-training support for corporate change initiatives, as well as personal development programs for individuals who want to define and achieve professional and personal goals.

Kimberly, thank you so much for being with us today on *Discover Your Inner Strength*.

GAYLE

Thank you.

About the Author

Kimberly D. Gayle is an executive and professional life coach for Executive Intervention LLC, a training and development company that designs and facilitates customized training programs in the areas of change management, employee performance development, and information technology. She creates and designs professional coaching programs in order to serve as post-training support for corporate change initiatives, as well as personal development plans specifically for individuals who want to define and achieve professional and personal goals.

She has earned a Bachelor of Science degree in Business Administration from Bowling Green State University, and a master's degree in Public Administration from the University of Akron. She is a Certified Life Coach from the Institute for Life Coach Training and a member of the International Coach Federation, Central Ohio Coaches Association, and the Black Professional Coaches Alliance. She also volunteers her coaching service to MBA graduate students who attend Franklin University in Columbus, Ohio.

Kimberly Gayle

Executive Intervention, LLC
P.O. Box 112
Blacklick, OH 43004
Phone 614-866-6681
Fax 614-866-7467
info@execintervention.com
www.execintervention.com

Discover Your Inner Strength

DISCOVER YOUR INNER STRENGTH

2

A Values-Based Approach

An Interview With...
Dr. Stephen Covey

DAVID WRIGHT (WRIGHT)

We're talking today with Dr. Stephen R. Covey, cofounder and vice-chairman of Franklin Covey Company, the largest management company and leadership development organization in the world. Dr. Covey is perhaps best known as author of *The 7 Habits of Highly Effective People,* which is ranked as a number one bestseller by the *New York Times*, having sold more than fourteen million copies in thirty-eight languages throughout the world. Dr. Covey is an internationally respected leadership authority, family expert, teacher, and organizational consultant. He has made teaching principle-centered living and principle-centered leadership his life's work. Dr. Covey is the recipient of the Thomas More College Medallion for Continuing Service to Humanity and has been awarded four honorary doctorate degrees. Other awards given Dr. Covey include the Sikh's 1989 International Man of Peace award, the 1994 International Entrepreneur of the Year award, *Inc.* magazine's Services Entrepreneur of the Year award, and in 1996 the National Entrepreneur of the Year Lifetime Achievement award for Entrepreneurial leadership. He has also been recognized as one of *Time* magazine's twenty-five most influential Americans and one of *Sales and Marketing Management's* top twenty-five power brokers. As the father of nine and grandfather of forty-four, Dr. Covey received the 2003 National Fatherhood Award, which he says is the most meaningful award he has ever received. Dr. Covey earned his undergraduate degree from the University of Utah, his MBA from Harvard, and completed his doctorate at Brigham Young University. While at Brigham Young he served as assistant to the President and was also a professor of Business Management and Organizational Behavior.

Dr. Covey, welcome to *Discover Your Inner Strength*.

DR. STEPHEN COVEY (COVEY)

Thank you.

WRIGHT

Dr. Covey, most companies make decisions and filter them down through their organization. You, however, state that no company can succeed until individuals within it succeed. Are the goals of the company the result of the combined goals of the individuals?

COVEY

Absolutely—if people aren't on the same page, they're going to be pulling in different directions. To teach this concept, I frequently ask large audiences to close their eyes and point north, and then to keep pointing and open their eyes. They find themselves pointing all over the place. I say to them, "Tomorrow morning if you want a similar experience, ask the first ten people you meet in your organization what the purpose of your organization is and you'll find it's a very similar experience. They'll point all over the place." When people have a different sense of purpose and values, every decision that is made from then on is governed by those. There's no question that this is one of the fundamental causes of misalignment, low trust, interpersonal conflict, interdepartmental rivalry, people operating on personal agendas, and so forth.

WRIGHT

Is that primarily a result of an inability to communicate from the top?

COVEY

That's one aspect, but I think it's more fundamental. There's an inability to involve people—an unwillingness. Leaders may communicate what their mission and their strategy is, but that doesn't mean there's any emotional connection to it. Mission statements that are rushed and then announced are soon forgotten. They become nothing more than just a bunch of platitudes on the wall that mean essentially nothing and even create a source of cynicism and a sense of hypocrisy inside the culture of an organization.

WRIGHT

How do companies ensure survival and prosperity in these tumultuous times of technological advances, mergers, downsizing, and change?

COVEY

I think that it takes a lot of high trust in a culture that has something that doesn't change—principles—at its core. There are principles that people agree upon that are valued. It gives a sense of stability. Then you have the power to adapt and be flexible when you experience these kinds of disruptive new economic models or technologies that come in and sideswipe you. You don't know how to handle them unless you have something you can depend upon.

If people have not agreed to a common set of principles that guide them and a common purpose, then they get their security from the outside and they tend to freeze the structure, systems, and processes inside and they cease becoming adaptable. They don't change with the changing realities of the new marketplace out there and gradually they become obsolete.

WRIGHT

I was interested in one portion of your book, *The 7 Habits of Highly Effective People,* where you talk about behaviors. How does an individual go about the process of replacing ineffective behaviors with effective ones?

COVEY

I think that for most people it usually requires a crisis that humbles them to become aware of their ineffective behaviors. If there's not a crisis the tendency is to perpetuate those behaviors and not change.

You don't have to wait until the marketplace creates the crisis for you. Have everyone accountable on a 360-degree basis to everyone else they interact with—with feedback either formal or informal—where they are getting data as to what's happening. They will then start to realize that the consequences of their ineffective behavior require them to be humble enough to look at that behavior and to adopt new, more effective ways of doing things.

Sometimes people can be stirred up to this if you just appeal to their conscience—to their inward sense of what is right and wrong. A lot of people sometimes know inwardly they're doing wrong, but the culture doesn't necessarily discourage them from continuing that. They either need feedback from people or they need feedback from the marketplace or they need feedback from their conscience. Then they can begin to develop a step-by-step process of replacing old habits with new, better habits.

WRIGHT

It's almost like saying, "Let's make all the mistakes in the laboratory before we put this thing in the air."

COVEY

Right; and I also think what is necessary is a paradigm shift, which is analogous to having a correct map, say of a city or of a country. If people have an inaccurate paradigm of life, of other people, and of themselves it really doesn't make much difference what their behavior or habits or attitudes are. What they need is a correct paradigm—a correct map—that describes what's going on.

For instance, in the Middle Ages they used to heal people through bloodletting. It wasn't until Samuel Weiss and Pasteur and other empirical scientists discovered the germ theory that they realized for the first time they weren't dealing with the real issue. They realized why women preferred to use midwives who washed rather than doctors who didn't wash. They gradually got a new paradigm. Once you've got a new paradigm then your behavior and your attitude flow directly from it. If you have a bad paradigm or a bad map, let's say of a city, there's no way, no matter what your behavior or your habits or your attitudes are—how positive they are—you'll never be able to find the location you're looking for. This is why I believe that to change paradigms is far more fundamental than to work on attitude and behavior.

WRIGHT

One of your seven habits of highly effective people is to "begin with the end in mind." If circumstances change and hardships or miscalculations occur, how does one view the end with clarity?

COVEY

Many people think to begin with the end in mind means that you have some fixed definition of a goal that's accomplished and if changes come about you're not going to adapt to them. Instead, the "end in mind" you begin with is that you are going to create a flexible culture of high trust so that no matter what comes along you are going to do whatever it takes to accommodate that new change or that new reality and maintain a culture of high performance and high trust. You're talking more in terms of values and overall purposes that don't change, rather than specific strategies or programs that will have to change to accommodate the changing realities in the marketplace.

WRIGHT

In this time of mistrust among people, corporations, and nations, for that matter, how do we create high levels of trust?

COVEY

That's a great question and it's complicated because there are so many elements that go into the creating of a culture of trust. Obviously the most fundamental one is just to have trustworthy people. But that is not sufficient because what if the organization itself is misaligned?

For instance, what if you say you value cooperation but you really reward people for internal competition? Then you have a systemic or a structure problem that creates low trust inside the culture even though the people themselves are trustworthy. This is one of the insights of Edward Demming and the work he did. That's why he said that most problems are not personal—they're systemic. They're common caused. That's why you have to work on structure, systems, and processes to make sure that they institutionalize principle-centered values. Otherwise you could have good people with bad systems and you'll get bad results.

When it comes to developing interpersonal trust between people, it is made up of many, many elements such as taking the time to listen to other people, to understand them, and to see what is important to them. What we think is important to another may only be important to us, not to another. It takes empathy. You have to make and keep promises to them. You have to treat people with kindness and courtesy. You have to be completely honest and open. You have to live up to your commitments. You can't betray people behind their back. You can't badmouth them behind their back and sweet-talk them to their face. That will send out vibes of hypocrisy and it will be detected.

You have to learn to apologize when you make mistakes, to admit mistakes, and to also get feedback going in every direction as much as possible. It doesn't necessarily require formal forums—it requires trust between people who will be open with each other and give each other feedback.

WRIGHT

My mother told me to do a lot of what you're saying now, but it seems that when I got in business I simply forgot.

COVEY

Sometimes we forget, but sometimes culture doesn't nurture it. That's why I say unless you work with the institutionalizing—that means formalizing into structure, systems, and processing the values—you will not have a nurturing culture. You have to constantly work on that.

This is one of the big mistakes organizations make. They think trust is simply a function of being honest. That's only one small aspect. It's an important aspect, obviously, but there are so many other elements that go into the creation of a high-trust culture.

WRIGHT

"Seek first to understand then to be understood" is another of your seven habits. Do you find that people try to communicate without really understanding what other people want?

COVEY

Absolutely. The tendency is to project out of our own autobiography—our own life, our own value system—onto other people, thinking we know what they want. So we don't really listen to them. We pretend to listen, but we really don't listen from within their frame of reference. We listen from within our own frame of reference and we're really preparing our reply rather than seeking to understand. This is a very common thing. In fact, very few people have had any training in seriously listening. They're trained in how to read, write, and speak, but not to listen.

Reading, writing, speaking, and listening are the four modes of communication and they represent about two-thirds to three-fourths of our waking hours. About half of that time is spent listening, but it's the one skill people have not been trained in. People have had all this training in the other forms of communication. In a large audience of 1,000 people you wouldn't have more than twenty people who have had more than two weeks of training in listening. Listening is more than a skill or technique; you must listen within another's frame of reference. It takes tremendous courage to listen because you're at risk when you listen. You don't know what's going to happen; you're vulnerable.

WRIGHT

Sales gurus always tell me that the number one skill in selling is listening.

COVEY

Yes—listening from within the customer's frame of reference. That is so true. You can see that it takes some security to do that because you don't know what's going to happen.

WRIGHT

With this book we're trying to encourage people to be better, to live better, and be more fulfilled by listening to the examples of our guest authors. Is there anything or anyone in your life that has made a difference for you and helped you to become a better person?

COVEY

I think the most influential people in my life have been my parents. I think that what they modeled was not to make comparisons and harbor jealousy or to seek recognition. They were humble people.

I remember one time when my mother and I were going up in an elevator and the most prominent person in the state was also in the elevator. She knew him, but she spent her time talking to the elevator operator. I was just a little kid and I was so awed by the famous person. I said to her, "Why didn't you talk to the important person?" She said, "I was. I had never met him."

My parents were really humble, modest people who were focused on service and other people rather than on themselves. I think they were very inspiring models to me.

WRIGHT

In almost every research paper I've ever read, those who write about people who have influenced their lives include three teachers in their top-five picks. My seventh-grade English teacher was the greatest teacher I ever had and she influenced me to no end.

COVEY

Would it be correct to say that she saw in you probably some qualities of greatness you didn't even see in yourself?

WRIGHT

Absolutely.

COVEY

That's been my general experience—the key aspect of a mentor or a teacher is someone who sees in you potential that you don't even see in yourself. Those teachers/mentors treat you accordingly and eventually you come to see it in yourself. That's my definition of leadership or influence—communicating people's worth and potential so clearly that they are inspired to see it in themselves.

WRIGHT

Most of my teachers treated me as a student, but she treated me with much more respect than that. As a matter of fact, she called me Mr. Wright, and I was in the seventh grade at the time. I'd never been addressed by anything but a nickname. I stood a little taller; she just made a tremendous difference.

Do you think there are other characteristics that mentors seem to have in common?

COVEY

I think they are first of all good examples in their own personal lives. Their personal lives and their family lives are not all messed up—they come from a base of good character. They also are usually very confident and they take the time to do what your teacher did to you—to treat you with uncommon respect and courtesy.

They also, I think, explicitly teach principles rather than practices so that rules don't take the place of human judgment. You gradually come to have faith in your own judgment in making decisions because of the affirmation of such a mentor. Good mentors care about you—you can feel the sincerity of their caring. It's like the expression, "I don't care how much you know until I know how much you care."

WRIGHT

Most people are fascinated with the new television shows about being a survivor. What has been the greatest comeback that you've made from adversity in your career or your life?

COVEY

When I was in grade school I experienced a disease in my legs. It caused me to use crutches for a while. I tried to get off them fast and get back. The disease wasn't corrected yet so I went back on crutches for another year. The disease went to the other leg and I went on for another year. It essentially took me out of my favorite thing—athletics—and it took me more into being a student. So that was a life-defining experience, which at the time seemed very negative, but has proven to be the basis on which I've focused my life—being more of a learner.

WRIGHT

Principle-centered learning is basically what you do that's different from anybody I've read or listened to.

COVEY

The concept is embodied in the Far Eastern expression, "Give a man a fish, you feed him for the day; teach him how to fish, you feed him for a lifetime." When you teach principles that are universal and timeless, they don't belong to just any one person's religion or to a particular culture or geography. They seem to be timeless and universal like the ones we've been talking about here: trustworthiness, honesty, caring, service, growth, and development. These are universal principles. If you focus on these things, then little by little people become independent of you and then they start to believe in themselves and their own judgment becomes better. You don't need as many rules. You don't need as much bureaucracy and as many controls and you can empower people.

The problem in most business operations today—and not just business but non-business—is that they're using the industrial model in an information age. Arnold Toynbee, the great historian, said, "You can pretty well summarize all of history in four words: nothing fails like success." The industrial model was based on the asset of the machine. The information model is based on the asset of the person—the knowledge worker. It's an altogether different model. But the machine model was the main asset of the twentieth century. It enabled productivity to increase fifty times. The new asset is intellectual and social capital—the qualities of people and the quality of the relationship they have with each other. Like Toynbee said, "Nothing fails like success." The industrial model does not work in an information age. It requires a focus on the new wealth, not capital and material things.

A good illustration that demonstrates how much we were into the industrial model, and still are, is to notice where people are on the balance sheet. They're not found there. Machines are found there. Machines become investments. People are on the profit-and-loss statement and people are expenses. Think of that—if that isn't bloodletting.

WRIGHT

It sure is.

When you consider the choices you've made down through the years, has faith played an important role in your life?

COVEY

It has played an extremely important role. I believe deeply that we should put principles at the center of our lives, but I believe that God is the source of those principles. I did not invent them. I get credit sometimes for some of the Seven Habits material and some of the other things I've done, but it's really all based on principles that have been given by God to all of His children from the beginning of time. You'll find that you can teach these same principles from the sacred texts and the wisdom literature of almost any tradition. I think the ultimate source of that is God and that is one thing you can absolutely depend upon—"in God we trust."

WRIGHT

If you could have a platform and tell our audience something you feel would help them or encourage them, what would you say?

COVEY

I think I would say to put God at the center of your life and then prioritize your family. No one on their deathbed ever wished they had spent more time at the office.

WRIGHT

That's right. We have come down to the end of our program and I know you're a busy person. I could talk with you all day, Dr. Covey.

COVEY

It's good to talk with you as well and to be a part of this program. It looks like an excellent one that you've got going on here.

WRIGHT

Thank you.

We have been talking today with Dr. Stephen R. Covey, cofounder and vice-chairman of Franklin Covey Company. He's also the author of *The 7 Habits of Highly Effective People,* which has been ranked as a number one bestseller by the *New York Times*, selling more than fourteen million copies in thirty-eight languages.

Dr. Covey, thank you so much for being with us today.

COVEY

Thank you for the honor of participating.

About the Author

Stephen R. Covey was recognized in 1996 as one of *Time* magazine's twenty-five most influential Americans and one of *Sales and Marketing Management's* top twenty-five power brokers. Dr. Covey is the author of several acclaimed books, including the international bestseller, *The 7 Habits of Highly Effective People*, named the number one Most Influential Business Book of the Twentieth Century, and other best sellers that include *First Things First, Principle-Centered Leadership,* (with sales exceeding one million) and *The 7 Habits of Highly Effective Families.*

Dr. Covey earned his undergraduate degree from the University of Utah, his MBA from Harvard, and completed his doctorate at Brigham Young University. While at Brigham Young University, he served as assistant to the President and was also a professor of Business Management and Organizational Behavior. He received the National Fatherhood Award in 2003, which, as the father of nine and grandfather of forty-four, he says is the most meaningful award he has ever received.

Dr. Covey currently serves on the board of directors for the Points of Light Foundation. Based in Washington, D.C., the Foundation, through its partnership with the Volunteer Center National Network, engages and mobilizes millions of volunteers from all walks of life—businesses, nonprofits, faith-based organizations, low-income communities, families, youth, and older adults—to help solve serious social problems in thousands of communities.

Dr. Stephen Covey

www.stevencovey.com

Discover Your Inner Strength

Having What You Want is Easier Than You Think

An Interview With…
Jessica A. Haynes

DAVID WRIGHT (WRIGHT)

Today we're talking with Jessica Haynes. Jessica is a business and relationship consultant who specializes in helping individuals realize their goals. In the realm of maximizing one's potential, she is known and respected for her ability to help individuals find success, fulfillment, and inner strength. Jessica has been a motivational and self-empowerment speaker for the past twenty years. Using her psychology degree, marketing background, and business networking skills she consults with a steady clientele both nationally and internationally. She counsels

Fortune 500 business leaders, well-known personalities, entrepreneurs, and those seeking to improve the quality of their lives and their relationships. Her book *Get What You Want Now: Money, Love, Power, and More*... has received continued praise and highly supportive reviews from her clients and is now available to the general public. Jessica has been a speaker on panels with such authors and motivational speakers as Ram Dass, Dr. Raymond Moody, and Dannion Brinkley. From the State of the World Forum hosted by world leaders in San Francisco to as far away as Japan, Jessica inspires audiences.

Whether she's talking about relationships, careers, or finding your purpose, she connects you with your most valuable resource—You— that powerful part of you innately designed to prosper and thrive. In this chapter, Jessica will show you how to find life balance, overcome adversity, learn ways to deal with transition, develop inner courage, and utilize strategies that encourage you to walk away from going-nowhere situations. She will help you put the "elation" back into your relationships and open new doors to discovering your inner strength.

Jessica, welcome to *Discover Your Inner Strength.*

JESSICA HAYNES (HAYNES)

It is a pleasure to be here, thank you.

WRIGHT

So what led you to become a strategist in helping others discover their inner strength?

HAYNES

At the age of twenty-seven I had an experience that forced me to discover my inner strength.

In 1983, as a passenger in a car that crashed at accelerating speed, I sustained massive injuries. The driver walked away from the accident, but the impact on my side of the car crushed my face beyond recognition. The bones in my feet were shattered and my vertebrae suffered multiple fractures. I had lack of mobility and a prognosis of sustained disfigurement and nerve damage. My life literally turned topsy-turvy. I went from being a marketing executive working on national projects (offset with running and exercising) to lying in a hospital bed and looking at a future that was bleak. Also, the pain was excruciating.

After the surgery to reattach my jaw, rebuild my face, and close the multiple gashes from broken windshield glass, I had a near death experience. Lying in my hospital room, I felt a loving presence convey to me, "If you want to let go, it will be okay." I remember feeling a floating sensation; it was as if I were being gently lifted out of my body to a place of eternal time, indescribable love, and a "foreverness" of spiritual energy. I was now experiencing my ethereal body. I felt like a point of light, yet I was one with all. Earth was no longer a part of my new reality. In my ethereal body, I was able to reevaluate the choices I had made from a standpoint of looking back at my life as if it were a film clip.

In my life review I was shown possible futures that I could have created and lived, but didn't. It was a revelation for me to see all the possible directions my life could have taken had I made different choices. I recognized that I had some regrets. In recounting the choices I had made while I was alive, I could have enjoyed life more, I could have believed in myself more, and I could have more fully recognized my life's purpose. It was all so clear and obvious—why hadn't I understood this before?

I wanted a second chance. I wanted to go back and redo some of my life choices. But, I was dead. I didn't have a way to get back.

As I continued to review my life, I thought over and over, "There must be a way to have a second chance." A never-ending brilliance appeared around me. The message was, "Now you understand the value of life and the importance of creating a life well lived. Use this knowledge wisely." I felt myself being pulled back into my body. The excruciating pain returned. I was alive!

My recovery began immediately. The nurses were inspired with my optimism and my healing mindset. Despite the doctors' prognosis, I was getting better every day. The nurses asked me to visit other patients in critical care. I did, and these individuals improved and experienced their own healing.

Within five months I was noticeably healed. The doctors had no explanation. I was running up steep hills, hiking mountains, and looking like myself again. I embraced the knowledge I had gained in my near death experience and focused each day on further developing my inner strengths. People were drawn to me and I helped them find answers to situations that positively changed their lives.

With hundreds of success stories, I knew what my mission was. I left my marketing position and started my own business as a business and relationship consultant. My clients started calling me their "success and fulfillment coach."

Today I continue to teach how to effectively use the power of your mind.

WRIGHT

Your message of hope and inspiration supports the reality that building your inner strength offers great rewards. Will you briefly define inner strength and give our readers a few strategies to develop one's inner strength?

HAYNES

Inner strength is the driving force within you that defines and guides your thoughts, feelings, and desires so that you can become the person you really want to be. Inner strength defines who you really are. The more you know who you are, the easier it is to manifest what you want. People show up in your life at the right time, outcomes you desire easily fall into place, and positive possibilities surround you.

Here are a few strategies to enable you to maximize your inner strength(s):

1. You are in control of your thoughts.
2. Your thoughts can create tangible things.
3. Your thoughts are fluid—they're not static or rigid.

4. You are the source of your happiness.
5. Having a life with few regrets comes from making wise choices.
6. You have inner resources, talents, and intuitive capabilities.
7. Be yourself. Believe in yourself.

You alone control your thoughts. Each day you have the opportunity to make choices and follow through with actions that can better your life. Who are you right now? Is this the person you want to be? Are your thoughts working for you or are they hindering you from moving in the direction you desire? Are your thoughts mostly positive or do you slip into negative thinking?

You can change, improve, and better yourself at any time when you tap into your inner strength.

A few weeks ago, Tami called me for advice. She said she felt emotionally beaten down and drained. Her husband regularly found fault with her and she wanted a formula to bypass his criticisms and focus on her dreams and goals.

I suggested that she consider the seven strategies for reclaiming her identity and inner strength. These points proved to be a breakthrough for Tami. She realized that she was in charge of her thoughts. She wasn't stuck. She could find new ways to feel happy. She could make new choices.

The more Tami focused on her inner strengths, the more she wasn't affected by her husband's difficult moods. In fact, she began feeling secure enough to leave if he didn't value her wishes, concerns, or needs. When her husband realized she was serious about her newfound self-image, he began to change. He started looking at his own issues and internal anger. He began supporting her goals and stopped belittling her.

Tami remarked, "It took believing in me, taking charge of my thoughts, and valuing my inner strength to change things. The seven steps you described helped me to turn a seemingly impossible and going-nowhere situation into a genuine marriage."

To make change, you need to believe it is possible to make a shift in a new direction. Because many of us have been taught it's difficult to start over or initiate change, we overlook how important it is to take control of our thoughts and focus on a new or better goal.

Maximizing your inner strength(s) starts with knowing you are in control of your thoughts. What you desire can become your reality. Your thoughts can become tangible things. You choose your thoughts. You choose your moods. You choose what interests you. You are more in control of what you think and feel than you might imagine. The people you meet, the books you read, and the experiences you add to your life are under your control.

WRIGHT

So what makes your message unique from others who teach ways to develop one's inner strengths?

HAYNES

David, my message is one of hope and enjoying solid results. My message allows you to: Do what you love. Ask for what you want. Have the courage to take risks. Make time for what matters most. Dare to dream big. Let the child within you have fun. Find love. Reach your potential, and create a life well lived. Using your inner strength(s) is the most effective way to improve every aspect of your life—money, relationships, success, health, and more. It puts a powerful force into motion, one in which you gain the ability to influence and create outcomes that you desire.

1. My method works for people in all walks of life.
2. My approach helps individuals to fast-forward and create outcomes that are positive.
3. My techniques stretch one's perception.
4. My message endures the test of time.

Take a moment to reflect on qualities that most accurately describe you. For instance, I *am:*

Prepared	Committed
Imaginative	Self-affirming
Good at listening	Resilient
Powerful	Genuine
Humorous	Aware of my talents
Adventurous	Responsible
Self-assured	Passionate
Intuitive	Positive
Loyal	Creative
Persistent	Playful
Goal-Oriented	Independent
Courageous	Optimistic
Determined	Caring

This exercise brings into focus the qualities that are most important to you. It helps you define your identity. It helps you empower your thoughts in a positive way.

The goal of this exercise is to focus on "I ams" that help you develop a secure and empowered identity. Your "I am" list reflects the life you want to create.

If you weren't particularly optimistic, you may have written such things as, "I am someone who procrastinates. I am someone who gives up too easily. I am someone who enjoys pleasing others to my own detriment. I am too trusting. I am someone who rarely enjoys the current moment."

Every person has inner talents and intuitive capabilities. If you hold onto pessimistic thoughts, mental clutter, or self-deprecating emotional baggage, you will imagine less for your future and downgrade the potential within you.

Don't give up when faced with negative influences or negative internal programming. Reach deep down into your soul and believe that your life has purpose.

As I mentioned earlier, after the car accident, my face was disfigured. I didn't know if I would be able to do normal physical activities or exercise again. It was scary for me to look at myself in the mirror. My identity was challenged. I didn't give up. I chose to believe I could heal and create a better life for myself.

Give thought to and then answer the following questions:

- What outcomes do I want to create for myself?
- What benefits will I get by moving in this direction?
- With whom will I connect as I become my best self?

This exercise is helpful because it encourages you to look at solutions from various viewpoints, perspectives, and possibilities. Write down answers to these self-directed questions. Notice what comes up for you.

If you have experienced a setback, use these questions to focus your attention on building a more fulfilling life. For instance, if you are starting a new career, developing a new relationship, or developing a healthier lifestyle, these questions help you to focus on a goal, take action, assess what needs to change, and create positive results.

Think about ways of getting people interested and involved in what you love to do. What are you passionate about? By writing down empowering thoughts and "I ams" regularly, you will feel more confident and put a powerful force into motion—what I call a "you force." Your talent isn't to be ignored, underutilized, or wasted.

Having a positive "I am" list at your fingertips and looking at it regularly puts your "you force" into motion. By focusing on what is valuable and unique about you, your internal universal energy begins to go to work for you. Your thoughts start producing the tangible things that you want.

Even sublime goals can be reached when you put your "you force" to work.

WRIGHT

You've written a book that your clients are raving about. What makes your book so unique and so popular?

HAYNES

I have synthesized how to manifest what you want into five logical, practical, and highly effective steps. The presentation of ideas is based on real life success stories. One step overlaps the next, so that by the last chapter your perception of reality is vastly expanded. My clients have been telling me for years, "Jessica, put your techniques down on paper. You've helped so many people reach their dreams. Write your system down in a book." So I did.

By the time you finish *Get What You Want Now: Money, Love, Power, and More . . .* you will have a new perspective regarding the way the world works and how you can develop your inner strength(s). It's been a delight writing it. But even more so, I'm delighted in watching how people's lives have improved.

When you understand and develop your inner strengths, you can go from rags to riches. You can improve your health. You can find and experience committed and enduring love. You can build a successful and streamlined business.

WRIGHT

You've got me intrigued. What are the basic steps you've developed to help anyone develop their inner strengths?

HAYNES

Here are the basic steps I've developed:

Believe you can get what you want.

Become an asset thinker.
Use the power of your mind.
Maximize your personality.
Make your dreams come true.

I am an advocate of believing that you can get what you want. Events can rearrange themselves for you in the most unexpected ways.

Believe in yourself

It all begins with believing in yourself and that it is possible to realize your dreams. Where your attention goes, your future flows. Believing in yourself starts with recognizing that your thoughts hold great power.

Look at your "I am" list and prioritize the qualities as most important to least important. What are your top three? Maybe they are: humorous, playful, and creative. Or, maybe they are: powerful, resilient, and persistent. Or, maybe they are: loyal, good at listening, and committed. Notice the combination that you choose.

Attach these qualities to a goal. Then identify and pursue what you want using these qualities. Follow through. Take action. Practice these qualities until they become second nature. Find people who are like-minded and support your goals. Make these qualities a part of your identity.

The stronger your belief is in yourself, the faster you'll get results. Weak thoughts create weak outcomes. Jumbled or confused thoughts do the same. A Universal force goes to work for you, as well as your own "you force" when you get committed to implementing your "I am" inner strengths. Things will start falling into place.

Keep adding qualities that you have listed as important to you. Integrate these inner strengths daily. As you add more inner strengths, notice that what you desire will seem more obtainable and perhaps even inevitable. Notice what does and doesn't work for you.

Key questions for you to answer:

1. What is most important to me?
2. If I could have anything I wanted, what would I choose?
3. What inner strengths help me get what I want?
4. What inner strengths help me keep what I want?
5. Are these inner strengths congruent with my values?
6. What inner strengths attract the best people for me, to me?
7. What inner strengths help me to believe in myself?

For many people, imagining getting what you want isn't really that difficult. It's the "believing" part that takes practice. Positive inner mind-talk is another way of transforming negative habits into constructive actions. It takes you from feeling "out of power" to feeling "in power." Whenever you feel anxious about one or more challenges and wonder if you can achieve what you want, tell yourself positive affirmations. Tell yourself that the best in life is yet to come. Tell yourself that nothing can stop you. Tell yourself that your inner strength is stronger than your challenges. Believe that you can get what you want.

Believing you can get what you want is a mindset. Believing tells your conscious mind and your subconscious mind that you're ready to receive more and that your dreams have a chance. It allows you to move past doubt, external criticism, and uncertainty.

Try not to compare yourself unfavorably with others. Your inner strengths may be different from that of someone else. If you start comparing yourself to others, you can mistakenly think an asset you have is a liability. Notice what works for you and keep doing it.

Sometimes it helps to tape your voice on a recorder so that you can *listen* to your positive "I ams" and life goals. The spoken word is very powerful. By listening to yourself talking about ways you will succeed, you tend to draw positive events and outcomes to you in unexplainable ways.

Actually, David, how in your life have you used this technique? Obviously, you created your own publishing company. You're out there taking on the business world. You had to have believed in yourself when you got started. I mean, you must have had ups and downs and highs and lows and setbacks. I know everybody out there wants to know—how did you do it?

WRIGHT

I just kept on keeping on. I just wouldn't be denied, I wouldn't stop, I wouldn't let anybody stop me, and I just kept on going. It's been successful now for many, many years.

HAYNES

So when somebody said "you couldn't," "it's not possible," or "give up," you chose to believe in yourself. It sounds like you also chose to get people around you who believed in you and your mission. It is impressive to see how you have connected with so many noted authors and celebrities. I guess the magic word here is, *"believe!"*

I remember a client who came to me saying that his business couldn't be salvaged. I saw the opposite. I noticed that the only thing causing Doug's failing business was that he didn't believe he could turn it around. I pointed out that Doug had a difficult time controlling his top staff. They were regularly instigating confusion, dissention, and inner turmoil. I helped Doug set boundaries. I showed him how to move from being a "doormat" employer to a decisive "I am in control" employer.

Within a few months, he had replaced numerous highly ineffective employees. The production at his pasta company went up tenfold. Doug went forward to sell his company for a profit that allowed him to retire in style, buy expensive classic cars, and travel.

Keep updating your identity as you get more and more of what you want. This will help you stay on track as you set loftier goals. If a particular goal is taking longer than you expected, believe that events are rearranging themselves for you on an unseen level. It's an inner strength to have faith.

Don't be afraid to ask for what you want. Don't let other people push you in directions that aren't meaningful to you. This is your life and you want to get the most out of it. Be committed to your "I am" list. Use it every day. Keep on using it.

How to Choose Wisely

The next step is to become what I call an "Asset Thinker." An asset thinker is someone who focuses on adding assets, not liabilities. The predictable connection between having your actions result in positive outcomes starts with asset thinking. It forces you to continually look at your options, make wise choices, and follow through in logical yet optimistic ways.

To become an asset thinker, you want to stay focused on bettering your life.

Here are some key questions to help you become an "Asset Thinker."

1. What must I give up or add to get the results I want?
2. What outcome is so important that I'll follow through?
3. What actions will I take so that others believe in me?
4. What contacts or resources must I have to reach my goals?
5. What are my short-term and long-term goals?
6. Do my choices have any possible negative consequences?
7. What skills must I develop to build the life I want?

This exercise is important because it focuses your attention on where you have been, where you are right now, where you want to go, and what you need to do to get optimum results. It helps you explore alternate choices so you can expand your sense of possibilities. Sometimes a solution may be right in front of you but you can't see it.

When Nick called me saying he was considering filing for bankruptcy and walking away from the business he had inherited from his family, I asked him why. He saw bankruptcy as his only choice. Over a period of months, I helped Nick see options that he had previously overlooked. By using the "Asset Thinking" approach, Nick found inner strengths within himself he'd previously overlooked. For instance, Nick developed creative ways to reduce his expenses. He networked and found individuals who wanted to invest in his business. He revamped his marketing team. He replaced advisors who had been giving him shortsighted advice, and he learned how to effectively manage his time, energy, and resources. Nick gradually turned his company around. His son was so impressed he said he wanted to get involved in the family business. To this day Nick uses asset thinking to improve and build his business.

For a moment, take a look at the individuals you admire most. Perhaps they came from humble beginnings and now they're doing what they love and getting far more of what they want. Imagine what it would be like to sit down with such a person and hear his or her story.

Probably after your introduction and some initial pleasantries, you would ask, "How did you do it? What tips could you share?"

He or she would invariably respond, "I noticed that certain actions enabled me to gain assets, while others brought liabilities. I began to divide my time, energy, mental thoughts, and imagery into two different categories: Assets and Liabilities. I clearly focused on patterns that worked for me and let go of patterns that resulted in nothing or set me back. It got easier and easier to say no to patterns that held me back."

What successful people are really saying is that they have learned how to make wise choices. They know how to ask the right questions. They understand when to move forward and when to walk away. They know what an asset is versus a liability.

This is one of the most powerful secrets for getting what you want sooner than later.

If you have a long list of assets and few liabilities, you tend to feel more secure. You have more options. You can easily create positive outcomes because you have a plenitude of choices. However, in comparison, if you have a great many liabilities and very few assets, then you are going to feel less secure, less powerful, less mobile, less confident, and your optimism can wane.

When Bailey came to me, she said she couldn't understand why she was rarely happy. Looking at the life choices she had made, she had very few assets. She also had mounting liabilities. I asked, "Why so few assets?" She said, "I don't know what it takes to be successful."

I helped Bailey take a deeper look at her inner strengths so she could see herself as her own best asset. She created an "I am" list and began using the inner strengths that came naturally for her. She reframed her thoughts and started on a career path that brought her a greater sense of purpose. She found it easier to ask for what she wanted. She dropped negative habits that no longer served her. This provided Bailey with more time to develop new inner strengths. Today Bailey is doing well. She likes her career, has quality friends, and says she's happy.

To become an asset thinker, bring the idea or mental picture you want to your mind often. In this way, your goal becomes an integral part of your life. But try not to push too hard or hold onto negative imagery from the past. Both tend to hinder rather than help your progress. As you think about your goals, say encouraging statements to yourself.

So David, how did you learn to become an "Asset Thinker?" Obviously you've had to experience this lesson yourself in making choices in your business.

WRIGHT

Yes, I had to recognize some weaknesses, no question about that. And I had to hire people who would cover my weaknesses.

HAYNES

Learning how to make wise choices is an essential inner strength. It's also about asking questions that propel you forward and motivate you. Notice what is and isn't working for you. Decide to use your time wisely. Reach out to a support system that covers your weaknesses and enhances your strengths. Give yourself the courage to be innovative and creative. Focus on how to add more meaning and purpose to your life. Don't let the cynics or naysayers bring you down!

Here are some questions to help you to make wiser decisions:

1. What is most important to me?
2. What must I add to my life to feel fulfilled?
3. Can I say no to situations that don't serve my needs?
4. Can I take one step at a time and still be satisfied?
5. Do I believe that I will get what I want?
6. What mistakes have I learned to never repeat?
7. What triumphs are helping me to further succeed?
8. How can I maximize these strengths to do what I love?

Don't get sidetracked or confused by others who offer detrimental feedback that could hold you back or compromise your future. Be smart and choose people who inspire you to be your best self. Always think in terms of adding assets and limiting liabilities. Have a clear picture of what you want and go for it!

By being an asset thinker, it's easier to attract highly successful people and join forces. It's also easier to ask for what you want. Doubt or uncertainty falls away and is replaced with confidence and competence.

Mastering the Power of Your Mind

It is important to note that your mind wants to support you, not hold you back. Your conscious and unconscious thoughts work together to be your best ally. When you truly understand the power of your mind, your life can change in positive ways without much effort.

There is a connection between your thoughts and creating tangible things. I used the power of my mind to heal my body after the car accident. I "believed" I could recover. I never doubted this outcome. There are many people who are unaware of the power of their mind. They think synchronicity is based on luck or a rare occurrence. However, the power of your mind is real. Using this inner strength turns the unlikely into the probable, and the probable into the inevitable.

Again, your mind wants to support you if you let it do so.

Here's a formula to use:

1. Set a goal.
2. Focus on it.
3. Mentally and emotionally experience what you want as something you *must* have.
4. Feel fully deserving of what you want and think of what you desire as being normal, inevitable, and real.
5. Believe that you have the power to rearrange events or situations to match your mental pictures.
6. Believe that a universal force is helping you to fulfill your desires.
7. Even if things don't show up immediately, stay focused.
8. Surround yourself with people who believe in your dreams and goals.
9. As events fall into place, don't stop visualizing. If anything, get even more focused on what you want and desire!

By focusing your mind on a desire and believing it will happen, synchronistic events begin to occur. In essence, you begin to "think your way to success!"

Here is an exercise to help you build added inner strength in your mind. It's a High/Low test.

Mark High or Low next to each inner belief below:

_____ I choose to believe that I can get what I desire.
_____ I accept that sometimes things go away in order to get more.
_____ I am willing to try new things to improve my life.
_____ I am persistent in following through on my goals.
_____ I notice and acknowledge things I need to change.
_____ I value my personality and let myself shine.
_____ I stay committed to what is most meaningful to me.

How many highs did you give yourself? How many lows did come up with? David, how many highs did you get?

WRIGHT

A lot more highs than lows.

HAYNES

Your subconscious mind responds to your mental commands like a chef preparing and serving up a meal. If you are not clear, the chef can't get your order right. If you send out mixed messages, you'll get mixed results. The goal is to focus upon and hold the belief that you will get what you ordered—or better!

Lofty goals may take a bit longer because you may need to get used to feeling deserving of having your goal. Choose to find goals that expand your sense of purpose. Choose to feel deserving of these goals. Choose to have fun in the process, even if things currently seem bleak. Choose to leave behind people, things, or situations that hold you back.

Where most people get lost is giving up too soon. As things start to rearrange themselves, people, jobs, or living situations can fall away causing a feeling of panic or "alert." These changes are part of the process for getting more of what you really want. Expect that the opportunity, job, lifestyle, or other is coming your way. Do you want a new job? Then accept that your current job has to go away.

Imagine what you want in your thoughts and don't get scared as things change to make this mental image a reality.

Do you want a better lifestyle? Then your current situation is going to change. Allow your mind to picture that having more is what you want. Don't let yourself be limited by current circumstances. If a thought of lack or doubt slips into your intentions, say to yourself, "There is nothing that can hold me back. I am getting what I want—this or something better!"

Try not to focus on scarcity. (This way of thinking is not an inner strength.) Avoid dwelling on past mishaps or failures that prevent you from feeling confident about moving forward. I can provide countless examples of clients who remained so focused on calamities or setbacks that their lives reflected their worries, fears, and emotional pain. Yet, when I was able to jump-start their perception to a new reality—one of hope and possibilities—positive things began to happen. Your constructive thoughts open positive possibilities.

If you are experiencing a situation that holds you back or causes emotional distress, it is up to you to change course. Notice alternative choice(s) that are available. Then take action. Take the necessary steps needed using the nine-step formula to create a life that makes you feel fulfilled.

Picture yourself living your dreams. (This way of thinking is an inner strength.) Imagine settling for nothing less. See yourself enjoying the outcome you desire as part of your purpose in life.

While you can't control other peoples' actions, beliefs, or values because everyone has free will, you can take greater control of your future by learning how to tune into the power of your intuition. You might say this skill bridges your conscious mind to your subconscious mind so that you get flashes of insight helping you to come up with excellent solutions.

If you ask any successful inventor, businessperson, researcher, or other creative individual, they will likely tell you that developing their intuition has played a major role in making wiser choices. Some people call this inner strength a "sixth sense." It involves recognizing the inner voice within you that often *knows* what direction to pursue and the best way to proceed. Here are some tips to help you develop your intuition.

1. Sitting quietly, relax your mind.
2. Allow yourself to connect with your "gut feelings."
3. Ask a question. Listen for a suggestion that fills your mind.
4. Don't judge what comes up for you.
5. Does this impression stay with you?
6. Does this impression feel right for you?
7. Follow up on any hunch that seems particularly meaningful.
8. Notice the events that happen as you follow your hunch.
9. Take action when you have a clear intuitive impression.
10. Resist letting other peoples' doubt affect your certainty.
11. Affirm yourself when you get positive results.
12. Keep repeating the process until it becomes second nature.

Once you tap into the beauty of this exercise, your intuition will grow stronger and more accurate. My clients tell me, "This technique changed my life. I rarely 'get it wrong' when I listen to my intuition. I feel more in control of my future and it helps me not settle for less."

Quiet slices of inner reflection can help you not give up too soon and turn the corner during moments of discouragement, lack of faith, or confusion. Your intuition helps you to not focus on scarcity. The more you practice these steps, the more you will feel confident that the right people, situations, and opportunities will show up in excellent timing to get what you need and desire.

It's rewarding when you decide to tap into the potential that lies within you. In my book, *Get What You Want Now: Money, Love, Power, and More* . . . I go into more detail. But I'm sure you are getting the picture that your thoughts hold tremendous power. You are innately created to live your dreams and feel "on purpose."

So I would imagine, David, that you've become good at this. Maybe you can validate that it's possible to put out a thought or desire, and then the phone rings with the perfect answer. Has that happened to you?

WRIGHT

Yes, surprisingly enough it has—just when I least expected it.

HAYNES

My client, Haley, was renovating her parents' mansion. She had hired a crew to come and sand the entry hallway. This was a fifteen-foot by forty-five-foot entry hallway. With a deadline to meet, she had to get this portion of the house sanded that day to be ready for the construction crew coming the next day. But the people who were supposed to redo the floor didn't show up. She sat in the pantry and focused on "creating a solution."

She made several phone calls and put forth the thought: the right person will show up. The doorbell rang a few hours later and a carpenter she had hired three months previously said he got a strong feeling that she needed help. He was in the area and decided to drop by. He professionally sanded the floor and Haley was able to keep her schedule on time. She paid him extra for his time and he was very pleased.

Haley manifested the solution she needed. That's the power of mind in action. It's real; it's authentic. Believe in it.

Here's another quick example. A company called me to boost its sales in the import/export business. Their connections abroad had disappeared and they heard about my method of using the power of one's mind to move forward. They wanted to connect with another firm but couldn't get an introduction or a lead into this sector. Using the technique described above, I asked my clients to focus on what they had to offer and hold a positive mindset.

I suggested they continue to take action in letters and phone calls, but to also focus on a specific intention. The principal of the company called me two weeks later saying that he had crossed paths unexpectedly with the person who was in charge of purchasing. It was a fluke. By mentally being prepared that synchronicity could happen, my client confidently presented his sales proposal. The encounter went well and a deal was sealed.

I invite you to discover this inner strength—that of harnessing the power of your mind!

WRIGHT

So will you give us some more examples of how you work with your clients and get such noticeable results?

HAYNES

I remember a client I consulted with who wanted to develop her talents as a television anchor. The station wanted her to change her looks, mannerisms, and speaking voice. I could see that her looks, mannerisms, and speaking voice were her greatest asset. She naturally exuded star quality. She listened to my suggestions and the station manager capitulated. She propelled the news station to top ratings. Today she's married to an international movie star. She's having the time of her life. She is now a cutting-edge role model for women.

A true feeling of fulfillment is experienced when you are doing what you enjoy. Living a life of mediocrity might be described as never daring to try the things you love. To make your intentions work, you need to dare trying what you love. Real freedom is being able to live your life the way you want.

Use the following affirmation for adding more plenitude to your life. "Each day and in every way, my thoughts have the power to attract the best people and events to me. The right situations find me, as if the details I need are falling into place. I find prosperity. I find love and inner joy. I find the career that most fulfills me. I have more to share with everyone else. Life is meant to be fun and I am willing to accept this. I feel abundant, well, and happy. My inner power is unfailing and unlimited."

Feel deserving when you repeat this affirmation. It boosts the energy a hundredfold!

How to Maximize Your Personality

There is no question that we are taught to filter our world though our parents' eyes, our teachers' guidelines, and our friends' opinions. Sometimes this works to our advantage, sometimes it doesn't. The goal is to become your authentic self. Try the following:

1. Take time to get quiet and meditate about the importance of your life and what you have to offer. This will help you diminish unwarranted fears about the future and give you patience for discovering what you truly want.
2. Reach deep down and picture what you really want. Set time limits for situations that no longer serve you. Do not fault yourself for leaving any situation that is detrimental to your personal growth or holds you back from reaching your goals.
3. Leverage your time. You can't concentrate on what's best for you if you are taking care of everybody else first. Give yourself the chance to figure out a new career, find a new relationship, lose weight, get healthier, or increase your business skills. The more you take care of yourself first, the faster you will attract situations that help you become your best, authentic, and successful self.
4. Remind yourself that life is too short to question your talents and skills. Your personality is within you. It can't go away. Through reading books,

attending seminars, or connecting with helpful friends, you can venture forward and break old patterns that hold you back.
5. What is your mission statement? If you let your talents shine, you will be noticed. In doing so, you give others permission to do the same. When you liberate yourself from thinking small or doubting your abilities, people will come forward to help you. In doing so, you simultaneously liberate others to notice their potential.

A lot of people waste years of their lives trying to imitate or copy high profile personalities thinking that this will get them ahead or find "the answer" to life's problems. Having good role models is wise, but if you give your power or identity away in the process, you can get off track. For instance, if you try to copy someone else's ideology or path of success without a clear "sense of self," you can inadvertently prevent yourself from developing your own special charisma and talents.

We each have our gifts. Whether you want to jump into the world with gusto or create a safe and nurturing home life, just be you. There's no wrong answer when you are doing what you enjoy and love. Please don't punish yourself or give yourself an F for telling others how you really feel. Individuals who feel comfortable being themselves often have the most fulfilling lives. Rich, poor, or in between, they understand—be yourself, believe in yourself, and express your innate personality.

Make Your Dreams Come True

Your goals are defined by you. You decide what is most meaningful to you. It's no secret that people with very few possessions are some of the happiest individuals on the planet. It's also true that people with great wealth are some of the happiest people on the planet. These people are happy because they understand the secret to joy and inner fulfillment.

The goal is to make *your* dreams come true. Maximize the inner strength of believing that your dreams can come true. The world is not against you—it is simply moving at its own pace and doing its own thing.

Think back to these seven strategies to fulfill your dreams:

1. You are in control of your thoughts.
2. Your thoughts can create tangible things.
3. Your thoughts are fluid; they're not static or rigid.
4. You are the source of your happiness.
5. Having a life with few regrets comes from making wise choices.
6. You have inner resources, talents, and intuitive capabilities.
7. Be yourself. Believe in yourself.

WRIGHT

That is very interesting. This whole conversation has been extremely interesting and I would like to thank you for taking all of this time to answer these questions for me. It's been absolutely fascinating and I know our readers are going to use a lot of this information to strengthen their own lives.

HAYNES

Thank you. That is the goal.

WRIGHT

Today we have been talking with Jessica Haynes. Jessica is a business and relationship consultant who specializes in helping individuals maximize their goals. She counsels Fortune 500 business leaders, well-known personalities, entrepreneurs, and those who are seeking to improve the quality of their lives and their relationships. Whether she's talking about career goals, relationships, or finding your purpose, she connects you with your most valuable resource—*you*.

Jessica, thank you so much for being with us today on *Discover Your Inner Strength.*

HAYNES

It has been a pleasure David, and thank you for participating.

WRIGHT

You're more than welcome.

About the Author

Jessica A. Haynes is a business and relationship consultant who specializes in helping individuals realize their goals. In the realm of maximizing one's potential, she is known and respected for her ability to help individuals find success, fulfillment, and inner strength. Jessica has been a motivational and self-empowerment speaker for the past twenty years. Using her psychology degree, marketing background, and business networking skills, she consults with a steady clientele both nationally and internationally. She counsels Fortune 500 business leaders, well-known personalities, entrepreneurs, and those seeking to improve the quality of their lives and their relationships. Her book *Get What You Want Now: Money, Love, Power, and More . . .* has received praise and highly supportive reviews from her clients and is now available to the general public. Her keynote message of "How to Create and Live the Life You Want" has helped many thousands to reshape their lives and live their dreams. She's proven that it is possible to get what you want.

Jessica A. Haynes
P.O. Box 1363
Carmel, CA 93921
831-455-2585
JessicaAHaynes.com
bcandjh@comcast.net

Discover Your Inner Strength

Keeping His Fire Alive Within

*As a deer longs for flowing streams,
so my soul longs for you, O God.—Psalm 42:1*

An Interview With…
Jeanne M. Harper

DAVID WRIGHT (WRIGHT)

Today we are talking with Jeanne M. Harper. Harper compassionately and effectively addresses issues of life, grief, and death in a participative, creative, and practical style for the public and professionals as a life coach, spiritual director, retreat director, professional speaker, and consultant. Before retirement as a psychotherapist in 2008, she specialized in trauma counseling for twenty-eight years. Since 2000, she has served as a Vincentian for the Society of St. Vincent de Paul. She has authored numerous published articles, a book, *Hurting Yourself: After an Attempt,* and a chapter in the acclaimed book, *Death & Spirituality.* Through thirty-three years of speaking, counseling, and coaching, she considers herself privileged to journey with others as they turn their "problems" into "creative opportunities for growth." Her Vincentian mission is to journey with and help those she works with to find the inspiration within themselves to move forward in life. Jeanne encourages the celebration and appreciation of life—every moment!

Jeanne, welcome to *Discover Your Inner Strength.*

When did you first discover your inner strength?

JEANNE M. HARPER (HARPER)

Historically, when I first discovered I had inner strength, I was about ten years old and my newest brother was just born. My mom had a difficult delivery during which she "put her back out" and was in traction for about three months after he was born.

During that time, I brought my baby brother, Jeff, to Mom for nursing. I changed his diapers and I did the best I could to take care of my three other siblings, ages two, five, and eight. Even then I realized that I needed to find time for myself. Some days I looked at the situation as a real problem and other days I was able to see the benefits—the opportunities for me to learn more and grow more as a person.

I remember Dad putting a hook lock on the inside of our closet door so that I could go inside and my little siblings could not bother me. The closet gave me what God knew I needed for His reasons—so that I could grow in my closeness to His Son. This experience was the beginning of a phenomenal relationship. This began my journey inward to truly discover my inner strength—my inner guide(s).

In that closet, I read many books about underwater adventure and saints' biographies. I also pictured myself in this special space, with my older brother, Jesus, who was interested in just being with me. I began my first journals in this closet. My innermost thoughts were on those many pages. I could tell when I was in a *"zone,"* with His Holy Spirit guiding as the words would fly onto the pages. Afterward, I would read them and wonder how they got written—lots of deep questions about life.

During this time, all I ever wanted to be was a nun, just like the visiting Sisters of St. Joseph of Carondolet. In eighth grade, I went to their motherhouse in St. Louis and they informed me I had to finish high school, then I could come back. Throughout high school, I continued journaling and spending time just going inside myself.

Now, as an adult, I look back on this important experience and I cannot even imagine being my mom with five children, a new baby, and unable to get out of bed! Can you imagine the "tapes" in her head? She had to watch me care for my baby brother, she had to see and hear the needs of the rest of my siblings, and through all of this she had to deal with her limitations of not being able to get up! Mom always said, "God was helping her all the time." I have a greater appreciation for that acute awareness of the presence of God that she spoke of during this experience.

I now realize what a tremendous gift my parents were as powerful role models of fire-filled living. My mom had great inner strength, warm enthusiasm, and genuine optimism as she wrote poems about her faith and raised the five of us children despite her many medical challenges. My dad was charismatic in his belief in the Lord, a hard worker and provider, as well as committed to having *fun* with his family. One example was Dad rebuilding my cousin's retired school bus into a "house on wheels" so that we could go camping every weekend throughout the summer.

WRIGHT

What did you discover as you journeyed inward?

HARPER

Discovering my inner strength started by discerning within myself what God wanted me to do with my life. In this process, which encompasses over fifty-two additional years, I discovered many articles, quotes, songs, and books that played a role in helping me with this process. Since I became a Vincentian in 2000—a member of The Society of St. Vincent de Paul—I have grown in my inner strength and found new ways to discern what God wants for me in my life. Maybe they will be helpful for others as well.

WRIGHT

How did you keep God's energy alive and growing within?

HARPER

Some of the articles and books that came into my life were read cover-to-cover and with others, just a few pages gave me what I needed. I would like to share some of the process I discovered as I went about keeping God's fire—God's energy—alive within my heart, mind, body, and soul.

One of the most recent books that was helpful in discovering my inner strength was *Hearing with the Heart: A Gentle Guide to Discerning God's Will for Your Life* by Debra K. Farrington. On page four, Farrington states, *"Hearing with the Heart is hearing with compassion and knowing God's will (the heart) is the center of the whole human being . . . emotions, feelings, moods, passions, thought, understanding and wisdom . . . a place where real knowledge and conversion take place."*

St. Vincent de Paul is often quoted on this subject: *"We must begin by establishing the kingdom of God in ourselves and only then in others . . . tend to our interior life . . . if we fail to do that, we miss everything!"*

Blessed Frederic Ozanam, charismatic founder of The Society of St. Vincent de Paul, wrote on November 4, 1834, to Leonce Curnier at Lyon in *A Life of Letters*, *"Besides, in such a work* [serving those living in poverty and/or desperate need] *it is necessary to give yourself up to the inspirations of the heart rather than the calculations* of the mind. *Providence gives its own counsel through the circumstances around you and ideas it bestows on you. I believe you would do well to follow them freely . . . it* [charity] *is a fire that dies without being fed, and good works are the food of charity"* (page 55).

Blessed Frederic is often quoted as well on the subject of interior discernment: *"Without the detachment and humility, which empties us of Self, we cannot truly live in Christ nor can Christ act in us. It is in the emptying of self that Christ not only dwells, but acts and bears fruit."*

St. Louise de Marillac would quote *Galatians 2:20*, *"I live now, not I, but Christ lives in me."* Mary, the Blessed Mother, gave *life* to Jesus *first* in her *heart* and then in her body. So we too can emulate this by giving life to Jesus in our *heart*, as St. Louise and the Blessed Mother did. We are called to serve the poor both corporally and spiritually, seeing Christ in them. St. Louise would say, *"The charity of Christ crucified urges us a call to do the will of God and call to imitate Jesus' ministry of loving service to one's neighbor."*

St. Therese of Lisieux teaches how she listened to the voice of God in *A little White Flower*, *"I know and have experienced that 'the Kingdom of God is within us,' that our Master has no need of books or teacher to instruct a soul. The Teacher of teachers instructs without sound of words, and though I have never heard Him speak, yet I know He is within me, always guiding and inspiring me; and just when I need them, lights, hitherto unseen, break in upon me. As a rule, it is not during prayer that this happens, but in the midst of my daily duties"* (page 173).

Mother Teresa, in *Words to Love By*, wrote, *"The beginning of prayer is scripture . . . we listen to God speaking . . . and silence . . . God speaking in the silence of the heart. And then we start talking to God from the fullness of the heart. And He listens. That is really prayer. Both sides listening and both sides speaking"* (page 40).

John O'Donahue, Irish poet/priest/philosopher, wrote about the importance of hearing with your heart your own "interiority:" *"You should belong* first *in your own interiority. If you belong there . . . then you will never be vulnerable when your outside belonging is qualified, relativized, or taken away."*

Henry J. van Dyke wrote the song about what happens in discovering your inner strength in the process of discovery and discernment:

"Joyful, joyful, we adore Thee, God of glory, Lord of love;
Hearts unfold like flowers before Thee, opening to the sun above.
Melt the clouds of sin and sadness; drive the dark of doubt away;
Giver of immortal gladness, fill us with the light of day!
. . . Teach us how to love each other. Lift us to the joy divine."

Henry's words truly release that *joy* within when sung with your heart and soul!

Finally, Dom Jean-Baptiste Chautard, OCSO, in *The Soul of the Apostolate*, writes about St. Gregory the Great who believed that "life is always essentially a mixture of contemplation [love of God] and action [love of neighbor]." Chautard writes about the deep call from within "to remain always united with Him who love me." Chautard writes about this "interior life" that we are to develop, discover, and/or discern: ". . . *Our 'word' is the interior spirit formed, by* grace, *in our souls. Let this spirit, then, give life to all the manifestations of our zeal, but, though poured out unceasingly for the benefit of our neighbors, let it be renewed likewise without ceasing, by the means which Jesus offers us for this purpose. Our interior life ought to be the stem, filled with vigorous sap, of which our works are the flowers! The soul of an apostle—it should be flooded first of all with* light *and* inflamed *with* love, *so that, reflecting that* light *and that* heat, *it may enlighten and give warmth to other souls as well. That which they have heard, which they have seen with their eyes, which they have looked upon, and their hands have almost handled,* this *will they teach to men [and women]"* (page 51).

WRIGHT

After reading these types of reflections, what do you find yourself doing?

HARPER

The first thing I do when wanting to discover my inner strength is to organize things around me and, in doing so, prayer becomes the reflection. Prayer and praying for me can occur in other ways as well—one word focus, a reflection prayer, reciting a memorized prayer, silence, in the middle of doing daily activities, nature (viewing or being in it—especially by water or watching a sunset or sunrise), Lectio Divina (Divine Reading), music, movement, dance, song, prayerful conversation with God, journaling, etc.

WRIGHT

How do you discover the "child of God" in yourself and in others?

HARPER

One of my prayer reflections is one written for a *"Vincentian heart"*—for me it is in hearing myself through the eyes of my heart that I am able then to witness God and feel His "fire within." Then, with joy, I am able to experience the compassion of God and begin to see, through the eyes of God, the face of Christ *within myself*—seeing me as a child of God as well as in the faces of those living in poverty or despair during the home visits that I go to as a Vincentian.

WRIGHT

What do you need to do to keep His "fire" alive within?

HARPER

One of the core values of Vincentians is to "grow in holiness" of life. Growth in intimacy with Jesus is experienced as a life-long process—prayer is essential—both personal and communal. Also in Lumen Gentium, it shares this "growing in holiness" as "the foundational challenge for all." Blessed Frederic said, *"The poor will disturb our consciences . . . it is* they *who can light a* fire, *which does not go out!"* St. Vincent de Paul says, *"Lord Jesus, teach me by your example. Make me, through the vigor of my efforts,* set the world on fire. *I want to give myself to You, body and soul, heart and mind, and spirit so that I may always do what gladdens You. In Your mercy, grant me the grace to have You continue in me and through me Your saving work."*

In order to set the world on fire—the fire must be within me—I must see and experience this within myself. Then, and *only* then, can I bring it to those I serve. St. Paul says this clearly—that we cannot give what we do not have. I remember a song that filled me and reconnected me to God—my inner strength: "Spirit of the living God, fall afresh on me. Spirit of the living God, fall afresh on me. Melt me, mold me, fill me, use me." If we do not believe we are a Child of God, then we cannot believe that those we visit are Children of God. I cannot give what I do not have.

There is a common prayer, *To Be a Disciple of Jesus Christ,* and it reflects this desire for the "fire in the belly" experience:

"Lord God, you who provide the fire *for a transformed life, I come before you this day and beg for* the fire of your love *and mercy to forgive my sins and free me from my self-imposed bondages. I pray for the* fire of your Spirit *to lead me in repentance and conversion so I may be faithful in following you. I pray for the* fire of your love *to ignite my heart with love for my brothers and sisters and lead me to intercede in faith for them. I pray for the* fire of faith *to be committed to you and your teaching as a servant to his Master. I pray for the* fire of Your desire *to save all mankind to inflame me so that I can witness to the Good News of Jesus Christ and be a channel for the salvation of mankind. Lord, I want to burn for you before all peoples. Amen."*

Through a variety of prayers, I reignite God's *fire within.* One such Vincentian prayer is written by Sr. Kieran Kneaves of the National Society of St. Vincent de Paul in St. Louis, Missouri:

"Lord, we ask for the grace to have a Vincentian heart. We give you our gifts and talents, our dreams and visions so that we may carry the mission of St. Vincent to the poor . . . Lord, we ask for the grace to have hearts of love and compassion, so that we may bring your mercy to the broken hearts of the poor . . . Blessed are You, God of Unconditional Love, help us to believe in ourselves as You believe in us. Help us to see our potential as You see it, as we work together as members of the Society of St. Vincent de Paul. Blessed are You, God of Providence, for You challenge us to constantly move beyond our pasts and call us into fresh possibilities for the future . . . And give us all a Vincentian heart, as we pray: Lord Jesus, you willed to become poor, give us eyes and a heart directed toward the poor; help us to recognize you in them—in their thirst, their hunger, their loneliness, and their misfortune. Enkindle within our Vincentian Family, unity, simplicity, humility, and the fire of love that burned in St. Vincent de Paul. . . . Amen" (Vincentian Celebrations and Rituals, pp. 151–152, Sr. Kieran, National SSVdP).

WRIGHT

Why is the heart so connected to the discovery of your inner strength?

HARPER

In *Awakening your Soul to the Presence of God* by Kilian J. Healy, Fr. Healy writes that *"God enters our hearts and inspires us to holy desires"* (page 56). Father quotes from Acts 16:14: *"And a certain woman named Lydia, a seller of purple, from the city of Thyatira, who worshiped God, was listening; and the Lord* touched her heart *to give heed to what was being said by Paul."*

Just as Farrington, in *Hearing with the Heart,* shared *"real knowledge and conversion take place—[in the heart]."* *"Thus,"* Father Healy writes, *"the Scriptures and the Church tell us that God* speaks to us in the silence of our minds and hearts. He speaks to all men [and women], *but all men* [and women] *do* not *hear Him . . . It is He who stirs up within us the desire to persevere against all adversaries."* So true has this been for me.

WRIGHT

What life experiences have helped you develop and discover your inner strength?

HARPER

My life experiences of cancer and treatment (twice) and more than twenty surgeries for arthritis, injury, biopsies, emergency, etc. have shown me that I will persevere if *"I dance in the darkness, slow be the pace, surrender to the rhythm of redeeming Grace"* (quoting Joe Wise). When I would lay in the hospital bed (once for three months), I would repeat this refrain, over and over so that I could get above the physical pain from the surgeries, the emotional pain of the depression, and the spiritual pain of not being able to be on my feet serving my husband and two little children.

My Spiritual director, then Fr. Robert Morneau (now Bishop Morneau), encouraged me to "take my scars and turn them into stars to shine light on the path for those who would follow." I truly believe that my hundreds of presentations throughout the last thirty-two years have done just that. This chapter has again offered me the opportunity to shine the light on those who read this chapter.

I remember talking with my daughter, Lisa, who was then in college, after some of the treatments with Dr. Thomas Stone, Mary, and Mary Ellen (his special gifted nurses). He was a world-renowned environmental specialist. Lisa and I would just talk about how God directed me to Dr. Stone and what a gift he was in my life and ultimately in my children's lives. During this time of painful treatments, my friend, Ellen Zinner, wrote to me during this time, *"Jeanne, you have an indomitable spirit that soars through adversities."* Her gift of this statement and her project to sending "round red and white blood cells" to all my friends throughout the world so that they could write and send me a message of courage and support" has truly gifted my life.

A few years later, I was named a keynote for the Chicago Conference of the Association for Death Education and Counseling (ADEC) after Ellen's card and project. Ellen, Rob Stevenson, and his high school students and the other ADEC members had truly helped me discover my inner strength through their support and love. I named the keynote *"Persevering through Adversity: Circles of Love, Rays of Hope, Winds of Life."* Rob and his students took up collections to assist with some of the medical bills. They would write me letters that moved my soul. They too sent me red and white blood cells. Their reaching out touched my heart and later I learned, for some, it was just as important to them. Some of my co-workers and clients covered my office with copies of red blood cells on white paper and vice versa—the ceiling, doors, windows, filing cabinets, and every inch of the walls—all were "decorated."

I was to go to Australia to present on "Reintegration After a Suicide" and Dr. Stone encouraged me to *persevere*—to hang on. He said if I gave up on the trip, my body might also give up on me, so I hung to the possibility of going. I did go and presented, knowing it was truly a gift from God to be there! I remember chancing everything and deep-sea diving on the Great Barrier Reef! It was so amazing! Perseverance had brought me to this place.

Another time in my life, I developed spinal meningitis and encephalitis and was out of work for six months. I was driven to Chicago by my son, Michael, who was on winter layoff from his construction job. We would go to the Chicago suburb, Palatine, for treatments with Nurse Mary and Mary Ellen and Dr. Thomas Stone during the week. Then, on the weekends, I was receiving home nursing care twice a day for intravenous treatments.

My exceptional doctor told me to *not* give up. "Work on the keynote," he would say, "it will help your mind focus." This was all very difficult, for some of the time I could not even talk in complete sentences or make any sense or remember anything. So to imagine I could stand in front of hundreds of attendees and present the keynote seemed absolutely absurd. But life is about making a *world* of difference.

About *choice* being the *"lifeblood of my soul."* Mother Teresa wrote, *". . . unless we change our hearts we are not converted. . . ."* Referencing Pope John Paul II's call to "live in a constant state of conversion," Mother Teresa wrote, *"All souls need to be converted. And if they accept God in their lives they are converted. To grow in holiness is a sign of conversion. To grow in likeness of Christ is a sign of conversion."* Jennifer, a friend who agreed to edit this material, suggests, "Mercy is always the motive for conversion."

For me, this is what occurred—a change of heart, a conversion, a growth in holiness, a positive attitude, and a gratitude for the experience. I had again discovered my inner strength! Tommy Newberry, in *The 4:8 Principle: The Secret to a Joy-Filled Life*, states, *"Gratitude is the cornerstone of an unstoppable attitude. Gratitude can be cultivated and then experienced at ever-deepening levels."* I became full of gratitude for everything, no matter what. I worked on the keynote daily—preparing PowerPoint slides, writing my speaker's notes—so that if I could not remember the words, the words would be written! The Scriptures exhort us to "give thanks and *praise in all things."*

The idea of choice being the *"lifeblood of my soul"* came to me while receiving my home nursing care treatments and realizing I had the *opportunity* to see my illness as a problem or to see it as a *"Creative Opportunity for Growth."* I had a *choice*, much as I had discovered when only ten and during other times in my life. My attitude was what was getting me through the adversities. My discovering my inner strength was the key to my positive attitude—my attitude of a cup being half full! The *choice* came in my prayerful reflections—the *choice* became the *"lifeblood of my soul."* I truly believe this was an incredible experience in *"hearing with the heart,"* of discovering my inner strength, of discerning what God wanted for me—being a Child of God, unconditionally loved and cherished and given *free will* to make this *choice* a positive one—one that would alter how I looked and experienced the world from that moment on, one that changed my heart forever. As Bishop Morneau had challenged me so many years before, to take these "scars" of living life and turn them into "stars" for those who follow.

I delivered that keynote and received two standing ovations! My sisters, Sue and Mik; brother, Jerry, and Kathy, his wife; nephews, Jon and Jeremy; godson, Dan; son, Michael; daughter, Lisa, and my husband (now of forty-three years), David—all were present in the front row to love and support me! It truly was a gift that I had that keynote to work on during a most difficult time in my life. The discovery of my inner strength did make a difference to those in the audience and to those who supported me throughout my life!

WRIGHT

How does "choice" affect your journey?

HARPER

Fr. Healy states that *"One way, then, to practice the exercise of the presence of God is to listen to God, to be aware that He speaks to us, to be ever conscious that God can use all things to communicate with us" ibid.,* p. 58. That is what I believe happened that day and many other days since then. God was using my illness experience to show me I had options as to how I experienced and understood this experience—the *choice* became the "*lifeblood of my soul.*" Father Healy continues*, "Day by day we must progress, seeing the hand of God in all things, being aware that He speaks to us, and manifests His will in the joys, sorrows, and circumstances of our daily life."* So true this has been for me! A. Heschel is quoted saying, *"It is through man* [and woman] *the cantor of the universe, that the secret cosmic prayer is disclosed."* Therefore, he is saying that God shares with us as partners, His prayer for us—His dream, His vision—and that it is in the "hearing with the heart" that this partnership becomes possible!

Pope John Paul II writes in Guaduim et Spes, "Man can fully discover his true self only in a sincere giving of himself . . ." I have been blessed ever since I was a child to experience that God's will for me has always been to serve others—husband, children, parents, neighbors, friends, church, community—so that serving the world as a Vincentian seems clear for me. This is what I am to be about. I pray daily and throughout the day for the gift Mother Teresa writes about: *"Just allow people to see Jesus in you, to see how you pray, to see how you lead a pure life, to see how you deal with your family, to see how much peace there is in your family. Then you can look straight into their eyes and say, 'This is the way.' You speak from life; you speak from experience . . . 'Love as I have loved you' "* (from *Words to Love By, page 15*).

In Vincentian work, we experience the suffering of those living in poverty and/or desperate need. We need to remember what Mother Teresa said, *"We will be judged by: 'I was hungry and you gave me to eat, I was naked and you clothed me, I was homeless and you took me in.' Hungry not only for bread—but hungry for love. Naked not only for clothing—but* naked of human dignity and respect. *Homeless not only for want of a room of bricks—but homeless because of rejection. This is Christ in distressing disguise."*

WRIGHT

What are some of the "gifts" you have experienced as your discovered your inner strength?

HARPER

I feel gifted by God to have been brought to the Vincentian mission work so that I too can imitate Christ in my daily living. Farrington, in *Hearing with the Heart*, writes, ". . . *in using our gifts we are following God's call. We gratefully use the gifts, given us by God, to be who we are called to be . . ." (page 77)*. This is in sync with my experience. She also writes, *"using our natural or inborn gifts . . . engages our joy, creativity, and energy."* Therefore, as Charles Bryant, in *Rediscovering Our Spiritual Gifts*, is quoted, we may *"wear out, but will never burn out . . ."* because, as Farrington writes, *"when we use our gifts . . . we feel alive and energized. The inner resources seem boundless and constantly refilled rather than depleted." After reading the first draft, my Aunt Joni suggested that it is better to "wear out" rather than "rust out" from not using our gifts!*

A "coincidence" that Farrington discusses for me is that Blessed Rosalie Rendu's birth name was *Jeanne Marie*. This is my birth name as well—Jeanne Marie. For me it is a unique confirmation of my path—it appears to me to be *"providential."* At the present time, like Blessed Rosalie, I meet with youth at the college, high school, and middle school levels. All are looking to grow in holiness—looking for ways to serve those living in poverty and/or desperate need. All desire commissioning as a Vincentian in April 2009.

Like the Rendu family, our home was a refuge for many priests and nuns, especially one poor soul, Fr. Bouche. My mother took him under her wings. He was very needy and appreciative of all the small things we did for him. With five children, we shared a meal anytime he stopped in. In retrospect, I believe he was very depressed. But he would always leave with a smile on his face and joy in his heart.

Like Sr. Rosalie, I taught catechism (religion, theology) from when I was in eighth grade. Throughout twenty years of our marriage, my husband and I together taught the high school students. As a child, the nuns felt I had a gift for witnessing my faith and sharing it with the young children. I also joined the convent, and was asked to leave because, true as it was, they felt I had too much energy and they did not feel my spirit would allow me to obey. Right they were! Thank goodness for their discernment of the situation, though it broke my heart at the time!

WRIGHT

How are you "keeping His fire alive" in your daily life?

HARPER

Sr. Rosalie experienced the conviction of St. Vincent that *"You will go and visit the poor ten times a day, and ten times a day you will find God there . . . you go into their poor homes, but you find God there."* I pray before, during, and after each home visit, that this will be the experience of my visits to those living in poverty and/or desperate need.

Doing Vincentian work, for me, has been discerned and continues to be discerned as a vocation, a calling, or as the Quakers call it, a "leading." Charlotte Fardelmann wrote in *Nudged by the Spirit: Stories of People Responding to the Still, Small Voice of God,* "A true leading touches a deep level in oneself. It resonates on the level with our deepest desires. When we talk about it to others, we show excitement."

As I present the Ozanam Orientation (a formation program for The Society), I have been told that "excitement" pours through my presentation as passion for the work!

Mother Teresa states *In the Heart of the World,* that once you have this calling, this vocation, *"the fullness of our heart is* expressed in our eyes, in our touch, in what we write, in what we say, in the way we walk, the way we receive, the way we serve. That is *the fullness of our heart expressing itself in many different ways . . ."*

Quoting Romano Guardini, Bishop Robert Morneau, my spiritual director during some of my earlier years, writes in *Mantras for the Morning,* in expressing to the next level what Mother Teresa is speaking, *"A man can look at another with a look that hardens the other's heart. A man can look at another with curiosity, with lust or malice, with a look that hurts and destroys, with a look that forces the other to resist. A man can look at another with cold indifference, humiliating and degrading the other. A man can also look at another with reverence, and when that happens, the other will be given freedom and opportunity to be himself. A man can look at another with kindness and goodness, with a look that encourages and loves, that opens up what is locked up inside the other, that awakens his powers and brings him to himself."*

Bishop Morneau also quotes Simone Weil on this subject, *"This way of looking is first of all attentive. The soul empties itself of all its own contents in order to receive into itself the being it is looking at, just as he is, in all his truth."*

WRIGHT

What recommendations would you give to others who want to discover their own inner strength?

HARPER

It takes a large step forward in holiness when you are discerning your vocation. Realizing that the way you look, walk, serve, receive—everything you do—*must* show the *love* of God and His Son, Jesus Christ, to those you are called to serve.

Internal Family Systems© (IFS) theory, developed by Richard Schwartz, is something that helped me along the way in discovering my inner strength. It helped me to understand how sometimes I could have such hardened ways with some, and with others I could show and reflect the face of Christ. To know I had these *"parts"* within me that could be so hurtful to others created anxiety within me. After numerous experiences of suffering in my life, I learned to listen to my parts and to "hear [them] with my heart."

I became so very grateful to the IFS process. A major assumption is the concept that our mind is *naturally* divided into parts. Parts demonstrate different beliefs, feelings, thoughts, sensations, behaviors, temperaments, talents, desires, ages, and gender. Dr. Schwartz writes, "another assumption is that the parts form an internal family system within *you*. Each part, in its non-extreme state, wants what is *best* for *you.*"

More on IFS Theory: Dr. Schwartz names the various parts. "Exiles" are usually very young, vulnerable parts that hold stories. "Managers" are those parts that may scare the Self into thinking it *needs* the Manager to protect us from feeling or experiencing other parts—either our exiles or our "firefighters"—and once we begin to feel our exiles, our firefighters are parts that get us to do things to avoid feeling the anticipated pain and suffering from the exile parts, such as using drugs or alcohol, shopping, gambling, cleaning, anything to avoid feeling or hearing the story of the exile parts. "Manager" parts may try to keep things in control—pushing or hard working. They may be very organized. They tend to be articulate, intelligent, and energetic. They may appear normal, successful, and independent, but they may not allow your other parts to *experience* the vulnerable burdens it may carry. Exiles can be easily overwhelmed and can carry *burdens*—worthlessness, perfectionism, sadness, pain, shame, responsibility, etc. Exiles may have positive, hidden, or expressed parts—joy, hope, playfulness, humor, freedom, creativity.

Dick gives us the following example of IFS: "It is like a well directed orchestra. Each part with unique talent, playing its special piece at the right time; in unison and harmony with others, discovering each its own vision and preferred roles, allowing the core Self—the Self leader—to be the conductor who has established credibility, trust, and a shared vision with each part."

Internal Family Systems is an applied systems thinking and technique to be used in the human system "within us." It is *more* than a set of techniques . . . it is a way of thinking about the world and people. The *"system,"* Dick says, is *"You"* and *"Your"* human system within. IFS therapy restores balance and harmony to our Self, releasing our Natural Healing Capacity.

WRIGHT

Are there different ways or thoughts of understanding "the Self" and of "hearing with the heart"?

HARPER

"The Self," Dr. Schwartz writes, "is natural . . . an innate resource we have within us from birth. The 'parts' develop as we encounter life." I see this innate resource as being developed as a result of our partnership with God, wherein the

Self becomes fully enflamed with the Love of God so that it becomes God's hands, feet, and voice to those we serve.

Speaking of the self-concept, Aldous Huxley said there is *"in the soul something similar to, or even identical with divine Reality."* Huston Smith (1989) expands on this, saying, *"Unconsciously dwelling at our inmost center; beneath the surface shuttlings of our sensations, precepts, and thoughts; wrapped in the envelope or soul . . . is the eternal and the divine, the final Reality; not soul, not personality, but All-Self beyond all selfishness; spirit enwombed in matter."* It is in this sacred space that we discover our inner strength.

Smith says *". . . spirit is the Atman that is Brahman, the Buddha-nature that appears when our finite selves get out of its way."* Fr. Thomas Keating says the practice of contemplative prayer *"begins to make us aware of the divine presence within us, the source of true happiness."* Grigg, in *The Tao of Zen* writes, *"Tso-wang, sitting with blank mind, finding the mind within the mind—the still place in the center of consciousness."* Habakkuk 2:1–2, is about how Habakkuk was going to *"open the eyes of his heart, and look into the spirit world to see what God wanted to show him."* Zechariah 7:11 says, *"Render the hearts of this people insensitive, their ears dull. And their eyes dim. Otherwise, they might see with their eyes. Hear with their ears. Understand with their hearts. And return and be healed."* So if we did come to *"understand with our hearts,"* we could be healed, according to Scripture.

"Hearing with the heart" (according to http://sfhelp.org/pop2/listen.htm) is to *"empathically sense what our partner* [God] *thinks, feels, needs, and perceives now without judgment."* What a powerful experience that can be—to sit in this *"cathedral"* space listening to our Lord and with our Lord listening to us speak.

WRIGHT

How does one truly listen to the inner self so to develop hope within?

HARPER

In prayer, in silence, I became aware of my "parts within." I was fortunate to have a spiritual director/guide through these processes, Sherry Graham Nelson—another Gift from God in my life! In *The Rule of the Society of St. John the Evangelist* she wrote, *"Silence is a constant source of restoration. Yet its healing power does not come cheaply. It depends on our willingness to face all that is within us, light and dark, and to heed all the inner voices [parts] that make themselves heard in silence."*

My authentic self for me is the self I am as a Child of God connected directly to the power of the Holy Spirit within my very own "cathedral." For me, listening—truly listening—in self energy (the co-creation of God and me) through the voices and into the silence, I was able to seek what IFS theory refers to as my exile parts and began recognizing my manager parts who were working overtime believing they were protecting me from these exile parts, as well as understanding the process of how and when my firefighter parts were being activated and how they thought they needed to derail my attention from the pain and suffering, hurt and anger of my exile parts.

Through this process, I recognized that in discovering my inner strength, when God and I become partners and I sit in the Self Energy (one of Curiosity, Compassion, Calmness, Clarity, Confidence, Courage, Creativity, Connectedness, etc.), my inner voices/resources can be heard. Ephesians 1:18, states that the inner Self comes alive, *"so that, with eyes of your heart enlightened, you may know what the hope to which He has called you is."*

Portia Nelson wrote a great *Autobiography in Five Short Chapters* about the process of listening and hearing our parts and coming to an understanding as to why they acted as they had in the past. It is amazing how this short poem catches the meaning behind parts, works, and the option of freewill given by God to us—*choice*. Choice is truly a gift from God to see things as Creative Opportunities for Growth instead of Problems:

Jeanne M. Harper

I

I walk down the street.
There is a deep hole in the sidewalk
I fall in.
I am lost . . . I am helpless.
It isn't my fault.
It takes me forever to find a way out.

II

I walk down the same street.
There is a deep hole in the sidewalk.
I pretend I don't see it.
I fall in again.
I can't believe I am in the same place
but, it isn't my fault.
It still takes a long time to get out.

III

I walk down the same street.
There is a deep hole in the sidewalk.
I see it is there.
I still fall in . . . it's a habit.
My eyes are open
I know where I am.
It is my fault.
I get out immediately.

IV

I walk down the same street.
There is a deep hole in the sidewalk.
I walk around it.

V
I walk down another street.

WRIGHT

What last reminders do you have for those beginning this journey to discovering their inner strength and learning to keep the fire alive within themselves?

HARPER

Benjamin Disraeli states, *"We are not creatures of circumstance, we are creators of circumstance."* So it is God and we as partners, as we listen in Self during the discovering or discernment process, we hear those inner voices/parts and it is by *choice* we become *creators* in this life we live—energized and peace-filled and no longer "creatures" reacting to our parts' needs. Marcus Aurelius is quoted saying *"Life is what our thoughts make of it!"* So *choice* is and can be the "lifeblood" of your soul! The choice is yours! An ancient Chinese proverb says, *"Whatever is Flexible and Flowing will tend to Grow. Whatever is Rigid and Blocked will Wither and Die."* So choosing to be flexible and flowing can become our practice in discernment.

Ira Progoff, in *The Well and the Cathedral,* talks about going deep within into the "Cathedral" that is within each of us, there is the presence of God, or a "higher power" as some may name. Through the discovery or discernment process, *"Disruptions that seem to be disasters at the time, end by redirecting our lives in a meaningful way,"* writes Bernie S. Siegel, MD, a physician who worked with living-dying patients.

Catherine Taylor in *The Inner Child Workbook,* states, *"It is our choice to become a student of our suffering, rather than a victim to our pain!"* My friend, Jennifer, in reflection on the "suffering," states ". . . as a Christian, it is in our weakness that God's power is most manifest." Jimmy Dean continues, "You cannot change the direction of the wind, but you can adjust your sails to always reach your destination." So it is that when disasters occur in our lives and we go within to discover our inner strength or to seek discernment, we have choices to continue in the same direction the storm of life has paved for us, or adjust our sail and get back on track to what we believe and know to be our path in life.

In *Hearing with the Heart,* Farrington talks about the body and how it needs to be noticed and to be heard, as well as, *"learn prayer practices and* attentiveness to our bodies, *dreams, gifts, all of which help us listen for, understand, and open up to God's call."*

In IFS, we recognize that our parts can create havoc within our body system, making them ill, creating feelings of pain, or just carrying the pain of the trauma within—an environment vulnerable to disease later in life.

Therefore, the process of going into discovery or discernment and "hearing with the heart" is clearly a way of healing our parts and getting all of them onto the same page so that we have the renewed energy that comes from using our gifts to better the world within us and around us! Learning to sit in Self—just you and God—listening to your inner voices (parts), it begins to feel like a metamorphosis is occurring. You are the same, yet different, from crawling around, lost in your own world to coming to know yourself better than ever before and feeling a sense of *freedom, peace, hope,* and renewed energy to continue the work of serving those living in poverty and/or desperate need.

WRIGHT

What are your closing beliefs or statements you would like to share?

HARPER

I recognize the path for my spiritual direction is in the hands of the Lord, and, as Mother Teresa said, *"I begin by picking up one person—maybe if I didn't pick up that one person I wouldn't have picked up 42,000."* Therefore, I begin by making one home visit as a Vincentian and measuring that against what I know true discovery or discernment is—that to which we are called, as listed in Galatians: *"love, joy, peace, patience, kindness, generosity, faithfulness, gentleness, and self-control."*

I believe wholeheartedly that serving those living in poverty and/or desperate need through the Vincentian mission is "the hope of God"! St. Vincent said, *"Let us love God, my brothers* [and sisters], *let us love God, but let it be through the works of your hands, let it be by the sweat of our brow."* Sr. Rosalie reminds us that the poor are our *"lords and masters."* She would say, *"The poor will insult you. The ruder they are, the more dignified you must be; Remember, Our Lord hides behind those rags."*

There is a prayer for the Fire of Vincentian Charism that I have come to appreciate. It speaks about the discovery of your inner strength—and His *fire* of renewed energy:

"O God, your love ignites our hearts, captures our imaginations, shapes our dreams, and awakens possibilities. Make us disciples on fire with your love so that we can become true followers of St. Vincent de Paul. Help us, O God, to enkindle in others a sense of hope that transformation is possible . . . and give us the Grace to transmit to others the Fire of the Charism of St. Vincent.

"When the heart is on fire, light comes from within. With the eyes of an enlightened heart we can see the hope to which we are called. By responding to the call to be a Vincentian, we proclaim that the quest to be a servant of the poor is the fire of our lives.

"The path to seeing with the eyes of the heart is discovered in the journey of discipleship. It is not an easy journey. It is an ongoing effort to live the Gospel with integrity—always trying, sometimes succeeding, often failing, recognizing the need for patience, and then trying again.

". . . We remember those in our lives today, whose flaming hearts have encouraged and touched us on our journey. God of Fire, fuel us into thankfulness.

". . . May God the Father who made us, bless us. May God the Son send His grace among us. May the Holy Spirit move within us and give us eyes that see, ears that hear, hearts that love, and hands that do God's work.

"May the God of peace watch over us and lead us as we walk together, as Vincentians, into the future. Amen" (*Vincentian Celebrations & Rituals* p. 150. Sr. Kieran, National SSVdP).

There is a song refrain in Babbie Mason's album, *The Finest Hour* (2000), written by Babbie Mason and Cheryl Rogers, *"We can make a world of difference, with the love of God we can change this world. We can shine the light that overcomes the darkness. Spreading* hope *across the land. Heart to Heart and hand in hand. We can make a World of difference."* I believe that the difference I am to make in the world is through The Society of St. Vincent de Paul, serving those living in poverty and/or desperate need.

How will you make a difference? The world is waiting! The world is your stage! Find your inner strength and move it into action to better our world! It can only become a reality one person at a time. The psalmist writes in Psalm 46:10, "Be still and know that I am God." And finally, Mother Teresa reflects the important process of moving "inside" to discover your inner strength:

> "In the silence of the heart, God speaks.
> Let God fill us, then only we speak.
> Do small things with great love.
> The Fruit of Silence . . . is prayer.
> The Fruit of Prayer . . . is faith.
> The Fruit of Faith . . . is love.
> The Fruit of Love . . . is service"

About the Author

Jeanne Harper compassionately and effectively addresses issues of life, grief, and death in a participative, creative, and practical style for the public and professionals as a life coach, adjunct faculty member, group facilitator, spiritual director, retreat director, professional speaker, and consultant. Before retirement as a psychotherapist in 2008, she specialized in trauma counseling for twenty-eight years. She has authored numerous published articles, a book *Hurting Yourself: After an Attempt* and a chapter in the acclaimed book, *Death & Spirituality*. Through thirty-three years of speaking, counseling, and coaching, she considers herself privileged to journey with others as they turn their "problems" into "creative opportunities for growth."

Jeanne is currently journeying with sociology students at Northeast Wisconsin Technical College as they learn about the filters through which they see the world and our social issues. She is also involved with the Wisconsin Department of Corrections and currently facilitates groups for those on probation or parole, helping them "discover their inner strength" so they can better their lives and the world around them.

Her mission is to journey with and help those she works with to find the inspiration within themselves to move forward in life. Jeanne encourages the celebration and appreciation of life—every moment!

Jeanne M. Harper, MPS, BCETS, FT, DAPA

Alpha Omega Venture
1113 Elizabeth Avenue
Marinette WI 54143-2514
715-923-9549
jmharper1964@gmail.com

DISCOVER your INNER Strength 5

The Secret to Sustainable Success

An Interview With...
Blaine Bartlett

DAVID WRIGHT (WRIGHT)

Today we're talking with Blaine Bartlett. Blaine is an internationally respected and sought-after executive coach, management consultant, and leadership and organizational development expert. His programs and processes are known for their practicality and applicability to the needs and objectives of his clients. He has consulted, developed training programs, and coached executives at some of the most successful companies on the planet. He is a guest lecturer at China's prestigious Tsing Hua University, been a featured speaker at numerous international world congresses, including the World Congress of Human Resource Management and the World Consortium for Research and Development of Training. He's also a member of the Transformational Leadership Council, a group of CEOs, thought leaders, and educators founded by *Chicken Soup for the Soul* author, Jack Canfield.

Blaine, welcome to *Discover Your Inner Strength.*

BLAINE BARTLETT (BARTLETT)

David, thank you for having me; it's a pleasure to be here.

WRIGHT

So sustaining success in life can seem like the ultimate in elusive grails. To begin with, how do you define it?

BARTLETT

I think I'll approach answering that question by focusing on the two pieces that really make it up—sustaining and success.

In approaching sustainability first, the question is really about how do we sustain anything in life? I think what happens with a lot of people and a lot of organizations is that once we've achieved some success in life we tend to look for what it was that got us that modicum of success. We begin to look for what the "secret sauce" is and what the code is. The thinking is that if we can just crack the code or learn the sauce's secret recipe, then we can just replicate it. That does not work in our experience. Literally, the way we define sustainability in our work with our clients is that it's about developing the capacity and the competencies necessary to *continuously start over*. If I really understand this definition of "sustainable," it makes it possible for me to continuously look for what I need to hold on to, let go of, or take on in order to start over (and I'll talk more about this in a moment). The starting over piece is really what we're paying attention to here. So that's part of the sustainability portion of your question.

The other part of your question has to do with success. I think success has been overly defined—everybody's got a definition of it. That being said, I will do my best to provide a definition that is consistent with our work with clients. I think that success is ultimately about the dual experiences of both mattering and fulfillment. The bottom line is I think the question that determines if I'm successful in life or not or successful in any endeavor is "was I used well"? Were we used well? "Used well" is a criterion that assesses both "did I matter?" as well as "am I fulfilled as a consequence of what I've done?" So being used well is what we track for. Success is sustainable in the sense that it happens when I am in the process of continuously starting over *in service of* answering the question am I (or are we) being used well by whatever endeavor I/we are involved with.

WRIGHT

That's a really different definition than I've heard.

So when you say "start over," what exactly are you talking about?

BARTLETT

I'll come back to that piece about the secret sauce or cracking the secret code. Life isn't static and while we would like it to be, once we've gotten some success in life most of us would like to hold on to it. But life just doesn't work that way. It's continuously changing—it's continuously in flux. To the degree that I'm willing to either hold on to what I think is actually useful now or let go of what isn't going to be useful in the future, and be aware of and open to looking at what I need next to learn, I'll be in synch with life. I'll be starting over and that keeps me moving.

The answers to the three questions of what I need to hold on to, what I need to let go of, and what I need next to learn, emerge against the backdrop of what meaningful reason(s) I have for them. What keeps me connected to what matters most for me, and what allows me to feel fulfilled in life as I move forward in life? The answers to those two questions—what matters and what allows me to be fulfilled—are going to change as I move through life. So I need to be in a position to be willing to entertain starting over, both in an abstract sense and in a very practical way.

WRIGHT

So what do you believe are the competencies necessary to do this?

BARTLETT

I think before competencies, there is also a concurrent need to develop capacity. So, if you'll give me just a moment I'll answer that question within the context of developing capacity. When I'm talking about "capacity" I'm referring to the breadth, depth, and variety of resources I have access to. Does the capacity that I currently have—my breadth, depth, and variety of resources—allow me to move in the direction that I'd like to move? Capacity is in many ways about my inner strength.

Now let me get a little bit more concrete. If capacity is about breadth, depth, and variety of resources, then developing capacity is a function of what I'm going to call the "for the sake of what" my life is being used for and what my goals and objectives are in service of. So if I'm developing capacity, one thing that aids the process is my ability to work with an expanded time horizon so that when I'm looking at what I'm trying to accomplish, it's more than can be done within my lifetime. Using this larger time frame allows for me to seriously expand considering the kind of, the amount, and the nature of resources I'll need to have available to make this goal or this objective occur beyond the natural span of my life.

When it comes to resources and capacity, many view both from a current time frame and, as a consequence, feel as if they aren't ready or capable to take on the next challenge. I'm reminded of a quote from *Women Who Run With the Wolves,* by Clarissa Pinkola Estes: "For the wildish woman, duration is one of her greatest strengths." Again, we can talk about this in more detail a little bit later. Simply put, when considering capacity my comfort with expanded time frames is a resource enabler that many don't consider.

So, coming back to your question, I consider capacity to be a critical component to developing the necessary competencies to start over. What we've identified with the clients we have worked with are what seems to be the core competencies that really make this possible. We've identified five of them and they are:

1. Self Awareness
2. Courage
3. Discernment
4. Practice
5. Inclusion

The first competency is self-awareness and I consider this to be the foundational competency. Am I aware of what it is that I'm doing from the standpoint of knowing why it matters to me? Why does this matter? What will be different as a

> And, for those who would argue "I know myself completely," I refer them to Oscar Wilde's statement, "Only the shallow think they know themselves!"

consequence of my taking this action? Is that valued and valuable and does it support the sense that I was used well and that my life's energy, which is a non-renewable resource, was actually spent in a wise way? Do I have the necessary resources to go to the next level? Am I using my resources wisely? This is where inner strength is discovered. As you may have discerned, there is a lot of questioning that comprises self-awareness. Socrates had it right when he said that the "unexamined life isn't worth living." Self-awareness is an enormously important competency, and is truly one of the core competencies that often most needs to be developed.

> "Courage is not the absence of fear, but rather the judgment that something else is more important than fear."
> —Ambrose Redmoon

The second competency is courage, and when you consider courage within the context of both letting go and learning anew, I believe that thinking of courage as a competency that can be developed makes eminent sense.

To be willing to let go of something I'm comfortable with, to let go of something that has worked historically for me, there has to be a certain amount of courage there. To trust the process, to be willing to step off the cliff, so to speak, and leap into that void of no guarantees is courageous.

For adults in particular, learning is a challenge requiring courage primarily because of our need for certainty in life. Most adults detest the feeling of being a beginner, which is part of learning.

I have four grandkids and I watch how they learn and how they absolutely revel in the learning process itself. What they don't have is something that has worked before, so they are willing to go out and explore and experiment.

As we become adults, we develop models for how to be successful when we get into our organizations and when we get into really living our lives. Based on these models we begin to do things, we're successful with them, and we try to replicate those over and over again, and learning has stopped. We become preoccupied with questions of right and wrong or good and bad. These questions are always asked within the context of our success models.

Among the things that enable the development of courage are different kinds of questions such as "is what I'm doing today working or not working?" This is a different type of question than one oriented around right/wrong or good/bad. If it's not working then I have the opportunity to do something different. But it will often mean letting go of my historic success model and that is a huge challenge for a lot of folks. In this sense, courage has less to do with bravery and far more to do with willingness to learn as a beginner.

This leads into the third competency that I call "discernment." This competency has its roots in a specific Buddhist tradition that involves mindfulness and is oriented around four levels of awareness. It is essentially a way of understanding how our viewing of the events in life actually conspire, or are structured to

> *"The ability to perceive or think differently is more important than the knowledge gained."*
> —*David Bohm*

affect, what it is that we're trying to do. The four levels of awareness are:

- Non-distinction
- Distinction
- Evaluation
- Judgment

The first level—the base level—is judgment. When I'm looking at understanding the competency of discernment, one way that I can look at life is through the filter or the lens of judgment. This entails seeing things and reacting to my world as though there is either a right or a wrong, or a good and bad in play. It's pretty black-and-white.

As the word "judgment" would imply, there is a values assessment that goes on that again comes back to right, wrong, good, or bad. Judgment is always used as a way of validating an existing belief system. In the extreme this can be paralyzing as well as exclusionary, as there is a polarizing dynamic inherent in judgment. Obviously, judgment can be useful as a values clarification tool and as a guidance mechanism for behavior. And, it's important to understand that it's a first level position.

The second level is evaluation. Evaluation is a little different from judgment in the sense that it's about orienting my world and life views so that I look for value. It's not that I'm looking with the intent of determining whether something is consistent with my beliefs and is therefore good, bad, right, or wrong; rather, I'm looking for the value in the event. The way I'm defining value is simply this: in what ways can what I'm viewing be utilized? So I'm looking for how it can be of value, how it can be useful and of service to something that, ideally, I've identified out there that is meaningful for me to participate in.

The second question that accompanies evaluation is focused on my intended response to an event. Is what I'm about to do generative? I'm not asking whether it's good or bad, right or wrong; but rather, is it adding value or taking value away from what I'm trying to have happen, both for myself and for others. So there's a quality to evaluation that is very different from judgment, it's got a much wider spectrum to it that is far more enabling.

Then we can move onto the third level, which is distinction. Distinction is literally the process of suspending both judgment and evaluation and just observing and noticing life's events and contents without assigning meaning to them. It's literally an observational state that puts me in the position of actually being a neutral observer. Being in a neutral position enables me to notice distinctions without judgment or evaluation; it is a practice that expands my overall awareness. The value in this is that an increase in awareness increases the variety of choices I recognize as being available—it increases my choice-making capacity. I am now in a position that, from a resource and capacity standpoint (there are more choices), literally frees me up to potentially make different kinds of choices than I've made before. And, because I now have more choices available I am in a position to develop greater competency.

The last level is non-distinction. I'll link this back to the Buddhist conversation around enlightenment. Non-distinction is where I'm approaching all things with a sense of unity and oneness—it and I are not separate. We don't generally go into a lot of conversation about this with our clients, as attaining this level is often the pursuit of a lifetime (or maybe more). And, it is an extremely exalted level of viewing the way the world is structured.

Where we primarily work with our clients from a capacity expanding and competency-building standpoint are in the areas of evaluation and distinction. If I can develop the practice of learning how to evaluate effectively and be able to move into an observational orientation that allows me to notice distinction I've not been aware of previously, I am positioned to have access to resources that I've not noticed before. Then starting over becomes a process of developing those underutilized resources. This is about intentionality and mindfulness.

> *"We learn by practice. Whether it means to learn to dance by practicing dancing or to learn to live by practicing living, the*

This leads to the fourth competency, which has to do with practice. Developing the competency of making distinctions (as well as the other competencies) doesn't happen automatically—I have to practice this.

There is an old phrase that suggests that practice makes perfect. We're not after perfection here, and I actually don't believe that practice makes perfect. I think that practice makes habits. This is the value of intentional practices and intentional practices are where success in life is built. It has to do with the kind of habits I've developed that either support where I want to go or inhibit where I want to go and that have become stumbling blocks in and of themselves.

So when I'm looking at practices and developing mindful practices—intentional practices—this is a challenging competency because it requires a high state of awareness and discipline. Is what I'm practicing on a daily basis going to enable what it is that I'd like to have from a behavioral standpoint, from an attitudinal standpoint, and from an experience of life standpoint?

When it comes to developing intentional practices I've found it very useful to keep in mind that the way I do anything is the way that I do everything. Do my practices provide me the ground from where I may be able to connect more effectively with others in a way that propels us to what it is that we want in our life?

This then leads to the final competency, which is the competency of inclusion. This competency has to do with my ability to tap into and utilize the power of social networks.

> *"After the game, the king and pawn go into the same box."*
> —*Italian Proverb*

The value and the power of social networks are irrefutable in terms of enabling change. When I'm looking at starting over—sustaining success in life—it's crucial to realize that I'm not going to do it by myself. I have to develop the competency to include others in a meaningful way in that process.

A key focus with this competency has to do with developing my ability to deliberately create and sustain high quality relationships over time. We and our lives are defined by our relationships, the quality of our social networks, and our ability to utilize them well.

If I'm effectively working at developing these five competencies: self-awareness, courage, discernment, practice, and inclusion, I will have developed a set of powerful tools that allows me to be in a position to sustain success in life—to be able to continuously start over.

WRIGHT

Is there one competency that is more important than the others?

BARTLETT

I think they're all important and, having said that, I believe they all rest on a bed of self-awareness. Without self-awareness, nothing else actually becomes possible, from my perspective. This is borne out from the observations that we've done with people who are highly effective and successful over long periods of time. They are very aware of what's important to them, how they're doing in feeling and being connected to it, and how whatever it is they're doing enables them to achieve what they want to have.

As an aside, self-awareness is also a critical competency in the development of high emotional intelligence. So, I believe that self-awareness is, as I said earlier, the foundational competency—not necessarily more important than the other four, but certainly their foundation.

And, while self-awareness is foundational, awareness by itself does little. I think practice is the great enabler of the group of five. Starting over begins with self-awareness, but then I must have the practices that allow for movement to consistently occur and effective "habits" to become integrated into my daily life.

WRIGHT

Are there any keys to developing these competencies?

BARTLETT

I'm compelled to use the word "vision," but I want to use something a little differently here, and it's the phrase *"for the sake of what"* that I talked about earlier. There needs to be a compelling "for the sake of what" to orient around. Otherwise I'm not going to be willing to start over. For the sake of what do I need to start over? For the sake of what am I trying to do whatever it is that I'm doing?

In businesses we use the word "vision." We've used the word "vision" with many of the coaching clients we work with at an executive level, but the power of what we're truly working with actually goes beyond what most people assume vision is about. Using the phrase "for the sake of what" is a way of making vision and goals personal. It's not abstract and vision can tend to be. I use this language very specifically when working in this area. So in terms of the keys used in developing these competencies, the question of what this makes possible is a very relevant question. I'm not going to be really willing to let go of what's been working, to put in the practice, be willing to take the risks, be willing to examine myself, and I'm definitely not going to be willing to move through fear, or include others unless I'm sure of, and unless I'm attached to and connected to, the value inherent in a clearly defined for the sake of what.

I think that another key has to do with the power of deciding. I must be willing to make and then act on the decision that this is something I indeed want to do and having it is more important than having what I am currently experiencing.

I'm under no illusion about the potential difficulties with this way of engaging life. The great management and leadership sage Peter Drucker once said that "Unless a decision has degenerated into work, it is not a decision; it is at best a good intention." I think one thing that helps activate this decision is literally contained in the nature of the decision itself—starting over. If I approach this whole idea as something to live into rather than live up to I can't fail at it. There will be stumbling blocks; there will be periods of disillusionment. That's part of the process just as it is part of life.

The German poet Ranier Maria Rilke said that "the purpose of life is to be defeated by greater and greater things." I believe we all have the inner strength to have success in life. It's made easier if we adopt the notion that success is in many ways achieved by slow degrees and requires a continual recommitment to the decision to continuously start over in order to be and have what I want.

WRIGHT

What do you think are the biggest obstacles in sustaining success in life?

BARTLETT

Simple answer to that question is attachment to what was. Memory is the great brake. I also think that the perception of failure is the result of limited awareness. What happens with people and organizations is that we will tend to look at failure almost always within the limited awareness of a very discreet time frame. I either succeeded or I failed within this narrow time frame. This is where the context of time becomes a very useful tool.

So an awareness of the effect of time frames is one piece of this, which is why I look at the question "for the sake of what?" Any event in my life can be looked at as a success or a failure. But if it's looked at within a larger context of time that holds this long-term "for the sake of what," both the seeming successes and failures in my life become learning opportunities. They are simply milestones on the path toward the realization of a greater for the sake of what. It takes a lot of inner strength for people to say, "I didn't fail here, I am actually on the road to success." Others may view this as a failure, but in the way that I'm looking at my life, and in the way in which we're looking at what we're doing, this actually was a learning experience that is invaluable to my next steps and I'm going to be leveraging it.

So an increase in awareness is a way—the most workable way—to overcoming the inevitable obstacles that life tosses at us. Very simply stated, because a perception of failure is the result of limited awareness, an increase in awareness is going to increase my choice-making capacity. When I increase the number of choices I have available to me, by definition I will increase the power that I have. By "power" I'm talking about my ability to effect change. Increasing my ability to effect change will ultimately result in expanding results. So when it comes to the biggest obstacles to success, I think the truly big ones are limited awareness and attachment to what was.

And then there is a limitation that creeps in from thinking and taking things too personally. This is the great paradox of self-awareness and I'll come back to it in just a minute.

What keeps me moving in my life is that I've actually developed a thousand-year vision for myself. Now, a thousand years! How accurate can this be? Well, not very accurate at all. But a thousand-year vision is completely outside of me. By definition, there is no way in the world I will be there when it's realized. At the same time, there is no way that I can be "failing" as I move toward its realization. The power—the leverage—is inherent in the for the sake of what do I do things in my life? For the sake of having that thousand-year vision realized, and that picture of a thousand-year future is huge and compelling. I want it to begin to take form every day.

It's a very interesting process to do, and when I talk about this with clients—that I'd like them to develop a thousand-year vision—they look at me as though I'm crazy. It's something that everybody can do. It's definitely different than a one-year vision. It's different than a three- or five-year vision. With a thousand-year vision there is something that begins to spark imagination and it takes me out of the realm of thinking too personally.

As I mentioned a moment ago, part of the paradox inherent with self-awareness is that there is often too much focus on myself and when there is too much focus on myself it limits me. Too much focus on self actually constrains awareness. Awareness is defined, in the way that we work with our clients, within a larger picture. We look at developing an awareness of "what am I contributing to, how am I making things happen, and for the sake of what?" This way of holding self-awareness has the benefit of helping insure that I'm aware of "self" within a larger context—how is the self being well used? So this competence of self-awareness is literally the key to moving beyond obstacles; it can also be one of the biggest obstacles people face in moving forward.

WRIGHT

It's been said that all people want ultimately to be happy. Where or how does this pursuit of happiness fit into what you're saying?

BARTLETT

As a general rule, people do whatever they do based on an expectation that their experience of being alive will be better for it. Essentially, everything that we do, as individuals and as a people, is in service of having a great experience of being alive. The desire for that experience is the catalyst for all of the actions we take. We don't do things in order to have bad experiences.

I think for too many people, being happy lives outside of themselves. In other words, the pursuit of happiness is often about the pursuit of symbols that represent happiness. The illusion is that if I can only get the symbol I'll have happiness. This is where we need to start looking at how we define success. We chase the symbols thinking that attaining the symbol is success. If I get the house, if I get the car, if I get the job or the right relationship, if I get the money, or whatever it may be out there symbolically, then I will have whatever great experience of being alive might be associated with that—power, fulfillment, whatever it may be. It almost never works; we feel unfulfilled and we then start looking for the next great symbol. What many tend to do in life is chase the symbols and during the pursuit, lose connection with the experience that these symbols are intended to enable. Happiness is achieved when meaningful and fulfilling experiences are internalized.

Sustaining success, the act of starting over, is oriented around clarity of experience inherent in a meaningful for the sake of what, and not with identifying the symbol as the end all, be all. So when I'm talking about people ultimately wanting to be happy, the pursuit of happiness is not about pursuing a thing, it's about going back to the original definition that I work with. It's about the answer to the question of was I used well? It's about that deep abiding sense of fulfillment, the sense that what you are doing matters.

Those are the experiences that people seek when they talk about happiness—the duel experiences of fulfillment and doing something that matters. When experienced together, this is where people begin to feel as though life is worth living, that they've been successful, and there is happiness involved with that. A simple way to think of happiness is that it is an emotion that is generated as a consequence of being used well.

WRIGHT

So how does this perspective on success influence the work you do with your clients?

BARTLETT

Most of my work is with organizations and the people who run them—generally the top levels in these organizations. All organizations, and I mean this literally, were originally founded on an ideal that in some way included having others feel as though their lives would be improved as a consequence of using the products and services the organization provided. As organizations mature I think they get away from those ideals.

Most organizations were originally founded on the desire for people to have a positive experience, both internally (those who work with the company) and externally (those who purchase products or services from the company). So when we're looking at this, the focus on experience gets to be interesting in the context of time as it relates to business and product cycles and life cycles.

Organizations are simply a collection of people who are in relationship—with each other, with the organization, with their jobs, with customers, suppliers, and so on. If the relationships are working well, then the organization will likely work well. Unfortunately, relationships aren't static. Times change, people's expectations of what an enjoyable and fulfilling experience is change. What is meaningful changes over time. So because I've stumbled onto something that allows me to be successful today doesn't mean that it's going to be working next year, next month, or even tomorrow in some instances. So the idea of sustaining success—developing the capacity and the competencies to continuously start over—is absolutely paramount if we're going to have long-term success in life, in the way that we're defining success.

My experience suggests that there is a need for people and organizations to really look at how they're defining success. What's the life-enhancing experience, what's the ideal that we want to set in motion, what's the ideal that we're striving for? How do we continuously reinvent our relationships—with our customers, with our employees, with our products—in order to achieve sustainable success?

WRIGHT

Are there organizations or individuals you have worked with or know that are examples of what you're talking about?

BARTLETT

Definitely—there are a number of organizations I've worked with that I think exemplify this in many ways.

One in particular is Nokia, the mobile phone manufacturer and the network supplier for mobile phone services. I've worked with them for a number of years as an external consultant. Nokia is over one hundred and forty years old as a company. When I started consulting with them they were essentially a Scandinavian conglomerate that sold rubber boots, tires, television sets, and cable, and not IT cable or Internet cable—it was big, round cable that was used in construction. They have certainly changed in the years that I've been associated with them. They are continuously starting over. They have this in their "DNA." It's a willingness to look at what's working, what's not working, and what needs to be learned next. Learning is one of their formal core values and they strive to continuously live into that value as well as other ideals that they say matter to them.

On the personal side, my father and mother come to mind. He was a serial entrepreneur and, in my experience, was always "successful" in the way we've been looking at it here. Some of his business successes lasted longer than others but he always held them as ways to move a step closer to an ideal that was important to him. More than most, he had mastered the art of continuously starting over and did so with grace and exuberance.

My mother captured this in a very dramatic fashion when she had a heart transplant at the age of fifty-seven. She was very clear that she was not done living yet and, when we talk about discovering inner strength, she was an exemplar of this. The courage and strength she exhibited in making the decision to go forward without guarantees and her clarity about the "for the sake of what" continued to be a part of her life and her lifestyle until she died eighteen years later at the age of seventy-five.

WRIGHT

So have you applied this perspective to your own life?

BARTLETT

Yes, I think my life in many ways is a model of this perspective. I've lived in countries all over the world. I've had different careers—I've worked in advertising, I've worked in communication, I've worked in consulting, I've managed large organizations, and founded a number of businesses. There are a lot of areas in my life in which I am continuously starting over. I think one that many of our readers can identify with is physical exercise. Exercising regularly is very difficult for a lot of people, so being willing to continuously start over when I stop the process is one way that this actually shows up in my exercise practice.

WRIGHT

When we get it down to a practical application, then exercising would be a perfect example because I quit exercising all the time.

BARTLETT

Yes, so you're well positioned to continuously start over! You exercise and it's likely that the motivating question that is missing is for the sake of what am I doing it? This is different than a goal. If I exercise just to lose weight, then that is a fairly short-term goal and one that's not particularly compelling. If I can develop a for the sake of what that's compelling to me in ways that just losing weight isn't, then it has the potential to make exercising a very different experience. And that difference changes my approach to exercise. For me, the for the sake of what changes over time when it comes to exercising. I think this is an important point. The key has to be, is the for the sake of what currently meaningful to me?

At one point in time I exercised an enormous amount to get in shape for my daughter's wedding *for the sake* of looking as proud externally as I was feeling internally. At another time I exercised to be in shape to run in a mini marathon for the sake of accomplishing a personally meaningful milestone I'd set for myself. Now, those may seem like goals and they are, but the consideration of a "for the sake of what" was what enabled my willingness to keep at it. I wouldn't have done it just because somebody told me I needed to exercise thirty minutes a day.

Meditation is another great example. Most people who try to meditate give it up because of the way the mind tends to wander. Meditation can be a very frustrating experience for many. I use meditation as a way to practice mastering the process of continuously starting over!

WRIGHT

This is very, very interesting and I especially appreciate these five competencies, those are great; I will remember them for a long time. I want to tell you just how much I appreciate the time you've spent with me on this important subject, and you've done such a great job explaining it.

BARTLETT

Well, I appreciate the opportunity. I wish we had more time and I think that we've got a good start here.

WRIGHT

Today we've been talking with Blaine Bartlett, who is an internationally respected and sought-after executive coach, management consultant, and leadership and organizational development expert. His programs and processes are known for their practical application to the needs and objectives of his clients. I don't know about you, but I have sure learned a lot here today. I think you will too.

Blaine, thank you so much for being with us today on *Discover Your Inner Strength*.

BARTLETT

David, my pleasure, and again thank you for the opportunity.

About the Author

Blaine Bartlett is President and CEO of Avatar Resources, Inc., a leadership consulting firm he founded in 1987. The firm has affiliate offices in four countries.

Blaine sits on the Advisory Board of the All Nippon Management Coaching Institute based in Osaka and is the Director of Business Strategy and Development for InVision Global Group in China. He was certified as an executive and leadership coach by The Hudson Institute of Santa Barbara, certified by Strozzi Institute, as a somatic coach and he has been a member of the International Coach Federation since its inception. He has lectured on Enterprise Leadership Development at China's prestigious Tsing Hua University in Beijing. Blaine has been a featured speaker at numerous international symposiums including the World Congress of Human Resource Management and was a past panel member of the World Consortium for Research and Development of Training. He's an active member of the Transformational Leadership Council, a group of transformational CEOs, thought leaders, and educators founded by *Chicken Soup for the Soul* author, Jack Canfield. Blaine's second book, *Three Dimensional Coaching,* is scheduled to be published in Japan and China in late 2009.

Go to his blog Ideals in Motion (www.idealsinmotion.com) to read his commentary and musings on life, leadership, and success.

Blaine Bartlett

3011—263rd Place SE
Sammamish, Washington 98075
Phone: 425.557.5800
bbartlett@avatar-resources.com
www.avatar-resources.com

Secrets of Discovering Your Inner Strength: The Seven Paths to Success

An Interview With...
Mary Wayne Bush

DAVID WRIGHT (WRIGHT)

Today we're talking with Mary Wayne Bush, an internationally-known speaker, author, and professional coach. She works with organizations and individuals to develop leadership, communication skills, and team productivity. Dr. Bush is a well-known speaker, author and scholar, and has been a featured presenter at professional conferences, including American Psychological Association, International Coach Federation, Organization Development Network, Academy of Management, and the American Society for Training and Development. She holds a doctorate in Organizational Change from Pepperdine University and is here to talk with us today about discovering our inner strength.

Dr. Bush, welcome to *Discover Your Inner Strength*.

MARY WAYNE BUSH (BUSH)

Thanks, David! I'm delighted to be here with you. As a professional coach, I have had the opportunity to help people discover their inner strength, reach their goals, and live the life of their dreams. I am continually inspired by examples of people overcoming obstacles, claiming all that life offers, and achieving the success and happiness they deserve. Success is a destination, and discovering your inner strength is the key to getting there!

WRIGHT

So, what is inner strength?

BUSH

Inner strength is actually a combination of qualities. Our intention, our will, our self-confidence, and courage are all based on inner strength—and these qualities can be discovered and developed. Inner strength can be our greatest gift, our greatest ally.

Most of us are blessed with different types of strengths. We have the physical strength to walk or run or lift heavy things. Our emotional strength helps us feel joy, recover from loss or disappointment, and gives us the capacity to encourage and inspire ourselves and others. Mental strength lets us learn facts and apply concepts, as well as imagine possibilities for the future.

These are "outer" strengths. But we all have "inner" strengths as well—strengths that can enable us to meet tough situations with courage and confidence, strengths that can help us stay on track and accomplish a goal. Inner strengths are pathways that help us to get where we want to go. Once we discover these inner strengths, and learn to use them, we can call on them any time that we need them. And just as we exercise to keep our muscles healthy and strong, we can also develop our inner strengths to be stronger and more useful throughout our lives.

Discovering our inner strengths can give us the competitive advantage we need—the extra "edge" to get us where we want to go in life. People who know and rely on their inner strengths have the assurance that they can get through challenges and leverage the opportunities and choices that come to them.

WRIGHT

Why do you think it's so important to discover your inner strength?

BUSH

David, I believe that success is a destination—not just something that happens to us, randomly, or if we wish for it hard enough. If we want to be successful, we need to have a plan to navigate our way toward it—just like we would with any physical journey that we take. If we are in California, and want to go to Chicago, that is our destination and we need a path to get there. Success is no different—success is a goal that is ours to define and design. We set our own destination and arrive at it!

When we are choosing success as our destination, inner strength can be our path. Whether we walk, run, take a train, car, bicycle, boat or plane, there are paths that can help us get to our destination. These paths don't decide where we are going (or if we are going at all!). That is totally up to us. And, depending on where we are going, we may have to take several different pathways to get there!

With success as our destination, inner strengths are the paths that help us get what we want, go where we want to go, and do what we want to do. Our inner strengths help us focus our intentions, turning dreams into reality. Knowing how to call on them and use them gives us the courage and confidence face even the most difficult times and still arrive at our destination. Inner strengths are paths that help us reach our goals.

WRIGHT

How can our readers use their inner strength?

BUSH

Strengths help us overcome obstacles or successfully meet challenges. They can also help us dream, define, and design our lives to achieve the goals that we want in life. Each time we face a new situation, we have a chance to call on our strengths—for an exciting new opportunity or in a demanding crisis. We can use our inner strengths to help resolve, restore, and reinvent the situation, and ourselves, to create a successful outcome.

Many of us only call on our inner strengths when there is a problem or a disappointment. Inner strengths can get us through very difficult times—divorce, bankruptcy, illness—but they can also help define and design our lives to get what we want and live our dreams. Inner strengths can help us create opportunities as well as overcome challenges. I want our readers to think of their inner strengths as pathways to get where they want to go in life—to their Destination of Success.

WRIGHT

Do you think there are different kinds of inner strength?

BUSH

Yes! I have discovered that there are at least seven kinds of inner strength that can be called on to get what we want in life. These inner strengths can be used separately or together to help us accomplish our goals. They are truly the pathways to our Destination of Success! And they all start with the letter "P:"

- The Path of Purpose
- The Path of Passion
- The Path of Power
- The Path of Possibility

- The Path of Perspective
- The Path of Persistence
- The Path of Promise

All of these Paths help us get what we want, but the first three—Purpose, Passion, and Power—help us identify the Destination: where we want to go, or what we need to do. The last four—Possibility, Perspective, Persistence, and Promise—help us get there and reach our goals.

WRIGHT

Will you discuss them?

BUSH

I'd be glad to tell you more. Let's start with the Path of Purpose

The Path of Purpose

To reach any destination, we need to know what we want, what we need to do, or where we have to go. The Path of Purpose helps us identify, define, and move toward a goal or a result. Purpose helps clarify the steps or milestones that are necessary to get us what we want in life. And Purpose helps us stay strong and focused even if there are detours and difficulties along the way to our destination. As the philosopher Nietzsche wrote, "He who has a *why* to live for can bear with almost any *how*."

Victor Frankl wrote eloquently about the Path of Purpose in his best-selling book, *Man's Search for Meaning*. A prominent Viennese psychiatrist before the war, Dr. Frankl lived through the Holocaust and spent years in a concentration camp. From that experience, he was uniquely able to observe the way that both he and others coped (or didn't cope) with the experience. Frankl came to believe that man's deepest desire is the search for meaning and purpose.[1]

The inner strength of Purpose can change lives. It did for John Walsh. John's life changed forever the day his son, Adam, was abducted and killed. From that personal tragedy, John and his wife pledged to turn their grief into action. They found a new focus for their lives—to help missing and exploited children. John used the strength of Purpose to recreate, redefine, and re-identify his life mission. With his wife, Reve, he helped create two Senate bills: the *Missing Children Act of 1982* and the *Missing Children's Assistance Act of 1984*. In 1988, John went on to host a television show, *America's Most Wanted*, which has helped find fugitives and missing persons as a direct result of viewer tips to the program. Through John and Reve's strength of Purpose, thousands of people have been helped.

Dr. Anthony Lazzaro discovered his inner strength of Purpose to work with sick, destitute children in the foothills of the Andes Mountains in Peru. Over twenty years ago, he left a tenured post at Emory University in Atlanta, Georgia, where he supervised high-tech children's wards at two of the University's hospitals. The Path of Purpose led him to work at a clinic for poor and abandoned children halfway around the world.

Why did he leave his work in the United States to go to a country he had never seen and knew very little about? "I felt an unease," he says, "a feeling that I was not where I was supposed to be—that the Lord would have me elsewhere." Now, "Dr. Tony" has sixty-five children at the clinic, and has established the Villa La Paz Foundation to help them. He says "We are the only hope that these children have."[2]

A former coaching client of mine had a similar sense that he was not moving toward the right destination in his life. Robert F. was a successful corporate executive who realized that his purpose did not lie within a corporation, but in a congregation. He discovered his inner strength of Purpose, and changed his career and his life by becoming a minister. Starting out with a small congregation, he helped the church grow and thrive, and then taught at the denomination's seminary. Robert's Path of Purpose helped him reach a completely new destination, where he also met and married the love of his life!

The Path of Passion

Passion is the inner strength of excitement, energy, joy, and engagement. The Path of Passion is a motivating force that helps us accomplish difficult things, make changes in our lives, or overcome barriers and obstacles. Passion reminds us that we care about something very much or that something important is at stake in the situation—whether it is a personal interest or the desire to make a difference in the world.

Discovering our inner strength of Passion helps us clarify what is important in our lives, what we enjoy, and what we want to spend more time doing. The Path of Passion can open up possibilities and keep us motivated toward a goal because we are enjoying what we are doing.

Gary S.'s story is an example of this inner strength. In 1989, Gary was working as an electrical engineer at a high-tech company in Southern California. With a young wife and growing family, he was an active father and good provider. On weekends, he volunteered for the local search-and-rescue team. Over the years, he became well known as a hero in the community for helping to find people who were lost or injured in the surrounding mountains. The work was hard and dangerous, but it was Gary's Passion. He loved being out-of-doors, in nature, and the physical challenge of hiking and climbing in the mountains, as much as he liked helping those who were lost or hurt.

During the technology downturn of 1991, Gary lost his job. He continued to report for search-and-rescue duty, and when the local sheriff found out that he had been laid off, Gary was immediately offered a new job working for the Sheriff's Department. Gary did well and passed all of the mental and physical tests to become a Deputy Sheriff.

After several years as a Deputy Sheriff in Southern California, Gary moved to Tucson, Arizona. There, Gary combined his technical skills and passion for the outdoors to develop the police department's communications and information technology network. Using his knowledge and skill, he expanded their search-and-rescue capabilities. Today, Gary has a job he enjoys and he still volunteers for the search-and-rescue team. The Path of Passion led him to a new career, doing what he loves the most!

The Path of Power

WRIGHT

You say that the third inner strength is the Path of Power. When you say "Power," what do you mean in this context?

BUSH

The inner strength of Power is about belief and conviction. The Path of Power can help us in situations where we know what needs to be done and we put ourselves in the place to do it. Power gives us the fortitude and the belief in ourselves to do what we know is right. Power can help us identify solutions or opportunities that we could not have seen before. Power can also help us stand firm in difficult situations, or see a way forward to success in situations that seem ambiguous or hopeless.

We can each discover our inner strength of Power, and use the Path of Power to get where we want to go in life. For some of us, the inner strength of Power comes from a belief in ourselves and our abilities. For others, the inner strength of Power is a reflection of the love, faith and confidence placed in us by others. Often, the Path of Power is related to our religious or spiritual connections. Oprah Winfrey, one of the most successful and powerful women in the world today, says "For me, there is no power without spiritual power. A power that comes from the core of who you are and reflects all that you were meant to be. A power that's connected to the source of things. When you see this kind of power shining through someone in all its truth and certainty, it's irresistible, inspiring, elevating."[3]

We can draw our inner strength of Power from confidence, a sense of destiny, or our belief that something is the "right thing to do." Power can also come from the knowledge that someone believes in us strongly, or has faith in us. Thomas Edison is considered one of the most prolific inventors in history, holding 1,093 U.S. patents in his name. He is the inventor of the phonograph and the electric light bulb. His sense of inner strength of Power may have come from his mother's faith in him. He was quoted as saying, "My mother was the making of me. She was so true, so sure of me; and I felt I had something to live for, someone I must not disappoint."[4]

Some find Power in focusing on the present moment, contemplating and being present to what is happening in the "now." Phil Jackson, head coach of the Los Angeles Lakers and perhaps one of the greatest basketball coaches of all time, finds the Path of Power through focusing on the present moment. In his 1996 book, *Sacred Hoops*, he wrote, "In basketball–as in life–true joy comes from being fully present in each and every moment, not just when things are going your way. Of course, it's no accident that things are more likely to go your way when you stop worrying about whether you're going to win or lose and focus your attention on what's happening right this moment"[5] Author Eckhart Tolle says, "Through the present moment, you have access to the power of life itself. In his best-selling book, *The Power of Now* (2005), he writes "Only when you align yourself to the present moment do you have access to that power."[6]

The inner strength of Power can also be linked to strongly held values of justice, integrity, compassion, or faith in a "higher power." Sometimes, the Path of Power is simply an unexplainable sense of "knowing"—knowing that things will turn out all right. The Bible calls it the "peace that passes all understanding."

Diane B. told me about her experience of discovering this inner strength of Power as a new wife. She said, "My husband and I were married in September of 1978. About nine months later, after months of suspecting something was not quite right, we learned my husband had a brain tumor. I was twenty-two years old. Our friends were having babies and celebrating their lives. We were trying to understand the severity, size, and implications of the tumor. We were both registered nurses and we had a good understanding of the technical terms and treatments. I vividly recall meeting with the young neurosurgeon who said something like, "The tumor is about the size of a grapefruit. If this were me, I would want Dr. M. to do the surgery." (Translation, "This is a lot worse than we think.")

"We decided to take a vacation before the surgery, as we anticipated a long recovery afterward if my husband survived. We temporarily forgot about the impending surgery and enjoyed our time away. We drew strength from each other and our faith in God. I remember being afraid, but moving out of the fear and staying focused on being strong for my husband.

"My husband was first on the surgery schedule, which meant he was prepped and ready to go to the operating room about 6 AM. I walked alongside his bed until we got to the operating room doors. We said goodbye and I went to the family waiting room. The operating room was in the basement of the hospital. The waiting room was a small area with no windows, one door, and a red telephone that was used to communicate to family members letting them know when surgery was over.

"With me that day were my husband's mother, sister, and two aunts. My parents also came to the hospital later in the day, as surgery went on much longer than expected. Nine hours after my husband's surgery began, Dr. M. came to the door of the waiting room. We went into the hall to hear his report. He said, 'The surgery is over. The tumor was wrapped around the brain stem and it was a lot bigger than we thought. I don't know if he will walk, talk, see or hear again. We won't know until/*unless* he wakes up.'

"I will never forget the look on this neurosurgeon's face. He was notoriously burly and arrogant, but I could see that he was as devastated by what he was saying as I was by what I heard. I reached up, hugged him, and said, 'I know he will be all right.' I really *did* know my husband would be all right. I had a sense of calm and peace that told me not to worry.

"The rest of the family was crying and there was a good bit of panic and yelling around me. One of my husband's aunts took me to the chapel to get away from everyone else. We stayed in the chapel for probably half an hour, reflecting and praying in silence. We returned to the waiting room. About thirty minutes later, I heard the automatic doors from the operating room open, then footsteps running up the hall. I instinctively knew it was Dr. M. I ran out to meet him. He was beaming when he said, 'He's awake. He can hear! He can see, and he's talking!' This time Dr. M. hugged me and tears were streaming down both of our faces.

"In follow-up, Dr. M. said that, statistically, my husband should not have survived the surgery, and if he had survived, there should have been severe damage to his cranial nerves. Dr. M. said he knew there was a greater Power with him in surgery that day. That Power was with me, too, and I knew it would all be okay."

Diane's inner strength of Power helped her get through a very difficult time and focus on helping her husband. He is now healthy and they are both enjoying life with their daughter!

The Path of Possibility

Possibility is the inner strength of imagination. Possibility helps us to see what needs to change in order for us to be successful in a new situation or to overcome a challenge. It helps us to think "out of the box," and to see new ways of approaching problems and opportunities. The Path of Possibility opens us up to new experiences and opportunities.

Stacey H. changed her life by discovering her inner strength of Possibility. She took a leap of faith into a better life in a new location, propelled and motivated by her inner strength of Possibility. She told me, "I grew up in a small town in southwestern Pennsylvania—a town with its own 'gravitational pull.' Most people lived their whole lives in the general area and I assumed that I would as well."

Stacey tried many different ways to adapt to the life she had in her hometown, which she assumed was her fate.

"My first attempt," she said, "was a fairly straightforward approach—just stay on the path I was already on and let inertia carry me forward to the happy life I envisioned for myself. I can only describe the years that followed as a 'square-peg-round-hole' experience—a constant struggle to make things fit together. Despite repeated efforts and thoughtful changes to my approach, I always found myself back at the same place, feeling unfulfilled, dissatisfied, and disappointed."

But Stacey didn't let her story stop there. By using her inner strength of Possibility, she realized that there was more to life than what she was experiencing in her small town. Stacey knew that she could have the life she wanted. Her inner strength of Possibility helped her see that the life she wanted could be possible somewhere else, if not in her small town.

"Then it hit me," she said. "No matter what I did, no matter how hard I tried, the road that I was on wasn't going to take me where I wanted to go. I needed a new road. In short order I quit my job, left graduate school, packed up a carload of belongings and headed west. I had a destination but not a plan."

To expand her options, Stacey chose a city in a different part of the country where she knew someone. She was confident that she could get work with her skills as a waitress and bartender. "It was a frightening experience," she said, "and there was a lot that could go wrong. But day by day, I built my new life from scratch and built the road to take me where I wanted to go. I'm happy to say it was worth the effort."

Relying on her inner strength of Possibility, Stacey staked her future on her belief that there was more for her in life than she had experienced in her hometown. And she was right! She now has the rich, full life she could only dream of back in her hometown. The Path of Possibility led her to earn a doctorate degree, getting a fulfilling job, and a having a husband and thriving family. Stacey's success *was* her destination—quite literally!

The Path of Perspective

Perspective enables us to think about a situation or person in different ways. This inner strength can help us see more potential in a situation, or help us understand it from another point of view. The Path of Perspective allows us to imagine how someone else would deal with the same situation that is currently facing us. For example, if there is someone else who is aware of the situation, ask the person about how he or she sees it. Find out why the person sees the situation that way, and ask yourself if you have taken all of those points into consideration.

If no one knows about the situation, or we cannot reach someone to ask, the inner strength of Perspective can help us imagine what someone else would tell you or advise you to do. The Path of Perspective invites us to look at things from different angles, to take a step back and see ourselves as others do. Think of a hero of yours, or a role model. Ask yourself, if that person were with you now, what advice or encouragement would you receive?

Johnny M. uses his inner strength of Perspective by talking to himself out loud, giving himself advice and encouragement. "When I know I should have done a certain thing, a certain way," he says, "and decided not to, for one reason or another, I then chastise myself out loud. I discuss a remedy with myself out loud, and then describe the plan to remedy the situation, again out loud. Speaking to myself out loud gives me more of a three-dimensional look at the situation. It helps me see things from a different perspective."

The inner strength of Perspective can also help us break the goal or challenge into parts or pieces or steps, helping to manage anxiety that can come when we are faced with a large or lengthy project. Focusing on small parts of a task one at a time can help us concentrate on what is needed, and what is next. Accomplishing those small steps helps build and sustain momentum, and increases confidence in knowing that we will get the whole thing done in time.

The Path of Perspective can also help us picture ourselves in the future, having already overcome or successfully achieved our goal. We can imagine what our life will be like when the challenge is over and we have already arrived at our destination: SUCEESS! Our inner strength of Perspective enables us to use these ideas and mental pictures to boost our confidence and motivate us to move through any current challenges in our situation.

Here is an example of how I used the Path of Perspective to complete my doctorate degree. When I had finished my classes and started working on research for my dissertation, I felt as though time had stopped and I would never reach my goal and get my degree. I loved the experience of being a student and learning in class, but the research process was lonely and rigorous. I felt that it would never end! This is when I came up with the idea of using a different Perspective to help me finish! Using my inner strength of Perspective, I imagined what I would do when I had actually completed my degree. My first thought was that I would want to have a party to celebrate, and I actually started planning the event. It was enjoyable to think about being with my friends and sharing my joy and success. I started making detailed plans, thinking of all the people I wanted to invite, where I wanted to hold the party, and what it would feel like. This may sound like procrastinating—a waste of my time thinking about my fantasy party—but taking this Path of Perspective helped renew my energy, and inspired me to complete the research project, and to get on with my new life as *"Dr.* Mary Wayne." The power of Perspective helped me envision the goal more clearly, and gave me the momentum and clarity to finish the dissertation in record time. The party was wonderful, and the celebration marked the end of one chapter of my life—and the beginning of the next!

The Path of Persistence

The Path of Persistence is the inner strength of determination, tenacity and endurance. The dictionary defines Persistence as "continuing to exist despite interference."[7] The inner strength of Persistence comes to our aid when we are losing hope, energy, or our ability to see a desired goal.

An important aspect of Persistence is about continuing to do what we need to do—not giving up, not letting ourselves become defeated or distracted from the outcome we want. Persistence involves believing in ourselves so much that we aren't focused on external rewards and so that we don't need others to believe in us or give us encouragement. There are many stories about writers or artists or actors who draw on the Path of Persistence to overcome failure and rejection before they become successful. Author J. K. Rowling's first Harry Potter novel was rejected eight times before being published! But Ms. Rowling did not give up writing because of these rejections. Her stories of Harry and his adventures at Hogwart's School of Witchcraft and Wizardry were published and gained worldwide success and critical acclaim, making Rowling one of the richest writers in history!

Another aspect of the Path of Persistence is discipline—doing what needs to be done, day after day, over and over again, like clockwork. It is taking the first step, and then the next step, and then the step after that, until the journey is complete. It is mustering time and energy to move toward a goal, even when that goal seems unreachable, or when we can't see the finish line, and even when no one notices or congratulates us on our progress. The inner strength of Persistence helps keep us going even when we do not see evidence of progress or accomplishment. Persistence helps us keep on doing what we know is right, what we know is important, even if we do not get external confirmation or validation.

Michele Hoskins used her inner strength of Persistence to become a multi-millionaire with her great grandmother's syrup recipe. After she formulated and packaged the syrup recipe, she started by taking it to local grocery stores, asking them to stock the product. She offered to only ask for payment if the syrup sold well. This worked so well that she got bigger ideas. Her goal was to get the syrup into Denny's restaurants.

She got in touch with the right people at Denny's and they told her no. But that did not stop her. She made it a habit to call them every single Monday at 10:30 a.m. for *two years!* When Denny's hired a new CEO, they told him about this woman who called every Monday at 10:30. "What does she want?" the CEO asked. "She wants us to use her product," they replied.

This was during the time that Denny's was suffering from a blow to their reputation after being sued for treating African Americans poorly in their restaurant in past years. Michelle Hoskins happened to be African American. The CEO was baffled that these people had turned her down for so long, as this is exactly the kind of business partnership they needed! Not long after, Michelle had the contract with Denny's and now she is a multi-millionaire. This is not about Michelle getting a lucky break because she is an African American, but being persistent enough to wait for the right time to come.[8] Michelle used the Path of Persistence to get to her destination: Success!

The Path of Promise

Promise is the strength of intention, will, and commitment. The Path of Promise involves deciding and declaring that something will happen, or that you will do something *no matter what the circumstances*. The dictionary defines Promise as "a declaration that one will do or refrain from doing something specified" and "ground for expectation of success, improvement, or excellence."[9] The inner strength of Promise can help us create opportunities as well as help us get through very difficult times, whether the Promise is one that is made to yourself or someone else.

In 1961, President John F. Kennedy made a Promise that our nation would "commit itself to achieving the goal, before this decade is out, of landing a man on the Moon and returning him back safely to the Earth." It would take inner strength for everyone involved in the project. As Kennedy went on to say, "No single space project in this period will be more impressive to mankind, or more important for the long-range exploration of space; and none will be so difficult or expensive to accomplish."[10] Kennedy's promise was fulfilled on July 20, 1969, almost six years after his death, when Project Apollo's mission successfully landed men on the Moon and returned them to Earth safely within a decade of his declaration.

Rob N. gives us a more personal example about how he discovered his inner strength of Promise as his mother was dying: "We had 'short notice,' so to speak," he said, "and her death followed surgery and a several-month stay in the hospital. I held her power of attorney, and was executor of her will. I never asked for those responsibilities and never wanted them. Regardless, I took them as honor-bound, and always felt that was the way it was meant to be.

"With my sister's counsel, that of my wife, that of my mother's friends who remained alive, and that of my extended family, I tried to wade through the numerous ethical challenges (and conflicts) that seemed to increasingly crop up. When decisions needed to be made, I made them, with or without 100 percent buy-in and consent from people whose perspective I needed to weigh.

"With but two weeks left in her life (we didn't know that at the time), my wife and I 'miraculously' walked into the hospital one day, en route home from a weekend away. A bed had been made 'available' in the hospital's palliative care unit. I knew, deep down, it would be one of the last important decisions I'd have to make concerning my mother's life. So she was sent [to the unit]. Over the next several days, I was practically on call as my mom's condition deteriorated. In every case—advice and counsel in tow—I made the decisions that I felt best for my mom. She died after a bedside vigil of some twenty hours."

Rob's story illustrates the Path of Promise. Rob made a commitment to his mother, and she counted on him to make the difficult decisions surrounding her passing. By calling on his inner strength of Promise, Rob fulfilled that duty to her—and to himself. Rob discovered his inner strength of Promise and honored his final responsibility as her son.

WRIGHT

That's great: Purpose, Passion, Power, Possibility, Perspective, Persistence, and Promise. So how do we discover these inner strengths?

BUSH

One way is to take an inventory of the strengths you think you currently have. Write a list of what you think your top strengths are. Then ask three of your close friends, family, or colleagues to write a similar list about you, and compare their answers with yours. You may be surprised at their answers—they may validate some of the strengths you listed, or they may even add other strengths you had not considered!

Another way to discover your inner strengths is to read the descriptions of the seven inner strength paths in this chapter (see below) and identify examples of when you have used each one in your own life For instance, look at the Path of Passion and ask yourself, "What have I done before in my life that was motivated by Passion or our of a desire to do it? What do I love about my life? What gives me joy and excitement? What energizes me?" The answers you get may help you identify what is already present in your life that you love, and what may be missing. This information can provide a direction, a motivation, and even give you new ideas about what else you want to do in your life.

You may also want to talk with a friend or family member about how they have seen you these inner strengths. There are also books and Web sites that help you identify your strengths, such as www.strengthsfinder.com and http://literacyworks.org/mi/assessment/findyourstrengths.html.

WRIGHT

And how do you use these inner strengths?

BUSH

As we've said, all of these inner strengths are paths that can help you reach your goals—your destination of success! Once you identify your inner strengths, you can think of them as paths to help you achieve a goal or make a change that you want. The destination is yours to choose! You may want to ask yourself these questions:

- What is it that I want to do, be, or have?
- Is there a particular issue or situation that is troubling me, and do I want to change it?
- Is there a challenge I have to meet or a choice I need to make?
- Do I have a vague sense of wanting "something better," but I don't know what it is?
- Am I facing a situation that seems overwhelming?
- Have I forgotten about an important goal or dream that I once had for myself?

Here is a list of Guiding Questions for each of the seven Paths. The questions will help identify which inner strength to draw on for any specific situation you face. They may also help you to discover other Paths that could be useful in the situation, and can point the way to develop other strengths that you may not have used successfully in the past.

Guiding Questions for the Seven Paths to Success

Path of Purpose:
- What do I want from this situation (or from my life)?
- What is the outcome that I will get from being a success in this situation?
- What is the benefit that I will see from successfully accomplishing this goal or overcoming this obstacle?

Path of Passion:
- What do I like or love—and how can I use it to create a new opportunity or help me in this situation?

- What gives me joy and excitement?
- What is fun and energizing to me?

Path of Power:

- What is the right thing to do in this situation? What needs to happen here?
- What is my role, my responsibility in this situation?
- What do I know to be true for me in this situation

Path of Possibility

- If money, time, and health posed no issue, what would I like to do (or have happen)?
- What could happen in this situation (both positive and negative)?
- How could I get more information, resources, or ideas (from what, where, from whom)?

Path of Perspective

- How would someone (a personal hero, role model, or yourself from the past or the future) deal with this situation?
- Are there smaller segments, parts (or timeframes) that I can accomplish to get to the goal?
- What is the best thing about this? What is the worst? What am I grateful for in this situation?

Path of Persistence

- How can I link every action, every day, to my overall goal or desire?
- What do I need to keep my energy and enthusiasm at its peak while I achieve this goal or resolve this issue?
- How can I plan or automate the steps I need to take toward the outcome I want, so that they become habits or routines?

Path of Promise

- Why is this goal or outcome important to me?
- Which of my strongest personal values are important in this situation?
- How am I fulfilling a duty or honoring others by meeting this commitment?

WRIGHT

So we've talked about discovering your inner strengths, but once you discover them, how do you develop them?

BUSH

All of us have inner strengths, and most of us have some that are stronger than others. In any journey, we may take a familiar path and then repeat that path so often that we hardly realize there are also other ways to get to our destination. But, to be well rounded and be able to leverage all our resources, it is good to develop as many of the Paths, or inner strengths, as we can draw on.

I have outlined an eight-step process for helping to develop an inner strength as a path to reach any goal. The process starts with choosing an inner strength to develop. Then, identify times in your life when you've used that strength, and rate yourself on how successful you have been at using that strength. Use a "one to ten" scale (with ten being the highest or most successful). To get additional input, ask other people what they have noticed about you in terms of that strength. You can also read biographies of successful people to get ideas about how they have used this specific strength or pathway in their life.

Next, ask yourself if there is a current situation in your life that would be a good place to practice using this strength. If you can identify one, create a list of some ideas or activities that would provide a good opportunity to develop the strength you have chosen. Brainstorm with a friend, pastor, mentor, or coach if you have one. Once you have a list of ideas for using this inner strength in your specific situation, choose one of the ideas and make it into a regular practice. (A practice is a regular ritual or a habit.) By adding this new practice, you create an opportunity to develop the inner strength you want to have.

When you start feeling comfortable with the practice and notice that you are getting results using the specific inner strength that you are developing, go back to your original list of ideas and choose another idea from your list to add as a practice.

This will help you develop even more competence with the particular inner strength that you are developing. At regular intervals—once every month or two—check to see if you are making progress in your situation.

- Are you applying the particular strength more often and/or more easily?
- Do you feel more comfortable or confident using that strength?
- Do you think that using the inner strength is helping you in the situation or goal?
- Are other noticing or commenting on your use of this strength?
- Are you getting closer to a resolution of the situation or to achieving your goal?

If you can answer "Yes" to these questions, then you'll know you are truly developing that specific strength.

Here is the step-by-step process to develop your inner strengths:

1. Pick a strength that you want to get to know better and develop in yourself.
2. Identify times in your past when you have used that strength and received good results, or learn about others who have used that strength to get positive results in their lives. Read biographies of historic figures or ask your friends and family if they know stories that involve this strength.
3. Look for a current situation that would be a good practice ground for this particular strength.
4. Create a list of several actions or practices that leverage this strength and could be helpful in this situation. If you can't think of any, ask your family or friends or a trusted advisor or coach for ideas.
5. Choose one or two of the actions or practices to focus on as a way to practice using this strength in the situation you have identified. Keep a log or journal of how you are doing, and any results you see.

6. When you feel confident and comfortable that you are getting results from these actions or practices, try adding one or two more (from the same strength) to develop even more competence with it.
7. Look at the descriptions of the other six strengths to see if any of them could help you be more comfortable or confident with the strength you are developing.
8. At regular intervals—weekly or monthly, depending on the situation—look back at how you are using your new strength and compare it to how you remember yourself from before you started developing it. Ask your close friends, family, or coach to help assess how you are doing. And, of course, look to see what results you are getting and how comfortable and confident you feel!

WRIGHT

So how can I know which strength or strengths to use in a particular situation?

BUSH

Many people know instinctively which paths to take in a given situation, but it is also important to look at all the strengths and decide which others could apply. It's like having tools in a toolbox—perhaps you always reach for the hammer or the screwdriver or wrench, but once in a while it helps to look at all the tools and ask yourself, "What else could I be using to make my life better or easier?"

Use the Guiding Questions to determine what situation or outcome could come from using each of the strengths. Where would each particular path take you? Then determine if that strength, or path, would benefit you in your current situation. I have included a chart of some particular situations to show which of the strengths would be most helpful. (See Table 1). Use it to match the appropriate path to the goal or destination you desire.

For instance, if you are starting a new job, you might want to call on your Paths of Purpose, Passion and Possibility. Determine how the job fits with your Life

Purpose. Have you selected the job or applied for it with the intention of living your Purpose more fully? Use the Path of Passion to increase your enjoyment and energy by asking, "What parts of this job energize me the most? How can I make the other parts of the job just as interesting?"

Use the Path of Possibility by asking:

- How can I make more out of this job?
- How can this job help to get me where I want to go in life—to my Destination Success?
- What else is possible from working in this job—who else can I meet?
- Can I travel or live in interesting places on assignment for the job?
- Are there opportunities to learn new things, take classes, and get more education through this job?
- How will this job prepare me for a more responsible, higher-paid job in the future?
- Will this job prepare me to be a leader or manager?

By learning to ask yourself questions from all the Paths, you will increase your awareness of the opportunities you have in any situation.

WRIGHT

I'm always interested in continuity of new information or spatial learning. Can any of my strengths help the others?

BUSH

Yes. There is a lot of synergy among these Paths. They actually build on each other. Each of the Paths, or inner strengths, can enable and assist the others. Depending on our destination, we may want to use several of the Paths. For instance, the Path of Possibility can increase both Power and Purpose by helping us identify different solutions or ways to approach a goal. Then Power and Purpose can give us the Persistence that we need, and may be able to help us imagine more

Possibilities or Perspectives to help us succeed. The Path of Persistence can also help us open up more Possibilities over time.

The Path of Promise is about committing to something, being able to stand up for something, saying "I'm going to make this happen!" and then following through. The Path of Promise can help deepen and support the Paths of Purpose, Power, and Persistence as well.

Three Practices to Develop Your Inner Strength

WRIGHT

So what else is important in getting what I want or developing those strengths further?

BUSH

Many of us know our goal—we know that we are destined for success, but when the time comes to call on our inner strengths, we're not sure which Path will get us there the soonest, and the best. So I want to highlight three Practices that can help with discovering and developing our inner strengths.

The Practice of Pleasure

The first practice that will help develop inner strengths is Pleasure. Pleasure is about discovering and doing what you like, creating time to enjoy life, and having fun with friends. There will always be challenges and obstacles to deal with, from petty annoyances to real tragedy and crisis. But even in the midst of problems and challenges, you can practice Pleasure—notice the laughter, beauty, and joy that life brings your way. Practice Pleasure to reward yourself for accomplishing milestones along the way toward your goals. Relaxation, beauty, love, and friendship can help tap into your inner strengths of Passion and Power and Purpose. A little Pleasure can go a long way in helping you achieve your goals and the life of your dreams! Whether it's walking in nature, taking a long soothing bath, hanging out with friends, sharing a great meal, or enjoying your family, practice Pleasure in your life while you're developing all your inner strengths. Then you will enjoy the journey as well as the destination!

The Practice of Partnership

The practice of Partnership is about developing a strong network that supports you in reaching your destination and overcoming any obstacles along the way. Partners can be friends, rabbis, ministers, coaches, counselors, mentors, or family. We can talk with our partners about our goals and dreams, to help make our destination more real, to get feedback about how we are doing, and to talk over our ideas and hopes, and our strategies for getting what we want in life.

The Practice of Partnership can also help us to be accountable for our actions and acknowledge our progress towards the destination, letting us know how we are seen by others, and what we are accomplishing. This practice helps us develop a wide and deep network of support for our goals, dreams, and desires—as well as inspiring those who follow us on the journey to our destination.

The Practice of Patience

A third practice that helps us master all seven of the inner strength Paths is Patience, defined as "being firm in belief, determination, or adherence, despite opposition, difficulty, or adversity."[11] Even when things are going well, and we are using all our inner and outer strengths, it can take time for our situations to change or for us to reach our destination. Patience is the practice of confidence that we will reach the desired goal, even if we don't see immediate results or if we don't get much encouragement from others.

The practice of patience allows us to wait for the outcome to occur when we have done everything in our power to make it happen. Patience is the art of the "long view"—not expecting to get instant gratification or to see immediate results for every effort we make. But Patience only works if we exercise it while taking action toward achieving our goals. If we are not doing what we need to do to reach our destination, our "Patience" is merely wishful thinking! Whether we cultivate Patience in order to develop our inner strengths or as a daily practice to be a better person, it is a way to reduce stress, gain wisdom, and get more enjoyment out of life in the long run.

WRIGHT

Is there anything else you want to tell our readers in closing?

BUSH

David, I've had such a good time discussing all the different paths that we can take to reach our destination of success on the journey of life. These paths, our inner strengths, are like untapped resources that we can call on to help us get what we want in life. I want to encourage all our readers to discover their own inner strengths so that they can design their own futures and be true leaders in their lives. Don't just *live* your life, *lead* your life!

WRIGHT

Well, what a great conversation! I've really learned a lot today; I've been taking notes like crazy! I've written Purpose, Passion, Power, Possibility, Persistence, Perspective, and Promise, and Partnership, Patience, and Pleasure!

I really do appreciate the time you've taken with me to answer all these questions. You have taught me a lot here today, and I know that our readers will enjoy this chapter.

BUSH

Thanks so much, David. It was good to have the opportunity to help people know about how their inner strengths can be the pathways to success. Our readers can log on to my website at www.marywayne.com and share their own stories about discovering their inner strengths.

WRIGHT

Today we've been talking with Mary Wayne Bush, an internationally known speaker, author, and executive coach. She coaches groups and individuals on leadership, communication, and team effectiveness; and she is a world leader in coaching-related research. I don't doubt that at all, based on her conversation with me today!

Mary Wayne, thank you so much for being with us today on *Discover Your Inner Strength*.

BUSH

It has been my pleasure, David!

SITUATION	PATH OF PROMISE	PATH OF PERSISTENCE	PATH OF PERSPECTIVE	PATH OF POSSIBILITY	PATH OF POWER	PATH OF PASSION	PATH OF PURPOSE
You are thinking of retirement and do not know what you want to do			✓	✓		✓	✓
You inherit money and want to invest or use it wisely				✓		✓	✓
You get promoted or have an opportunity to do something new in your job	✓	✓		✓		✓	✓
You have lost a loved one	✓	✓	✓	✓	✓		
You are facing a health crisis for yourself or a loved one			✓	✓	✓		✓
You have lost your job	✓	✓		✓	✓		
You are in a new job				✓	✓	✓	✓
You have just graduated and need to discover what to do with your life						✓	✓

References:

1. Frankl, V. (1966) *Man's Search for Meaning: An Introduction to Logotherapy.* New York, NY: Washington Square Press.
2. St. Anthony Messenger Feature Article. Retrieved June 18, 2009, from http://www.americancatholic.org/Messenger/Jan2004/Feature1.asp#F1.
3. Winfrey, O. (2009, September). "What I Know For Sure," *Oprah Magazine,* 10(9), 232.
4. "Edison Family Album," U.S. National Park Service. Retrieved June 15, 2009, from http://www.nps.gov/edis/home_family/fam_album.htm.
5. Jackson, P. (2006). *Sacred Hoops: Spiritual Lessons of a Hardwood Warrior.* New York, NY: Hyperion.
6. Tolle, E. (2004) *The Power of Now: A Guide to Spiritual Enlightenment.* Novato, CA: New World Library Press.
7. Merriam Webster's Online Dictionary. Retrieved April 12, 2009, from http://www.merriam-webster.com/dictionary/persistent.
8. "A Story About Persistence That Paid Off Big Time." Retrieved June 12, 2009, from http://createbusinessgrowth.com/marketing/a-story-about-persistence-that-paid-off-big-time.
9. Merriam Webster's Online Dictionary, retrieved April 12, 2009, from http://www.merriam-webster.com/dictionary/promise.
10. Historical Resources of the John F. Kennedy Presidential Library & Museum. (1961) *Special Message to the Congress on Urgent National Needs Page 4.* Retrieved September 6, 2009, from http://www.jfklibrary.org/Historical+Resources/Archives/Reference+Desk/Speeches/JFK/Urgent+National+Needs+Page+4.htm
11. Merriam Webster's Online Dictionary. Retrieved April 12, 2009, from http://www.merriam-webster.com/dictionary/patience.

About the Author

Dr. Mary Wayne Bush is an internationally recognized author, speaker, and coach who specializes in helping people get the results they want. She works with organizations and individuals around the world to develop leadership, manage change, build strong teams, and plan for successful futures. Mary Wayne has consulted for multinational, Fortune 100 companies, and is a sought-after speaker and professional coach.

Mary Wayne Bush
Info@marywayne.com
www.marywayne.com
(408) 882-6099

Attitude is Everything

An Interview With...
Dr. Kenneth Blanchard

DAVID WRIGHT (WRIGHT)

Few people have created a positive impact on the day-to-day management of people and companies more than Dr. Kenneth Blanchard. He is known around the world simply as Ken, a prominent, gregarious, sought-after author, speaker, and business consultant. Ken is universally characterized by friends, colleagues, and clients as one of the most insightful, powerful, and compassionate men in business today. Ken's impact as a writer is far-reaching. His phenomenal best-selling book, *The One Minute Manager*, coauthored with Spencer Johnson, has sold more than thirteen million copies worldwide and has been translated into more than twenty-five languages. Ken is Chairman and "Chief Spiritual Officer" of the Ken Blanchard Companies. The organization's focus is to energize organizations around the world with customized training in bottom-line business strategies based on the simple, yet powerful principles inspired by Ken's best-selling books.

Dr. Blanchard, welcome to *Discover Your Inner Strength*.

DR. KENNETH BLANCHARD (BLANCHARD)

Well, it's nice to talk with you, David. It's good to be here.

DAVID WRIGHT (WRIGHT)

I must tell you that preparing for your interview took quite a bit more time than usual. The scope of your life's work and your business, the Ken Blanchard Companies, would make for a dozen fascinating interviews.

Before we dive into the specifics of some of your projects and strategies, will you give our readers a brief synopsis of your life—how you came to be the Ken Blanchard we all know and respect?

BLANCHARD

Well, I'll tell you, David, I think life is what you do when you are planning on doing something else. I think that was John Lennon's line. I never intended to do what I have been doing. In fact, all my professors in college told me that I couldn't write. I wanted to do college work, which I did, and they said, "You had better be an administrator." So I decided I was going to be a Dean of Students. I got provisionally accepted into my master's degree program and then provisionally accepted at Cornell because I never could take any of those standardized tests.

I took the college boards four times and finally got 502 in English. I don't have a test-taking mind. I ended up in a university in Athens, Ohio, in 1966 as an Administrative Assistant to the Dean of the Business School. When I got there he said, "Ken, I want you to teach a course. I want all my deans to teach." I had never thought about teaching because they said I couldn't write, and teachers had to publish. He put me in the manager's department.

I've taken enough bad courses in my day and I wasn't going to teach one. I really prepared and had a wonderful time with the students. I was chosen as one of the top ten teachers on the campus coming out of the chute!

I just had a marvelous time. A colleague by the name of Paul Hersey was chairman of the Management Department. He wasn't very friendly to me initially because the Dean had led me to his department, but I heard he was a great teacher.

He taught Organizational Behavior and Leadership. So I said, "Can I sit in on your course next semester?"

"Nobody audits my courses," he said. "If you want to take it for credit, you're welcome."

I couldn't believe it. I had a doctoral degree and he wanted me to take his course for credit—so I signed up.

The registrar didn't know what to do with me because I already had a doctorate, but I wrote the papers and took the course, and it was great.

In June 1967, Hersey came into my office and said, "Ken, I've been teaching in this field for ten years. I think I'm better than anybody, but I can't write. I'm a nervous wreck, and I'd love to write a textbook with somebody. Would you write one with me?"

I said, "We ought to be a great team. You can't write and I'm not supposed to be able to, so let's do it!"

Thus began this great career of writing and teaching. We wrote a textbook called *Management of Organizational Behavior: Utilizing Human Resources*. It came out in its eighth edition October 3, 2000, and the ninth edition was published September 3, 2007. It has sold more than any other textbook in that area over the years. It's been over forty years since that book first came out.

I quit my administrative job, became a professor, and ended up working my way up the ranks. I got a sabbatical leave and went to California for one year twenty-five years ago. I ended up meeting Spencer Johnson at a cocktail party. He wrote children's books—a wonderful series called *Value Tales® for Kids*. He also wrote *The Value of Courage: The Story of Jackie Robinson* and *The Value of Believing In Yourself: The Story of Louis Pasteur.*

My wife, Margie, met him first and said, "You guys ought to write a children's book for managers because they won't read anything else." That was my introduction to Spencer. So, *The One Minute Manager* was really a kid's book for big people. That is a long way from saying that my career was well planned.

WRIGHT

Ken, what and/or who were your early influences in the areas of business, leadership, and success? In other words, who shaped you in your early years?

BLANCHARD

My father had a great impact on me. He was retired as an admiral in the Navy and had a wonderful philosophy. I remember when I was elected as president of the seventh grade, and I came home all pumped up. My father said, "Son, it's great that you're the president of the seventh grade, but now that you have that leadership position, don't ever use it." He said, "Great leaders are followed because people respect them and like them, not because they have power." That was a wonderful lesson for me early on. He was just a great model for me. I got a lot from him.

Then I had this wonderful opportunity in the mid-1980s to write a book with Norman Vincent Peale. He wrote *The Power of Positive Thinking*. I met him when he was eighty-six years old; we were asked to write a book on ethics together, *The Power of Ethical Management: Integrity Pays, You Don't Have to Cheat to Win*. It didn't matter what we were writing together; I learned so much from him. He just built from the positive things I learned from my mother.

My mother said that when I was born I laughed before I cried, I danced before I walked, and I smiled before I frowned. So that, as well as Norman Vincent Peale, really impacted me as I focused on what I could do to train leaders. How do you make them positive? How do you make them realize that it's not about them, it's about who they are serving? It's not about their position—it's about what they can do to help other people win.

So, I'd say my mother and father, then Norman Vincent Peale. All had a tremendous impact on me.

WRIGHT

I can imagine. I read a summary of your undergraduate and graduate degrees. I assumed you studied Business Administration, marketing management, and related courses. Instead, at Cornell you studied Government and Philosophy. You received your master's from Colgate in Sociology and Counseling and your PhD from Cornell in Educational Administration and Leadership. Why did you choose this course of study? How has it affected your writing and consulting?

BLANCHARD

Well, again, it wasn't really well planned out. I originally went to Colgate to get a master's degree in Education because I was going to be a Dean of Students over men. I had been a Government major, and I was a Government major because it was the best department at Cornell in the Liberal Arts School. It was exciting. We would study what the people were doing at the league of governments. And then, the Philosophy Department was great. I just loved the philosophical arguments. I wasn't a great student in terms of getting grades, but I'm a total learner. I would sit there and listen, and I would really soak it in.

When I went over to Colgate and got into the education courses, they were awful. They were boring. The second week, I was sitting at the bar at the Colgate Inn saying, "I can't believe I've been here two years for this." This is just the way the Lord works: Sitting next to me in the bar was a young sociology professor who had just gotten his PhD at Illinois. He was staying at the Inn. I was moaning and groaning about what I was doing, and he said, "Why don't you come and major with me in sociology? It's really exciting."

"I can do that?" I asked.

He said, "Yes."

I knew they would probably let me do whatever I wanted the first week. Suddenly, I switched out of Education and went with Warren Ramshaw. He had a tremendous impact on me. He retired some years ago as the leading professor at Colgate in the Arts and Sciences, and got me interested in leadership and organizations. That's why I got a master's in Sociology.

The reason I went into educational administration and leadership? It was a doctoral program I could get into because I knew the guy heading up the program. He said, "The greatest thing about Cornell is that you will be in the School of Education. It's not very big, so you don't have to take many education courses, and you can take stuff all over the place."

There was a marvelous man by the name of Don McCarty who eventually became the Dean of the School of Education, Wisconsin. He had an impact on my life; but I was always just searching around.

My mission statement is: to be a loving teacher and example of simple truths that help myself and others to awaken the presence of God in our lives. The reason I mention "God" is that I believe the biggest addiction in the world is the human ego; but I'm really into simple truth. I used to tell people I was trying to get the B.S. out of the behavioral sciences.

WRIGHT

I can't help but think, when you mentioned your father, that he just bottom-lined it for you about leadership.

BLANCHARD

Yes.

WRIGHT

A man named Paul Myers, in Texas, years and years ago when I went to a conference down there, said, "David, if you think you're a leader and you look around, and no one is following you, you're just out for a walk."

BLANCHARD

Well, you'd get a kick out of this—I'm just reaching over to pick up a picture of Paul Myers on my desk. He's a good friend, and he's a part of our Center for FaithWalk Leadership where we're trying to challenge and equip people to lead like Jesus. It's non-profit. I tell people I'm not an evangelist because we've got enough trouble with the Christians we have. We don't need any more new ones. But, this is a picture of Paul on top of a mountain. Then there's another picture below that of him under the sea with stingrays. It says, "Attitude is everything. Whether you're on the top of the mountain or the bottom of the sea, true happiness is achieved by accepting God's promises, and by having a biblically positive frame of mind. Your attitude is everything." Isn't that something?

WRIGHT

He's a fine, fine man. He helped me tremendously. In keeping with the theme of our book, *Discover Your Inner Strength,* I wanted to get a sense from you about your own success journey. Many people know you best from *The One Minute Manager* books you coauthored with Spencer Johnson. Would you consider these books as a high water mark for you or have you defined success for yourself in different terms?

BLANCHARD

Well, you know, *The One Minute Manager* was an absurdly successful book so quickly that I found I couldn't take credit for it. That was when I really got on my own spiritual journey and started to try to find out what the real meaning of life and success was.

That's been a wonderful journey for me because I think, David, the problem with most people is they think their self-worth is a function of their performance plus the opinion of others. The minute you think that is what your self-worth is, every day your self-worth is up for grabs because your performance is going to fluctuate on a day-to-day basis. People are fickle. Their opinions are going to go up and down. You need to ground your self-worth in the unconditional love that God has ready for us, and that really grew out of the unbelievable success of *The One Minute Manager.*

When I started to realize where all that came from, that's how I got involved in this ministry that I mentioned. Paul Myers is a part of it. As I started to read the Bible, I realized that everything I've ever written about, or taught, Jesus did. You know, He did it with the twelve incompetent guys He "hired." The only guy with much education was Judas, and he was His only turnover problem.

WRIGHT

Right.

BLANCHARD

This is a really interesting thing. What I see in people is not only do they think their self-worth is a function of their performance plus the opinion of others, but they measure their success on the amount of accumulation of wealth, on recognition, power, and status. I think those are nice success items. There's nothing wrong with those, as long as you don't define your life by that.

What I think you need to focus on rather than success is what Bob Buford, in his book *Halftime,* calls "significance"—moving from success to significance. I think the opposite of accumulation of wealth is generosity.

I wrote a book called *The Generosity Factor* with Truett Cathy, who is the founder of Chick-fil-A. He is one of the most generous men I've ever met in my life. I thought we needed to have a model of generosity. It's not only your *treasure,* but it's your *time* and *talent.* Truett and I added *touch* as a fourth one.

The opposite of recognition is service. I think you become an adult when you realize you're here to serve rather than to be served.

Finally, the opposite of power and status is loving relationships. Take Mother Teresa as an example—she couldn't have cared less about recognition, power, and status because she was focused on generosity, service, and loving relationships; but she got all of that earthly stuff. If you focus on the earthly, such as money, recognition, and power, you're never going to get to significance. But if you focus on significance, you'll be amazed at how much success can come your way.

WRIGHT

I spoke with Truett Cathy recently and was impressed by what a down-to-earth, good man he seems to be. When you start talking about him closing his restaurants on Sunday, all of my friends—when they found out I had talked to him—said, "Boy, he must be a great Christian man, but he's rich." I told them, "Well, to put his faith into perspective, by closing on Sunday it costs him $500 million a year."

He lives his faith, doesn't he?

BLANCHARD

Absolutely, but he still outsells everybody else.

WRIGHT

That's right.

BLANCHARD

According to their January 25, 2007, press release, Chick-fil-A was the nation's second-largest quick-service chicken restaurant chain in sales at that time. Its business performance marks the thirty-ninth consecutive year the chain has enjoyed a system-wide sales gain—a streak the company has sustained since opening its first chain restaurant in 1967.

WRIGHT

The simplest market scheme, I told him, tripped me up. I walked by his first Chick-fil-A I had ever seen, and some girl came out with chicken stuck on toothpicks and handed me one; I just grabbed it and ate it; it's history from there on.

BLANCHARD

Yes, I think so. It's really special. It is so important that people understand generosity, service, and loving relationships because too many people are running around like a bunch of peacocks. You even see pastors who measure their success by how many are in their congregation; authors by how many books they have sold; businesspeople by what their profit margin is—how good sales are. The reality is, that's all well and good, but I think what you need to focus on is the other. I think if business did that more and we got Wall Street off our backs with all the short-term evaluation, we'd be a lot better off.

WRIGHT

Absolutely. There seems to be a clear theme that winds through many of your books that has to do with success in business and organizations—how people are treated by management and how they feel about their value to a company. Is this an accurate observation? If so, can you elaborate on it?

BLANCHARD

Yes, it's a very accurate observation. See, I think the profit is the applause you get for taking care of your customers and creating a motivating environment for your people. Very often people think that business is only about the bottom line. But no, that happens to be the result of creating raving fan customers, which I've described with Sheldon Bowles in our book, *Raving Fans*. Customers want to brag about you, if you create an environment where people can be gung-ho and committed. You've got to take care of your customers and your people, and then your cash register is going to go ka-ching, and you can make some big bucks.

WRIGHT

I noticed that your professional title with the Ken Blanchard Companies is somewhat unique—"Chairman and Chief Spiritual Officer." What does your title mean to you personally and to your company? How does it affect the books you choose to write?

BLANCHARD

I remember having lunch with Max DuPree one time. The legendary Chairman of Herman Miller, Max wrote a wonderful book called *Leadership Is an Art*.

"What's your job?" I asked him.

He said, "I basically work in the vision area."

"Well, what do you do?" I asked.

"I'm like a third-grade teacher," he replied. "I say our vision and values over, and over, and over again until people get it right, right, right."

I decided from that, I was going to become the Chief Spiritual Officer, which means I would be working in the vision, values, and energy part of our business. I ended up leaving a morning message every day for everybody in our company. We have twenty-eight international offices around the world.

I leave a voice mail every morning, and I do three things on that as Chief Spiritual Officer: One, people tell me who we need to pray for. Two, people tell me who we need to praise—our unsung heroes and people like that. And then three, I leave an inspirational morning message. I really am the cheerleader—the Energizer Bunny—in our company. I'm the reminder of why we're here and what we're trying to do.

We think that our business in the Ken Blanchard Companies is to help people lead at a higher level, and to help individuals and organizations. Our mission statement is to unleash the power and potential of people and organizations for the common good. So if we are going to do that, we've really got to believe in that.

I'm working on getting more Chief Spiritual Officers around the country. I think it's a great title and we should get more of them.

WRIGHT

So those people for whom you pray, where do you get the names?

BLANCHARD

The people in the company tell me who needs help, whether it's a spouse who is sick or kids who are sick or if they are worried about something. We've got over five years of data about the power of prayer, which is pretty important.

One morning, my inspirational message was about my wife and five members of our company who walked sixty miles one weekend—twenty miles a day for three days—to raise money for breast cancer research.

It was amazing. I went down and waved them all in as they came. They had a ceremony; they had raised $7.6 million. There were over three thousand people walking. A lot of the walkers were dressed in pink—they were cancer victors—

people who had overcome it. There were even men walking with pictures of their wives who had died from breast cancer. I thought it was incredible.

There wasn't one mention about it in the major San Diego papers. I said, "Isn't that just something." We have to be an island of positive influence because all you see in the paper today is about celebrities and their bad behavior. Here you have all these thousands of people out there walking and trying to make a difference, and nobody thinks it's news.

So every morning I pump people up about what life's about, about what's going on. That's what my Chief Spiritual Officer job is about.

WRIGHT

I had the pleasure of reading one of your releases, *The Leadership Pill*.

BLANCHARD

Yes.

WRIGHT

I must admit that my first thought was how short the book was. I wondered if I was going to get my money's worth, which by the way, I most certainly did. Many of your books are brief and based on a fictitious story. Most business books in the market today are hundreds of pages in length and are read almost like a textbook.

Will you talk a little bit about why you write these short books, and about the premise of *The Leadership Pill?*

BLANCHARD

I really developed my relationship with Spencer Johnson when we wrote *The One Minute Manager*. As you know, he wrote, *Who Moved My Cheese*, which was a phenomenal success. He wrote children's books and is quite a storyteller.

Jesus taught by parables, which were short stories.

My favorite books are *Jonathan Livingston Seagull* and *The Little Prince*. Og Mandino, author of seventeen books, was the greatest of them all.

I started writing parables because people can get into the story and learn the contents of the story, and they don't bring their judgmental hats into reading. You write a regular book and they'll say, "Well, where did you get the research?" They get into that judgmental side. Our books get them emotionally involved and they learn.

The Leadership Pill is a fun story about a pharmaceutical company that thinks they have discovered the secret to leadership, and they can put the ingredients in a pill. When they announce it, the country goes crazy because everybody knows we need more effective leaders. When they release it, it outsells Viagra.

The founders of the company start selling off stock and they call them Pillionaires. But along comes this guy who calls himself "the effective manager," and he challenges them to a no-pill challenge. If they identify two non-performing groups, he'll take on one and let somebody on the pill take another one, and he guarantees he will outperform that person by the end of the year. They agree, but of course they give him a drug test every week to make sure he's not sneaking pills on the side.

I wrote the book with Marc Muchnick, who is a young guy in his early thirties. We did a major study of what this interesting "Y" generation—the young people of today—want from leaders, and this is a secret blend that this effective manager uses. When you think about it, David, it is really powerful in terms of what people want from a leader.

Number one, they want integrity. A lot of people have talked about that in the past, but these young people will walk if they see people say one thing and do another. A lot of us walk to the bathroom and out into the halls to talk about it. But these people will quit. They don't want somebody to say something and not do it.

The second thing they want is a partnership relationship. They hate superior/subordinate. I mean, what awful terms those are. You know, the "head" of the department and the hired "hands"—you don't even give them a head. "What do I do? I'm in supervision. I see things a lot clearer than these stupid idiots." They want to be treated as partners; if they can get a financial partnership, great. If they can't, they really want a minimum of a psychological partnership where they can bring their brains to work and make decisions.

Then finally, they want affirmation. They not only want to be caught doing things right, but they want to be affirmed for who they are. They want to be known as individual people, not as numbers.

So those are the three ingredients that this effective manager uses. They are wonderful values when you think about them.

Rank-order values for any organization is number one, integrity. In our company we call it ethics. It is our number one value. The number two value is partnership. In our company we call it relationships. Number three is affirmation—being affirmed as a human being. I think that ties into relationships, too. They are wonderful values that can drive behavior in a great way.

WRIGHT

I believe most people in today's business culture would agree that success in business has everything to do with successful leadership. In *The Leadership Pill*, you present a simple but profound premise; that leadership is not something you do to people; it's something you do *with* them. At face value, that seems incredibly obvious. But you must have found in your research and observations that leaders in today's culture do not get this. Would you speak to that issue?

BLANCHARD

Yes. I think what often happens in this is the human ego. There are too many leaders out there who are self-serving. They're not leaders who have service in mind. They think the sheep are there for the benefit of the shepherd. All the power, money, fame, and recognition move up the hierarchy. They forget that the real action in business is not up the hierarchy—it's in the one-to-one, moment-to-moment interactions that your frontline people have with your customers. It's how the phone is answered. It's how problems are dealt with and those kinds of things. If you don't think that you're doing leadership *with* them—rather, you're doing it *to* them—after a while they won't take care of your customers.

I was at a store once (not Nordstrom's, where I normally would go) and I thought of something I had to share with my wife, Margie. I asked the guy behind the counter in Men's Wear, "May I use your phone?"

He said, "No!"

"You're kidding me," I said. "I can always use the phone at Nordstrom's."

"Look, buddy," he said, "they won't let *me* use the phone here. Why should I let you use the phone?"

That is an example of leadership that's done *to* employees, not *with* them. People want a partnership. People want to be involved in a way that really makes a difference.

WRIGHT

Dr. Blanchard, the time has flown by and there are so many more questions I'd like to ask you. In closing, would you mind sharing with our readers some thoughts on success? If you were mentoring a small group of men and women, and one of their central goals was to become successful, what kind of advice would you give them?

BLANCHARD

Well, I would first of all say, "What are you focused on?" If you are focused on success as being, as I said earlier, accumulation of money, recognition, power, or status, I think you've got the wrong target. What you need to really be focused on is how you can be generous in the use of your time and your talent and your treasure and touch. How can you serve people rather than be served? How can you develop caring, loving relationships with people? My sense is if you will focus on those things, success in the traditional sense will come to you. But if you go out and say, "Man, I'm going to make a fortune, and I'm going to do this," and have that kind of attitude, you might get some of those numbers. I think you become an adult, however, when you realize you are here to give rather than to get. You're here to serve, not to be served. I would just say to people, "Life is such a very special occasion. Don't miss it by aiming at a target that bypasses other people, because we're really here to serve each other."

WRIGHT

Well, what an enlightening conversation, Dr. Blanchard. I really want you to know how much I appreciate all the time you've taken with me for this interview. I know that our readers will learn from this, and I really appreciate your being with us today.

BLANCHARD

Well, thank you so much, David. I really enjoyed my time with you. You've asked some great questions that made me think, and I hope my answers are helpful to other people because as I say, life is a special occasion.

WRIGHT

Today we have been talking with Dr. Ken Blanchard. He is coauthor of the phenomenal best-selling book, *The One Minute Manager*. The fact that he's the Chief Spiritual Officer of his company should make us all think about how we are leading our companies and leading our families and leading anything, whether it is in church or civic organizations. I know I will.

Thank you so much, Dr. Blanchard, for being with us today.

BLANCHARD

Good to be with you, David.

About the Author

Few people have created more of a positive impact on the day-to-day management of people and companies than Dr. Kenneth Blanchard, who is known around the world simply as "Ken."

When Ken speaks, he speaks from the heart with warmth and humor. His unique gift is to speak to an audience and communicate with each individual as if they were alone and talking one-on-one. He is a polished storyteller with a knack for making the seemingly complex easy to understand.

Ken has been a guest on a number of national television programs, including *Good Morning America* and *The Today Show*. He has been featured in *Time, People, U.S. News & World Report*, and a host of other popular publications.

He earned his bachelor's degree in Government and Philosophy from Cornell University, his master's degree in Sociology and Counseling from Colgate University, and his PhD in Educational Administration and Leadership from Cornell University.

Dr. Kenneth Blanchard
The Ken Blanchard Companies
125 State Place
Escondido, California 92029
800.728.6000
Fax: 760.489.8407
www.kenblanchard.com

DISCOVER YOUR INNER STRENGTH

8

Principles of Resilience

An Interview With...

Renee Robinson Sievert

DAVID WRIGHT (WRIGHT)

Today we are talking with Renee Robinson Sievert. Renee provides training, team-building, workshops, and coaching to individuals and groups nationally. She serves on the faculty of the University of California Davis Northern Training Academy, San Diego State University Academy of Professional Excellence, and the William R. Mead Academy for Counselors. Renee is a 2009 Tribute to Women in Industry (TWIN) Honoree in San Diego, California, for her work as a training and leadership consultant with Mental Health Systems, Inc. In 2006 she was honored as Mental Health Nurse of the Year by San Diego's North County Civic Association.

Renee, welcome to *Discover Your Inner Strength*.

RENEE SIEVERT (SIEVERT)

Thank you. I'm very happy to be here.

WRIGHT

How do you define resilience and why do you think it's so important?

SIEVERT

Resilience, from a psychological perspective, is the capacity to cope with change, stress, and difficult times. It can be described as emotional resourcefulness, hardiness, and effective coping skills. It is a concept that indicates the cumulative strategies or protective factors a person can nurture in order to remain emotionally healthy and resourceful on an ongoing basis.

WRIGHT

Are you referring to personal or professional hardiness and staying power?

SIEVERT

It really is both. I will present *Ten Principles of Personal and Professional Resilience,* which I hope will enhance resourcefulness strategies. Think of them as strategies for bouncing through life's challenges with power and purpose.

I have always believed that it is imperative to have strategies in both personal and professional life, and they're very much interrelated. However, I think you could agree that there are those who seem to have one and not the other. I know some people who seem to have professional staying power and their personal lives seem to be a mess. In addition, you can probably bring to mind people who are wonderful individuals and their personal lives seem fine and steady, but they can't seem to obtain professional success.

In her book, *The Art of Original Thinking,* Jan Phillips states, "One of the biggest illusions we suffer from is the notion that what goes on inside of us has little to do with who we are on the outside." I believe that we are mind, heart, body, and soul, all together. Our work affects our personal life and our personal existence can affect our work life. To be a leader, we have to trust our experiences and personal knowledge. And if we wish to remain resilient, we need strategies.

WRIGHT

Would you talk to our readers about some occasions in your life when your resilience was tested?

SIEVERT

It seems as though you never know how much you can survive until you're tested to the core. Three experiences come to mind.

One of the most difficult times in my life was when my first husband died in a car accident in 1980. I was twenty-three years old, I had been married only five years, and, of course, I was completely unprepared for facing that kind of a tragedy. The next two years of my life were very, very difficult for many reasons. But I was able to face the challenge and I was able to work through my grief. Somehow in the process I also kept my job, my home, and my sanity.

The second huge loss occurred when my mother died of cancer six years after I was widowed. Other losses in my life followed, and I realized at some point that I indeed had a capacity to weather the pain of those losses. Of course, my strategies were not well formulated. In fact, back then, it was purely instinctive survival mechanisms. Subsequently, after reflecting on that journey, I began to understand that there were specific principles that helped me survive, and they have now become a part of how I live.

I later went on to work in AIDS research and treatment. My own experience of grief and loss prepared me in many ways to help others face devastating life experiences. As a result of my own losses, plus years of working with persons with HIV/AIDS, I learned a lot about life and living. I did a great deal of soul-searching about what I believe, who I am, and how I want to live my life.

Third, I have experienced job loss twice in my career: once because it wasn't a good fit for my skill and knowledge; the other time because an entire training department was eliminated, with me included! I was forced to rely on my own skills and resilience at that point. And, in fact, that's when I started my own company, Sievert Services Consulting and Training Solutions. So it worked out to my advantage that I had some resilience working in my life.

Now I know that this is my purpose and my path in life—reaching out, speaking, coaching, and teaching strategies to be resilient. It also sustains me and makes me learn more from helping others through their experiences.

WRIGHT

So you had to utilize both personal and professional strategies to get through those challenging times in your life?

SIEVERT

Yes I did, and the strategies helped, even though early on I didn't realize they were working.

I had the support of good friends and family, and I was in a very supportive work environment at the time. There were excellent leaders and managers who modeled appropriate responses to my situation. They encouraged me to self-monitor and self-evaluate both my responses and my ability to perform my job. I was able to rely on some really important principles that have become a significant part of my success today.

WRIGHT

What are the first few principles?

SIEVERT

Let me start with personal resilience factors.

Principle One: Learn and Maintain Healthy Self-Care Habits

This principle is all about the biological ways that we can decrease stress, change brain chemistry, and help our bodies to reach optimal functioning. Take care of tension with exercise, relaxation, or meditation. Pay attention to nutrition, get adequate sleep, and spend time out in the fresh air.

We've been seeing more and more about nutrition and exercise and how they contribute to our self-confidence and self-esteem. One very simple thing we can do to boost our health is to increase our time in natural light. Get outside for just ten to fifteen minutes at least two or three times a week! Sunshine helps our body produce vitamin D, and studies suggest vitamin D assists our immune system. Along with calcium, vitamin D is also essential in bone health. Sunshine and light also have mental health benefits and can reduce symptoms of depression by activating endorphins. In fact, light is a proven treatment for seasonal depression. Sunlight, fresh air, and exercise combined have an incredibly positive effect upon the brain and nervous system.

Sleep is very critical as well. Our bodies depend on the sleep cycle in order to rest and repair. We can go without food for days and weeks, but we can't go without sleep for more than a few days. We really don't know exactly why people need sleep, but we know that lack of sleep can be very damaging. Humans deprived of sleep have difficulty concentrating, can't make decisions, and, if sleep deprivation continues, may begin hallucinating or become delusional. Sleep allows our neurons to rest and repair damage so we are better able to function.

Ask yourself honestly if you are getting enough sleep. Find a way to add even one or two hours of sleep and you will notice a difference after just a week or two. Pay attention to your nutrition and treat yourself to some sunlight and fresh air a few minutes every day.

Principle Two: Maintain a Positive Outlook

Creating and sustaining a positive outlook doesn't just happen to us; it takes time and attention. Useful strategies include seeing the humor in life, keeping things in perspective, nurturing a positive self-view, and maintaining hope. There are wonderful books written about this subject. Some of my favorites include *If Life is a Game, These Are the Rules*, and the collections of *Don't Sweat the Small Stuff* and *Chicken Soup for the Soul*.

Laughter, music, meditation, quiet time, inspirational reading, and helping others can all contribute to a positive outlook. And while you are at it, look for the best in everyone. It will help with your positive outlook.

Principle Three: Create and Nurture Connections with Others

Having the skills to form healthy attachments, nurture relationships, and maintain a support system are important aspects of resilience. When we're feeling unsure, fragile, or depressed, or when a crisis occurs, we need to know whom we can turn to and rely on. From time to time we also need to take an inventory to determine whether we're spending time with those who support and nurture us or with those who drain us and exhaust our energy.

In a book I co-authored called *Feeling Terrific: Four Strategies for Overcoming Depression Using Mood Regulation Therapy*, there is an exercise that I've used for years to help a person take a closer look at his or her support circle and examine the network and relationships that might either drain or nurture. In this exercise I ask you to draw two circles (an inner circle and an outer circle).

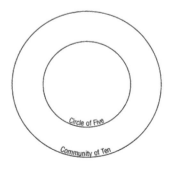

In the inner circle, think of the first five people you might call or turn to if you were in a crisis or in distress and wanted to talk to someone you trust. They also might be the same people you would call if something wonderful happened to you. Write their names down in the inner circle. We will call these your "Circle of Five."

Let's say you got a voicemail or answering machine when you called each of them. Who would be next on the list? Write the names of the next five people in that second circle. Now you can see your "Circle of Five" and "Community of Ten."

Next, review your Circle of Five and Community of Ten. Do you have enough people in your network? Are these people you can depend on? Are these people who will be there for you and with you? When is the last time you saw or talked to these people? What have you done lately to appreciate, honor, or acknowledge these people in your life? Consider a phone call or a card to let them know how you feel and how important they are. Nurture these connections.

This is a useful exercise to do from time to time. It can help you identify people you can depend upon and it can help you recognize the wealth—or the void—in your support system.

Principle Four: Strive for Balance

Strive for balance in work, home, and play. This is easier said than done for many of us. These days, demanding jobs may leave us feeling stressed out and in a state of imbalance. We may have lost sight of the benefits of "down time." Relaxation is as important as working.

When suffering from stress or fatigue, remove yourself from your usual environment to gain a different perspective. Take time to replenish, reflect, relax, and play. Do you make time for yourself away from work? Do you step away from your desk or workstation for even ten minutes a few times per day? If your answer is no, it is time to begin to pay attention to this area of your life and find ways to add this to your daily routine.

If you are self-employed, ask yourself when you last took time off. If you work at home, when is the last time you got away? If you work for a company, take an honest look at your vacation hours, sick hours, the amount of time that you've missed from work and why. This will give you an idea if you have created a balance. Some employees, managers, and executives have massive amounts of vacation time built up and never take time off. Then there are others who have used up so much of their sick and vacation time for illness, stress, or taking care of others that they haven't left any for themselves.

Frequently, I speak at workshops and conferences and coach people who are in the helping professions—such as nurses, counselors, therapists, and social workers—careers that really call for resilience. Professionals in these kinds of careers must carefully guard against burnout, vicarious trauma, and compassion fatigue.

Burnout is a cumulative response to constant levels of high stress. The workload can create a state of physical, emotional, and mental exhaustion and can deplete our ability to cope. Lack of attention to the first four principles can also contribute to burnout.

Secondary traumatic stress can occur when a person cares for or is exposed to another person's experience of trauma or extreme events. This "bearing witness" to those stories of traumatic events can create vicarious trauma and may lead to compassion fatigue, described as the convergence of burnout, stress, and secondary traumatic stress.

Caregivers must pay attention and take care of themselves so that burnout doesn't happen. And for those in a helping profession, resilience strategies are very important. Clinical supervision and assistance in guarding against vicarious trauma and compassion fatigue are crucial here.

Time away from work and making time for activities you enjoy contribute to a healthy balance in life. The key word here is "balance."

WRIGHT

These are four very important principles for taking care of one's self, but these are not new concepts. Why is it important to mention them here?

SIEVERT

Doesn't it seem that the simplest things are what we often forget during challenging times? We take care of everything and everyone else around us, and then—if there is time—we take care of our own needs. In actuality, we need to place ourselves first, and then we will be better able to confidently and competently attend to everything and everyone else in our lives.

WRIGHT

True. So you've addressed four of the ten principles. Can we move on to the next four?

SIEVERT

Principle Five: Clarify Expectations, Set Realistic Limits, and Accept Help

Many of us have been disappointed in both personal and professional relationships simply because we didn't state our expectations out loud. Perhaps we didn't clarify or check out the expectations that others might have for us. For example, when providing counseling or coaching for couples, one of the first things I ask is, "Have you ever sat down and told each other what your unsaid expectations are?" These people are often disappointing the other person simply because the expectations were not said out loud or the expectations were never clarified verbally.

Expectations are not bad and often they're needed. They help us know what we will be held responsible for. People being hired for a job need to know what the expectations and duties of the job are. An important part of leadership is setting the vision and goals and then communicating these to the team and the organization. This helps clarify expectations.

Being realistic about how much to take on is also important. Unmet deadlines, getting in over your head, being resentful after you have a project—all of these will contribute significantly to increased stress and decreased happiness. Know when to ask for help, accept help, and let go if you can. The need to control is a huge contributor to stress and can decrease resilience.

Principle Six: Be Open and Flexible

This relates to expectations, but more importantly it is about intention. Live and work with intention and strive to be accepting and allowing. If your intention is to be open and flexible, then you will guard against rigidity and inflexibility, two huge contributors to stress.

If you're working within or leading a team, it is essential to be open to other ideas and input. Remember that there are many different paths to the same goal. Sometimes you might even reevaluate or redefine the goal after receiving input from other people.

Author Wayne Dyer advises us to be "gentle, soft, and allowing." I really like this concept; I encourage people to embrace it, and I incorporate it into workshops on communication and listening.

Principle Seven: Don't Put Off Difficult Decisions or Critical Conversations

Brian Tracy speaks about this concept in leadership. Avoidance will significantly increase stress and chip away at resilience. What are one or two difficult personal or work-related situations that you have been avoiding? How much stress is this avoidance causing in your life or your work? We have ultimate control over stress. As Wayne Dyer states, "Stress is one of the few things that does not exist on its own—we create it." And avoiding difficult decisions creates stress.

Face it! Make an honest appraisal of the situation, collect information, evaluate concerns, seek guidance from trusted people, consider the options, think it through, and get on it. Take action. Then move on. Celebrate the good decisions and learn quickly from the ones that aren't so good.

Another central concept that will help when facing difficult decisions and critical conversations is to speak from your heart. This reminds me of Randy Pausch, the professor at Carnegie Mellon who gave *The Last Lecture* after having been diagnosed with terminal cancer. His complete lecture was on YouTube and several news programs. Do you remember him?

WRIGHT

Oh, yes.

SIEVERT

Randy Pausch said that if he could give only three words of advice, they would be: "tell the truth." Then he said if he could have three more words, he would add, "all the time." Excellent advice, don't you agree? I try to live and work in the truth, from the heart.

Author Martha Beck, in life coach training, taught us the "TAO of Coaching: Transparent, Authentic and Open." These simple guidelines are crucial to my work and integral in being a successful coach and consultant. I believe that one of the key qualities of a great leader is the ability to gracefully and compassionately tell the truth in a strategic manner—not bulldozing people, but just gently laying things out on the table and saying, "We need to talk about this, we need to look at this, we need to make a decision about this."

Face the critical conversations—those exchanges at work or in your relationships that you may dread. You may not like having to do this but when you avoid it, things usually get worse. So, take the plunge—speak your truth. Initially, the first conversations may be nerve-wracking and anxiety provoking, but once you start to speak honestly, in a caring and compassionate way, you will walk away believing that it's better to put these things out in the open. It gets easier and will become a part of you. Speaking the truth contributes to self-confidence and resilience.

A wonderful resource for preparing for these exchanges is *Crucial Conversations: Tools for Talking When Stakes Are High*, by Kerry Patterson, Joseph Grenny, Ron McMillan, and Al Switzler. The book outlines a powerful seven-step approach to handling difficult conversations with confidence and skill. If you are someone who avoids saying what you think or discussing uncomfortable issues, the book is waiting for you.

Principle Eight: Stay Away from Negativity

This is related to the earlier principle of maintaining a positive self-view, but I believe it deserves its very own category. A negative attitude is catching; it can spread like wildfire. Be aware, and beware, of people who complain or feel miserable all the time. Be careful about connections with those who criticize or gossip about others with you or to you. Make a conscious effort to move away from negativity and increase your moments of grace. Practice gratitude and kindness. Simple actions such as writing what you are grateful for each day can significantly dissolve negativity in your life and increase resilience.

Surround yourself with positive people. There is a wonderful movement called A Complaint Free World. Visit their Web site, *AComplaintFreeWorld.com,* and take the twenty-one-day challenge!

WRIGHT

Who are the people who have inspired you and have served as role models for resilience, and which leaders in the field are teaching and talking about these concepts?

SIEVERT

I love to be inspired. I want to live an inspired life each day and moment, with intention, so I read, listen to CDs, and attend workshops to help me with clarity and focus. Some of my favorite authors are in this very book, *Discover Your Inner Strength*: Brian Tracy, Ken Blanchard, and Stephen Covey. Others with lasting influence from early in my career are Louise Hay, author of *You Can Heal Your Life*, Steven Levine who wrote *Who Dies?* and *A Year to Live*, and Jack Canfield who teaches *The Success Principles*. I also love Wayne Dyer's *Inspiration: Your Ultimate Calling* and *The Power of Intention*. I've been to several of his live workshops, including his 2009 live taping for PBS, *Excuses Begone*. Jon Kabat-Zinn has a CD titled *Mindfulness at Work* which is very insightful.

These are authors who have written many inspirational books and teach skills that are vital for personal and professional resilience. Reading any of these authors' works or attending conferences or motivational workshops will keep increasing one's self-awareness and therefore resilience. And this is a nice segue to principle number nine.

Principle Nine: Consistently Seek Opportunities for Growth

Reading this book, *Discover Your Inner Strength*, is certainly a step in the right direction! Dream big, set goals, and move toward them. Consider therapy if you have not resolved serious issues from the past. Face the things that hold you back or create barriers to your success. Sometimes just attending a workshop, reading a book, or listening to a CD will help change your perspective and help you grow. Martha Beck's *Finding Your Own North Star* or *Steering by Starlight* and Jack Canfield's *Ten Steps to Success* are brilliant works that can help create a shift in you—to open things up and help you reset your path.

Turn to others for guidance or mentoring. Call a life coach or executive coach if you are stuck or getting in your own way. Work on dissolving negative and limiting thoughts. I recommend Byron Katie's *The Work*. I frequently use this in my coaching practice; it is also an efficient tool for self-coaching when I'm stuck. *The Work* is a simple, yet powerful process of inquiry that teaches you to identify and question the limiting thoughts that are causing suffering or creating barriers. It provides a way to understand what is hurting you and to address those problems with clarity. In its most basic form, *The Work* consists of four questions and a turnaround, and it can create an incredible shift in your perception. Give it a try!

Stagnation contributes to stress and low morale. Self-appraisal, self-awareness, and consistently seeking opportunities for growth will contribute to staying power.

WRIGHT

So how can a leader contribute to the resilience of a team or an organization?

SIEVERT

As a leader, you have tremendous influence on the people you lead. Work to maintain personal and professional clarity, focus, and resilience. Practice these principles and model them for others. Embrace a philosophy of health, self-care, balance, and growth. Incorporate these into the core values, the mission, and the vision of your organization. Embrace these concepts in staff development and training, and create learning opportunities for employees where they can gain exposure to concepts that contribute to resilience.

Whether in hiring, supervision, or ongoing work with management teams or employees, strive to create an opportunity for personal mastery, team learning, and shared vision.

One of my favorite leadership authors, Peter Senge, in his book *The Fifth Discipline,* outlines these concepts and provides an excellent blueprint for a learning organization. An organization that values and nurtures individuals and teams, evaluates its systems, and creates a learning environment will be a resilient organization.

This brings us to the tenth and final principle. It is a simple one that will contribute to happiness and resilience.

Principle Ten: Give Back Whenever You Can

Mentor others, be a role model, and share what you know. It will make you feel good about yourself, it will contribute to your positive self-view, and it will help others. Your advice and your experience are of value and can help others along their path. Celebrate their success.

Take time to acknowledge your value and consider how you contribute to the big picture at work, in your community, and in the world.

WRIGHT

How do you use these concepts in coaching, team building, and leadership consulting?

SIEVERT

I welcome and congratulate individuals who want to remove barriers, embark on a new journey, and participate in designing the life they were meant to lead. This always begins with a set of questions designed for self-assessment, which includes uncovering dreams and goals, utilizing exercises to dissolve old and unhealthy beliefs, changing or eliminating ineffective habits, and laying the groundwork for healthy practices of resilience.

In leadership consulting and team building, the process is similar. I learn about the organization's values, vision, and mission. I meet with the leader or leaders, discuss the goals, and then begin to work through some thoughtful self-evaluation about the needs of the team and the organization. Often it is very simply one or two or three of these resilience principles that we start to work on immediately.

These principles are incorporated into most of the workshops and conference sessions I present. I find that, no matter what the topic, whether clinical work, management, or leadership, when I mention resilience and self-care, there is a shift in the energy in the room because it creates an opportunity for reflection. Many of us are accustomed to going to workshops for knowledge and skills and increasing our capacity for work, but so often we forget self-care or replenishing.

WRIGHT

The *Ten Principles of Personal and Professional Resilience* are listed at the end of this chapter. Will you provide advice or guidelines about how to begin incorporating these principles into our personal and professional lives?

SIEVERT

Yes. I have two simple suggestions. The first assignment is to consider the three most stressful things that you are dealing with in your work life or in your personal life right now. Write these down on a piece of paper. Then read through the *Ten Principles* at the end of the chapter and identify at least one or two principles that will help you with each stressful item on your list. I know you'll find a strategy to help with every stressful situation, event, or relationship.

The second assignment is to honestly rate yourself on a scale of zero (lowest) to ten (highest) for each of the *Ten Principles*. How well do you incorporate each of these principles or practices into your personal or professional life?

Congratulate yourself on the ones that you rated the highest, because you are doing well in those categories. Look at the ones that you rated lower or lowest. Make a commitment to yourself that you will begin to address these principles or suggestions underneath each principle and consciously increase your attention, your intention, and your practice in these areas.

These assignments will provide you with two ways to immediately grab hold of these principles and use them.

WRIGHT

So what is the takeaway message about resilience that you want our readers to remember?

SIEVERT

Think of resilience as your staying power and your capacity to weather leadership, management, and relationship challenges—indeed, all of life's challenges. Much like happiness and success, resilience does not happen by chance. We must seek strategies for resilience, and we must adopt these healthy practices in all facets of our lives. Just as there are steps to success, there are specific principles and habits to consistently practice and keep in the forefront in both our personal and professional lives in order to stay resilient.

You are the only one who can create, nurture, and maintain your own resilience through life's challenges, so the time is now. Pick up the principles and use them.

WRIGHT

Great information, Renee. I really do appreciate all the time you've taken with me this morning to discuss this important chapter in our book, and I want to thank you for the information that you've given to us. I've taken notes copiously, and maybe it will help me.

SIEVERT

Well, thank you, I hope so. These are principles that have helped me through the worst times in my life, and I use them in the best times in my life as well. It is my pleasure to contribute to this project!

WRIGHT

Today we've been talking with Renee Robinson Sievert. She provides training, team-building workshops, and coaching to individuals and groups throughout the country. Renee, thank you so much for being with us today on *Discover Your Inner Strength*.

Ten Principles for Personal and Professional Resilience

Principle 1

Learn and Maintain Healthy Self-Care Habits. Eat balanced meals, get adequate sleep. Take care of tension with exercise, relaxation, or meditation. Get outside in the fresh air and sunlight a few minutes each day.

Principle 2

Maintain a Positive Outlook. Keep things in perspective and maintain a hopeful outlook. Begin each day with positive intention. Look for the best in others.

Principle 3

Create and Nurture Connections with Others. Take an honest assessment of your "Circle of Five" and "Community of Ten" and evaluate your support system. Connecting with supportive people strengthens resilience.

Principle 4

Strive for Balance. Take vacations. Do things just for fun. Maintain a balance between work, home, and play. When suffering from stress, fatigue, or burnout, remove yourself from your usual environment to gain a different perspective.

Principle 5

Clarify Expectations, Set Realistic Limits, and Accept Help. Clarify expectations in relationships, review responsibilities at work. Many people find it difficult to say "no," yet this leads to overload, one of the leading causes of burnout. Setting limits is a valuable skill in both personal and professional life. Ask for help and accept it from others.

Principle 6

Be Open and Flexible. Stress can result from rigidity and inflexibility. Allow for the possibility that there is more than one path to any given goal. Focus on accomplishments and acknowledge progress.

Principle 7

Don't Put Off Difficult Decisions or Critical Conversations. Tell the truth. Make an honest appraisal of the situation, collect information from all sources, seek guidance from trusted persons, consider your options, and think it through—then take action. Celebrate good decisions and learn quickly from the others.

Principle 8

Stay Away from Negativity. Surround yourself with positive people. Beware of people who complain or feel bad all the time. A negative attitude is catching. Work on dissolving negative or limiting thoughts. Visit *AComplaintFreeWorld.com* and take the twenty-one-day challenge.

Principle 9

Consistently Seek Opportunities for Growth. Clear up your past. Practice self-awareness and self-appraisal. Turn to others for guidance or coaching when you hit barriers. Set goals and move toward them.

Principle 10

Give Back Whenever You Can. Share what you know. Be a role model and a mentor to others. Take time to acknowledge your values and consider how you contribute to the big picture at work, in your community, in the world.

About the Author

Renee Robinson Sievert brings a wealth of knowledge and insight to her work with individuals and groups. With over twenty-five years of experience in counseling, consulting, and training for social service agencies, business organizations, and executive teams, she designs and delivers presentations, team-building, and coaching workshops nationally.

Renee has a unique ability to make each person feel heard while still challenging the limiting beliefs or mental models that create barriers to success. She truly listens, engages team members in thoughtful dialogue, and skillfully guides them to find their own solutions.

Trained as a Master Life Coach by bestselling author and *O Magazine* contributor Martha Beck, PhD, Renee is a member of the International Speakers Network, the International Coach Federation (ICF) and the International Motivational Interviewing Network of Trainers (MINT). She is co-author of *Feeling Terrific: Four Strategies for Overcoming Depression Using Mood Regulation Therapy,* published by iUniverse.

Renee Robinson Sievert, RN, MFT

Sievert Services
Consulting and Training Solutions
10601 Tierrasanta Blvd. #G-240
San Diego, CA 92124
(619) 507-6683
(858) 560-1238 Fax
SievertServices@aol.com
www.SievertServices.com

Discover Your Inner Strength for Maximum Success

An Interview With...
Dr. Brian Williams

DAVID WRIGHT (WRIGHT)

We are pleased to have Dr. Brian Williams, also known as "Dr. B," as a contributing author of our discussions about discovering your inner strength. He is The Head Coach of College Success™ as he speaks to and coaches college students about college success. Dr. B is a motivational speaker, author, coach, and seminar leader. Since 1989, he has delivered hundreds of presentations, including keynote speeches, breakout sessions, seminars, and workshops in many parts of the United States. Along the way, he has inspired thousands of people to tap into their greatness so that they can maximize their potential and achieve all they can achieve. Dr. B, welcome to *Discover Your Inner Strength*.

DR. BRIAN WILLIAMS (WILLIAMS)

Thank you, David. It's a pleasure to be here with you today.

WRIGHT

Would you start today by telling our readers what this book has the potential to do for them?

WILLIAMS

Let me start by saying that I'm very excited to discuss the topic of discovering your inner strength. When I was asked to contribute to this book, I was certainly honored. I think that this book has the potential to do four major things for our readers:

1. People who read this book and apply its principles will come to realize that they have a unique inner strength—a power that lies within that needs to be discovered, unlocked, and unleashed so that it can be utilized to its fullest extent to benefit the world.
2. Everyone who peruses this book with a genuine desire to discover their inner strength will be empowered to uncover their purpose and potential and then maximize that potential so that they can achieve their personal and professional endeavors.
3. People will come to understand how to overcome the challenges and obstacles that stand in the way of their discovering, utilizing, and maximizing their inner strength.
4. Those who read this book will see a plethora of examples of people who have discovered their inner strength and then magnified that inner strength by making their mark. This will help our readers see themselves from a different perspective and gain a deeper understanding of themselves, which

can reveal their inner strength, their individual purpose, and their place in the world so that they can achieve maximum success in life.

WRIGHT

Great! I know that our readers will be able to benefit greatly from this powerful book. So, how do you define a person's inner strength?

WILLIAMS

People's inner strength is their talent, their ability, their inner power, and their individual greatness! It is a gift that all people possess that was bestowed upon them to make a significant difference in their lives and in the lives of those around them. There is something very special inside of everyone. That may be difficult to comprehend, but it is true. Orison S. Marden once stated, "There are powers inside of you, which if you could discover and use, would make of you everything you ever dreamed or imagined you could become." As simple as it may seem, a person's inner strength might be his or her talent to teach, to build, to play a musical instrument, to communicate, to make people laugh, to plan, to lead, to speak, to organize, to sing, to write, to uplift, to act, to inspire, to draw, to listen, to paint, and so many others!

Marden also said, "Deep within man dwell these slumbering powers; powers that would astonish him, that he never dreamed of possessing; forces that would revolutionize his life if aroused and put into action." This inner strength that each of us has is unique because we each express our inner strength in a different way than others express theirs.

I had heard of and seen other people's inner strength for many years, but the first time I pondered over the concept of "greatness" within myself was in the 1990s when I was working in Washington, D.C. I was really enjoying my job, had just received a bonus for my work on an important project, and I was invited to accept a leadership role that would require the use of all my abilities.

Shortly after I accepted the leadership role, I called an old friend and talked with him about how my professional career was progressing, and I explained to him my new leadership role. After expressing his congratulations to me, my friend mouthed six words that I will never forget. He said, "You are being groomed for greatness!" When he made that statement, it shocked me because I never thought of myself as great or having any form of "greatness."

After internalizing my friend's profound declaration, I came to realize that I did possess a form of "greatness"—an inner strength that had been entrusted to me to influence the lives of others and it was very exciting for me to realize that! Discovering your inner strength will really excite you because it's your passion! It's what you absolutely love to do! We have all been lighted to touch the world, and I believe that as we do this, we're going to find great joy, peace, and happiness within.

WRIGHT

Thank you, Dr. B. Who needs to discover their inner strength?

WILLIAMS

Every single person needs to discover his or her inner strength because everyone has a purpose in life, a unique assignment that is interconnected with his or her inner strength.

Years ago, motivational speaker Keith Harrell said, "The two most important days of our lives are the day we were born and the day we realize why we were born." Now, that's a powerful statement! But, why is it so significant? Because each of us has a purpose for being here, and that purpose is strongly tied to the inner strength that each of us possesses. Think for a moment. Of all the trillions of people who were ever born, you and I were chosen to be here at this particular time because we have a purpose to fulfill at this particular time. Robert Byrne has said, "The purpose of life is a life of purpose."

I believe that all human beings have been entrusted with at least one strength to fulfill their individual purpose, and in the process, significantly influence the world!

But, before we can affect the world, we must first discover what our inner strength is and then find our purpose or our "place" in this world.

The lyrics of the song, "Place in this World" by Michael W. Smith are relevant to discovering your inner strength. He wrote:

"The wind is moving, but I am standing still.
A life of pages waiting to be filled.
A heart that's hopeful, a head that's full of dreams.
But this becoming is harder than it seems.
Feels like I'm looking for a reason, roaming through the night
to find my place in this world, my place in this world."

Now, that's both fascinating and pertinent to our topic.

WRIGHT

Absolutely. So, why is discovering their inner strength so important for people today?

WILLIAMS

Discovering our inner strength is extremely important today because we live during an extremely important time in history! There are more medical advancements today, more technology today, and so many more opportunities to succeed today than there has ever been in the history of mankind! For instance, there are over a hundred thousand patents issued for new inventions each year in the United States alone, which adds value and ease to our lives. We live during a time that our ancestors of yesterday could only dream of. Their hopes, dreams, and visions for a better future are now our reality and we have a distinct responsibility to take full advantage of the opportunities that lie right before our very eyes. And a gigantic part of those opportunities is to discover our inner strength and then utilize it and magnify it to make our mark!

It is also important for people to discover their inner strength today because when we take a look around the world, many people are not living their dreams, following their passion, and doing what they love to do for a living. Many people are waking up in the morning dreading another day at work, but we weren't born to work for a living, we were born to live our work.

When people don't love what they do at work, it affects the type of attitude that they bring with them to work, it affects how their colleagues view them at work, and it affects so many other things, including their bottom-line performance at work. But, more importantly, when people lack passion and purpose for what they do professionally, it also negatively affects their personal life. It affects everything and everyone they come in contact with because they're not fully utilizing the inner strength that they possess. Maxim Gorky has said, "When work is a pleasure, life is a joy! When work is a duty, life is slavery."

As a result of people not fully utilizing their inner strength, the world is cheated out of benefitting from those gifts, talents, and abilities that were meant to be utilized and magnified for the benefit of the world. When this happens, the world is thrown out of balance because the inner strength that a person was entrusted with remains dormant and unutilized. It's like playing in the biggest game of the year unaware that your best player is sitting on the bench, and unfortunately, the team will likely lose the game because its best player was not identified, utilized, or maximized.

On the other hand, when people have identified their strengths, talents, and abilities, and are utilizing and maximizing them professionally, they are most likely doing what they love to do for a living. In the words of William Hazlitt: "Men of genius do not excel in any profession because they labor in it, but they labor in it because they excel." They've discovered exactly what their entrusted powers, gifts, and talents are, and they're magnifying them for others to see, which greatly benefits mankind! As a result, they are making a major difference in society, and the entire world is a more balanced place, where more people are benefitting from the inner strengths that are being utilized and magnified.

WRIGHT

Thanks for sharing that, Dr. B. Now, if discovering your inner strength is so important for people today, why aren't more people discovering their inner strength and then magnifying it?

WILLIAMS

Excellent question, David. I think there are five main reasons why most people are not discovering and magnifying their inner strength. First, most people just don't know that they have an inner strength within themselves, but they'll watch and listen to others who have discovered and magnified their inner strength. This is why *American Idol* has been the top rated television show in America since 2004 and it's why the Super Bowl has been the most watched television telecast over the last nine years. Most people want to watch those who maximize their talents and live their dreams, but as far as their own talents and abilities go, most people are oblivious to the fact that they too have strengths that need to be seen and heard. Consequently, they are as Benjamin Franklin described, "sundials in the shade" because they have not tapped into their greatness! It was Augustine who said, "People travel to wonder at the height of mountains, at the huge waves of the sea, at the long courses of rivers, at the vast compass of the ocean, at the circular motion of the stars, and they pass by themselves without wondering."

The second reason is that most people do not know how to discover their inner strength, which prevents them from truly magnifying their inner strength. There is an old maxim that says, "What you don't know won't hurt you," but is that really true in all cases? What we don't know can in reality hurt us, and in the case of not knowing how to discover our abilities and talents can hurt and affect not only us, but so many others in the world who are not benefitting from what we have been given.

Third, most people take their inner strength for granted. They use their talents and abilities all the time, and often these talents and abilities are so easy and simple for them to utilize that they typically overlook their value to themselves and to mankind. Earl Nightingale's words come to mind when he said:

> "Things that are given to us for nothing, we place little value on; things that we pay money for, we value. The paradox is that exactly the reverse is true. Everything that's really worthwhile in life came to us free: our mind, our soul, our body, our hopes, our dreams, our ambitions, our intelligence, our love of family, and children, and friends. All these priceless possessions are free, but the things that cost us money are actually very cheap and can be replaced at any time."

Most people take for granted, overlook, and undervalue their inner strength because they haven't paid any money for it and their quest to discover the inner strength within themselves is only as strong as how much they value it.

Fourth, most people are not willing to work hard and put forth the effort needed to magnify their inner strength. I'm reminded of the story in one of my favorite books, where a man gave three people talents. He gave the first person five talents, the second person received two talents from him, and he gave the third person one talent.

Over a period of time, the person with five talents worked very hard and smart by taking his five talents and magnifying those talents into five other talents, giving him ten total talents. The person who was given two talents also worked hard and smart and magnified his two talents into two other talents, giving him a total of four talents. But the person who received one talent did not magnify or maximize his talent. He simply buried his talent, probably hoping that it would grow, multiply, and prosper on its own without any effort on his part, but he was mistaken. When he uncovered the talent he had buried, it was still only one talent and the man who had previously given him the talent was displeased with him and took the one talent he had and gave it to the person who had magnified his five talents into ten talents, which now gave that person a total of eleven talents. As the old saying goes, "If you don't use it, you lose it."

The obvious moral to this story is that we not only have to receive our talent(s), but we have to do everything within our power to utilize them and magnify them, not only for our own benefit but for the benefit of our family, our friends, and everyone we come in contact with. Oliver Wendell Holmes has said, "Every calling is great when greatly pursued."

The fifth reason why more people aren't discovering and magnifying their inner strength is because most people use excuses to excuse themselves from living their dreams. George Washington Carver has said, "Ninety-nine percent of the failures come from people who have the habit of making excuses." The common excuses of "lack of time," "fear of rejection," "lack of education," "no support," "lack of resources," and "too old to start" limit our personal and professional potential. Someone once said, "Your potential is limited only by how many excuses you have." In my life, I have learned that our woulda's, coulda's, and shoulda's are no gooda's! It was George Bernard Shaw who once said, "People are always blaming their circumstances for what they are, I don't believe in circumstances; the people who get on in this world are the people who get up and look for the circumstances they want and if they can't find them, make them." So, instead of settling for excuses that we may use today, I think it's vitally important that we discover the inner strength that we've been given and then maximize it to the best of our ability.

WRIGHT

Thanks for that insight, Dr. B! Now, you're the Head Coach of College Success.

WILLIAMS

Yes, I am.

WRIGHT

Will you please tell us how discovering your inner strength relates to college students obtaining success in school?

WILLIAMS

Yes, and thank you for asking about that because I have a passion for speaking to and coaching college students about college success! I think that discovering your talents, abilities, and strengths has a lot to do with college students achieving college success.

When people think about college success, most of them think of how to get good grades in college. While getting good grades in school is important, it is just as important to be studying the right major and attending the right classes while in school, which relates to our topic of discovering your inner strength. David, just out of curiosity, what did you major in during college?

WRIGHT

I was a Fine Arts major in Music.

WILLIAMS

Music. That's fascinating! Now, did you begin your freshman year with that same college major?

WRIGHT

Absolutely. I entered into school in the Summer of 1957 in the University of Tennessee as a Music student in Fine Arts.

WILLIAMS

Wow! That's very rare for a person not to change college majors during their undergrad years. Music must be one of your inner strengths?

WRIGHT

Well, actually I went into business after college, but I have used music for years. I've been on a Church staff with Church music now for over 50 years. I direct the First United Methodist Church music program; and also I directed the Choral Society, which is a classical group, an orchestra; and I still write compositions and things—so I use my music as an avocation.

WILLIAMS

Great! That must feel wonderful, knowing what your inner strength is and then following through on it during your college years and throughout your life!

WRIGHT

Right.

WILLIAMS

Did you have any other interests while in college?

WRIGHT

I had a second interest, which was psychology. So, I really poured a lot into the music and also in psychology. It's the psychology that has helped me form so many businesses. I've actually been in the business world now since I was about twenty-two.

WILLIAMS

So, psychology and how it relates to running a business must be one of your talents as well.

WRIGHT

Business is all about psychology in my opinion.

WILLIAMS

That's great to know! Thank you for sharing that insight with me.

WRIGHT

So, how about you, Dr. B? Did you ever change your college major?

WILLIAMS

I changed my college major only one time, but it was a big change for me. When I started my freshman year, I was majoring in Business Management because it was the college major of my mentor. I had learned so much from him, and I had looked to him for so much direction. At the time, I figured that if my mentor majored in Business Management and was able to do the things he could do with that college major, then I should also major in Business Management.

As my sophomore year in college was coming to a close, I decided that majoring in Business Management was not for me. Then I was fortunate to make one of the best decisions during my time as a college student by changing my college major to Communications because that was where my talents, abilities, and strengths were.

I realized during my sophomore year that choosing the right college major can be just as difficult as getting good grades in college. Choosing the right college major is a very tough and frustrating process for so many college students for various reasons. One reason is because there are so many college majors to choose from. This, among other factors, can make the decision process a very difficult ordeal for many college students, especially those who face this challenge without expert advice or guidance.

Not long ago, I had a conversation with a friend who told me that if she could go back and do college over again, she would major in Biology and become a forest ranger because that's where her inner strength and her passion is! David, so many people have had similar experiences. Think for a moment—wouldn't getting good grades in college be that much better if you were studying a major that was in alignment with your individual, unique inner strength?

WRIGHT

Oh yes, it would be much better. Do you have any programs that are designed to help college students choose the right college major?

WILLIAMS

Yes, I do. I have developed an exciting program that specifically guides college students through that extremely important and sometimes difficult process. More information about this program can be found at ChoosingTheRightCollegeMajor.com. There are so many benefits to this great program, and I'm very excited about sharing it with college students who want to choose the right college major and put themselves in alignment with their assignment.

WRIGHT

That's a good way to put it, Dr. B. What a great resource for college students. I wish I'd had that when I was choosing my college major. I hope that many college students will go to that Web site and benefit from your exciting program. Would you share with our readers some examples of people who have discovered their inner strength and achieved success in the process?

WILLIAMS

I'd be happy to share some examples. One that comes to mind immediately is Berry Gordy, Jr. At the age of eight, he wanted to do something with his life that would make people happy. He eventually discovered his inner strength, like yours David, in music as a songwriter, and by the late 1950s, he was co-writing songs for the great singer and performer, Jackie Wilson. But, Gordy didn't stop there. He also possessed a gift for identifying musical talent, producing songs, and bringing people together, so he began discovering talented singers, musicians, songwriters, and artists. In 1959, Gordy borrowed $800 from a family member and founded what would later be known as Motown Records, and the rest is history!

Think of all of the artists that we saw and heard who signed with Motown Records years ago—Diana Ross, Stevie Wonder, the Supremes, Smokey Robinson, the Temptations, Marvin Gaye, the Four Tops, Michael Jackson, the Vandellas, Mary Wells, the Miracles, Lionel Richie, Gladys Knight and the Pips, the Marvelettes, Jr. Walker and the All-Stars, the Isley Brothers, the Jackson 5, and the Commodores.

Those names and groups may be familiar to you, but what about other not-so-familiar names that helped to make Motown Records what it eventually became? These include The Funk Brothers, Cholly Atkins, Maxine Powell, Maurice King, Eddie Holland, Lamont Dozier, Brian Holland, Barrett Strong, Mickey Stevenson, Suzanne de Passe, Norman Whitfield, Harvey Fuqua, Nick Ashford, Valerie Simpson, The Corporation, and so many others. When you finally take it all in, every single one of those artists, songwriters, choreographers, and musicians discovered their inner strength and magnified it for the world! All of this was made possible by the vision and leadership of Berry Gordy, Jr., who simply discovered his talent in music and then utilized it to create "The Sound of Young America," which some people referred to as, "happy music."

Helen Keller, one of the most prolific authors of all time, is another example of a person who discovered her inner strength and achieved success in the process. Here was a person who was born with eyesight and hearing, but eventually became blind and deaf because of an illness when she was nineteen months old. She was the first ever deaf and blind person to earn a Bachelor of Arts degree. Later in life, she went on to say, "I thank God for my handicaps, for through them, I have found myself, my work, and my God." It was through Keller's challenges and obstacles that she truly found her inner strength and her purpose. She lived her life in complete alignment with her unique talents, and we have all greatly benefited from the rare inner strength that she discovered.

Another example is Michael Jordan, one of the greatest basketball players of all time. I remember Game 5 of the 1997 NBA Finals between the Chicago Bulls and the Utah Jazz. Jordan was nauseated and had been vomiting throughout the day. Team doctors diagnosed him with a stomach virus and the Bull's trainer told Jordan that there was no way that he could play in the game that night. But Jordan refused to accept that as an excuse and he played. He couldn't even walk onto the court at times during the game. However, when the game was over, he had 38 points, 7 rebounds, 5 assists, 3 steals, and 1 blocked shot to propel his team to victory. He did all of this while having a stomach virus. His teammates had to carry him off the court because he was so weak and so tired. But Michael Jordan had discovered his inner strength. He was living his dream as a world champion, and nothing was going to stop him from magnifying his inner strength for the world to see!

A lot of people listen to that story and they think, "Well, Michael Jordan was simply born with that high level of talent and greatness." The way he played the game of basketball made it easy for people to forget that he had been cut from his high school basketball team during his sophomore year.

I mention Jordan here because it took him a long time to discover that playing basketball at an extremely high level was a talent—an inner strength he had been given to affect the world. But when he discovered it, he certainly maximized it! When I interviewed Jordan in November of 1996, he shared with me the extremely rigorous preparation and practice time that he invested not only on the court, but off the court in the film room to watch, understand, and master the game of basketball. During his era in professional basketball, I can't think of any player who worked harder, who practiced more, who played smarter, or who had more of a desire to win than him. Jordan performed at a level that is rarely seen because he was willing to find his inner strength. Once he found it, —he was willing to do the things today that others wouldn't do so that he could have the things tomorrow that others wouldn't have. Jordan would no doubt agree with what Michelangelo, the great artist, said on one occasion: "If you knew how much work went into it, you wouldn't call it genius." He was such a great example of discovering your inner strength!

There are scores of other examples of people who have discovered their inner strength and achieved success in the process. They include: Abraham Lincoln, George Washington Carver, Clara Barton, Albert Einstein, Elgin Baylor, Dr. Martin Luther King, Jr., Eleanor Roosevelt, Johnny Unitas, Jessie Owens, Venus and Serena Williams, James Brown, Ray Kroc, Frederick Douglass, Lucille Ball, Muhammad Ali, Pavarotti, Martha Stewart, Jackie Robinson, Roger Federer, Ella Fitzgerald, Usain Bolt, Jim Brown, Victor Borge, Rosa Parks, Charlton Heston, Kobe Bryant, Michael Phelps, Julia Child, Barack Obama, Hank Aaron, Babe Ruth, Harriet Tubman, Frank Sinatra, Duke Ellington, Wayne Gretzky, Susan B. Anthony, Tiger Woods, Jim Henson, Jack Johnson, Oprah Winfrey, Sammy Davis, Jr., George Lucas, John Legend, Carol Burnett, Oscar Robertson, Les Brown, Wilma Rudolph, Pelé, Earvin "Magic" Johnson, Karen Carpenter, Nelson Mandela, Vince Lombardi, Bill Cosby, Amelia Earhart, Thurgood Marshall, Tom Brady, Denzel Washington, Maya Angelou, Fred Rogers, Lena Horne, Bill Russell, Doris Day, Charlie "Tremendous" Jones, Shari Lewis, Sidney Poitier, Fred Astaire, Cheryl Miller, Ray Charles, Jerry West, Alicia Keys, Joe Louis, Colin Powell, Bjorn Borg, Jackie Joyner-Kersee, Charles Schultz, Satchel Paige, Cicely Tyson, Mel Blanc, Louis Armstrong, Sandra Day O'Connor, Darrell Green, Zig Ziglar, LeBron James, and frankly too many others to list! We could literally go on for days listing more names of people who truly discovered their inner strength and magnified it for the benefit of mankind!

WRIGHT

Wow! All of those names you mentioned, Dr. B, bring back so many memories. Will you help us understand how people can discover their inner strength?

WILLIAMS

Definitely. In order for people to discover their inner strength, I would encourage them to answer the following five questions:

1. What comes easy to you and is difficult to others?
2. What would you do for years and years and never get paid for it?
3. If you knew you were going to die soon, what would you regret the most if you did not accomplish it before you died?
4. What would your passion be if you already had all of the money you needed?
5. What do most people compliment you on?

You see, in that fifth question, there is an inference that our willingness to listen to others as well as listen to ourselves can greatly influence our discovering our inner strength. The old poem comes to mind that states:

"The wise old owl sat in the oak.
The more he sat, the less he spoke.
The less he spoke, the more he heard.
Oh, why can't we be like that wise old bird?"

The ability to listen is a major key that will help to open the door to reveal the inner strength that we all possess. It was William James who once said, "Seek out that particular mental attribute which makes you feel most deeply and vitally alive, along with which comes the inner voice which says, 'This is the real me,' and when you have found that attitude, follow it." That's a powerful truth!

One of the best kept secrets in life and in discovering your inner strength is the same counsel that many parents tell their children. It is to simply be yourself. Someone has said, "It's hard enough being who you is without being who you isn't." Another person said, "Be yourself. Who else is better qualified?" When we are truly ourselves, or our authentic self, we learn what our inner strength is and who we really are. Superstar singer, Mary J. Blige puts it this way: "Don't hold back, you just be yourself . . . Work what you got."

The profoundness in being yourself lies in the fact that one thing we all have in common is that we're all different. So when people discover their inner strength, they will realize it is something that makes them different, distinguishable, and unique in a very good way. If you notice, the real difference makers in the world are in fact different.

It is also important to know that discovering your inner strength can be thrust upon you without warning. A few years ago, I was working as a senior consultant with IBM, and while I was working on a project, my supervisor sent me an e-mail, stating that he wanted to meet with me the next morning. When we met together, he communicated to me that I was being laid off. During my long drive home, I thought to myself, "What do I do now to make a living to support my family and how do I move forward from this?" It was at that point when my inner voice began to remind me of who I really was and what my true inner strength was.

My thoughts took me way back to when I was participating in a ninth grade science fair project competition, which was primarily based upon an oral presentation of the project. When the science fair judges came over to inquire about my project, I was somehow able to freely express my thoughts and ideas vocally like I had never expressed them before. I remembered how the judges carefully listened to my words with astonishment, but their astonishment was nothing compared to how surprised I was at myself because I had a speech impediment when I was in the first grade. But during my ninth grade science fair project's oral presentation, my tongue was loosed and it was like time literally stood still as I was speaking. A short while after the judges left my area, it was announced that I won first place for the entire ninth grade class. I then realized that I had a talent and ability to articulate and communicate effectively. I had discovered my inner strength!

During my difficult drive home after being laid off, my inner voice had helped me to realize that it was time to embrace my inner strength, utilize it, and maximize it with every ounce of energy that I had. Just before I arrived home, I noticed that all of my questions had been answered; and fortunately, I was willing to listen to my inner voice. Then, I began planning how I could magnify this talent and ability I had been entrusted with to contribute to the world and make a significant difference.

My lay off from IBM brings to mind something someone has said, "In life, when you don't have enough insight or courage to know that you have outgrown a situation and it's time to move on, life will move on you!" Life certainly moved on me, and in a strange way—it put me back in alignment with my purpose in life, which was to inspire others to achieve all that they can achieve! My mentor, world-renowned motivational speaker, Les Brown has aptly stated, "You haven't been fired if they let you go on your job. You haven't been laid off; you've been released so you can live your purpose." And that's exactly what happened to me. I was released to be myself so that I could live my purpose as a motivational speaker, author, coach, and seminar leader. Shakespeare once said, "To thine own self be true." I now have the freedom to speak to and coach college students and other people all over the world, and they would not have heard my voice or benefitted from my coaching had I still been working as a senior consultant with IBM.

My experience of being laid off helped me to realize that I already possessed the talents, strengths, and abilities that were necessary for me to succeed in my professional career as a motivational speaker. Zig Ziglar, the great motivational speaker, has said, "You already have every characteristic necessary for success if you recognize, claim, develop, and use them." Ziglar's statement is reminiscent of *The Wizard of Oz* when the Scarecrow, the Tin Man, and the Lion found that they already possessed what they needed within themselves when they faced their biggest challenges. Orison S. Marden aptly stated, "The golden opportunity you are seeking is in yourself. It is not in your environment; it is not in luck or chance, or the help of others; it is in yourself alone." This is true of everyone on the planet! They already have within themselves the inner strength that is necessary for them to make their mark!

So, it's vitally important for us as human beings to search for and discover the inner strength that we have. Marcus Aurelius, the Roman Emperor, once said, "Look well into thyself; there is a source of strength which will always spring up if thou wilt always look there." Once we find our inner strength, we should focus our undivided attention on it because someone once said, "What we focus on the longest becomes the strongest." When we utilize our inner strength, focus our attention on it, and then magnify it for the world to see, it will bring purpose, true happiness, and fulfillment to our lives.

WRIGHT

Thank you for sharing that with us.

WILLIAMS

You're welcome, David.

WRIGHT

What would you say to our readers who have tried to magnify their inner strength to the world after they discovered it, but have not been able to?

WILLIAMS

My message to them is to never give up, because success is not convenient. Dr. Charles Udall has commented, "In life, you will always be faced with a series of God-ordained opportunities brilliantly disguised as problems and challenges." After we have discovered our inner strength, we have to go after magnifying our inner strength with persistence, patience, and perseverance! It's important to remember that Colonel Harland Sanders was sixty-five years old when he used $105 from his Social Security check to begin franchising Kentucky Fried Chicken (KFC) restaurants. He discovered his inner strength much earlier in his life, but it took patience and perseverance as he was rejected over a thousand times while trying to maximize his talent of cooking fried chicken by establishing his franchises.

Many others have encountered challenges, adversity, rejection, and obstacles before they were able to magnify their talents for the world to see. Screenwriter, director, actor, and film producer, Tyler Perry faced adversity that was so intense that he was forced to live out of his car for a period of time before maximizing his gifts, abilities, and talents. Walt Disney was not only rejected various times, he also went bankrupt before creating the world-famous Walt Disney Company.

Thomas Edison, the great inventor, experienced various setbacks before creating 1,093 U.S. patents, which included the light bulb, the motion picture camera, and the phonograph. Although it may seem as though the life of the richest self-made woman in America has always been easy, Oprah Winfrey has had to endure a series of very difficult challenges and obstacles in her life in order to maximize her great talents and abilities.

In February 1962, Decca Records refused to sign four musicians to a contract on the basis that they sounded too much like another band and that guitar groups were on their way out. But these musicians refused to give up and within two years, the Beatles were on their way to becoming one of the most successful rock/pop groups of all time!

No matter how many times you've tried to maximize your inner strength and have not achieved it, the key is to never, ever give up. On one occasion, Thomas Edison remarked, "I have not failed. I've just found 10,000 ways that won't work." My friend, motivational speaker Willie Jolley, often says, "A setback is a setup for a comeback." Dr. Robert Schuller has said, "Tough times never last, but tough people do." When people really go after magnifying their inner strength with persistence, patience, and perseverance, they will eventually magnify and maximize their inner strength and literally influence the world!

WRIGHT

Thanks, Dr. B. You've been speaking to audiences for over twenty years about how they can achieve success. Tell us how discovering your inner strength will help people achieve real success in life.

WILLIAMS

Discovering your inner strength and achieving real success in life are closely related to one another. All people have the opportunity today to make their mark and achieve whatever level of success they desire by discovering their inner strength, which will lead to their eventual success in life.

Les Brown has declared, "Find what you love to do and then find someone willing to pay you to do it, and that is true success." Thus, real success in life is tapping into our greatness by discovering our inner strength and then living our passion by doing what we love, which is also what we do best. As we live our dreams and express what we do best by utilizing our talents, we are achieving real success in life. This also has monetary benefits. Les Brown has also said, "Living our making will make our living." In other words, when people discover their inner strength and do what they were born to do, they're going to benefit monetarily from their talents and abilities because they'll be expressing their inner strength so well that people will want to invest in what they have to share with the world.

For example, let's take a look at teachers who have the talent to teach others. If they are teaching to the very best of their ability, they are achieving real success in their professional career.

I had an excellent first grade teacher, Ms. Thomas, when I was six years old. She had everything! She was smart, she was attractive, and she was single! But, more important than all of that was her beauty on the inside. She was so caring. The old cliché is true: "People don't care how much you know until they know how much you care." Someone else has said, "It is nice to be important, but it is more important to be nice." Because Ms. Thomas was caring and nice, she became important to me.

One day, my mother took me to see the doctor because I was not pronouncing my words correctly. The doctor told my parents that I had a speech impediment. When I went back to school, my mother told Ms. Thomas that I had a speech impediment. When my mother left the room, Ms. Thomas turned to me and said something that I will never forget. She bent down, looked me square in the eyes, and said, "Don't you worry about that; you just keep going, just keep going." Those words have served to strengthen me over the years, and they came from a teacher who had truly discovered her inner strength and was maximizing her talent to teach others.

Ms. Thomas wasn't just there to pick up a paycheck every two weeks. Teaching students was her work. She made the ordinary look extraordinary. No matter what we did in class—reviewing the alphabet, counting numbers, or reading books—she helped to instill confidence within me because she had the contagious positive attitude of "you can do it!" George Washington Carver once said, "When you can do the common things of life in an uncommon way, you will command the attention of the world." Because of Ms. Thomas' talent to teach, she commanded my attention and she will eventually command the attention of the world. She was truly achieving success in life because she had discovered her inner strength and she was doing what she loved to do. It was obvious.

When people tap into their greatness, discover their own unique inner strength, and then magnify it for the world to see, as my first grade teacher did, they will feel a sense of happiness and satisfaction in knowing that they are living their dreams and achieving real success in life! Johann Wolfgang von Goethe has said, "The man who is born with a talent which he is meant to use finds his greatest happiness in using it."

Just a few months ago, I attended a seminar and the speaker invited those with talents, strengths, and abilities to share them with the entire group. There were people who raised their hands and began sharing their inner strength with the group, and then all of a sudden, we were in amazement when one person stood up and said, "I've had the talent to sing my whole life, and now I'm ready to share it." She asked for the microphone and began to sing and we all looked at each other in astonishment because we knew that here was a person who had kept her talent inside for years and years. Her voice and performance were absolutely amazing! I was watching a person who had truly discovered her inner strength, and she was now utilizing her inner strength by willingly sharing it with our group! I could see her high level of joy and satisfaction as she sang the song because she was releasing the inner strength she had inside of herself for years, and I was inspired! She made the commitment that day that she would no longer hide her talent, but she would use her talent of singing to influence the world. When she fulfills that commitment, she will be achieving real success in life!

WRIGHT

Thank you for sharing those stories with us, Dr. B. As we conclude our discussion, what final thoughts do you have for our readers about discovering your inner strength?

WILLIAMS

I'd like our readers to remember the great advice that Dr. Myles Munroe has given: "The key to life is to live full, and die completely empty." While we are still breathing, it is extremely important for us to truly live our lives in a purposeful way so that we can have a positive effect on our family, our community, and the world. I say this because there are so many people who have gifts, talents, strengths, and abilities, but for some reason, their inner strength is not being shared with the world.

There are many painters in the world, but they aren't painting pictures. There are various writers around the globe, but they aren't writing songs, books, articles, and lyrics. There are plenty of speakers throughout the world, but they aren't speaking to audiences and influencing lives. There are various musicians in the world, but they aren't making music. There are lots of comedians around the globe, but they aren't making people laugh. There are so many people whose inner strength is not being utilized and maximized and the world is being cheated because it is not benefitting from those many talents that would have made a difference in the lives of others.

If we don't contribute to the world in ways that we know we should, we will have missed an opportunity of a lifetime to make a difference. Mother Theresa has said, "We ourselves feel that what we are doing is just a drop in the ocean, but the ocean would be less because of that missing drop."

Recently, one of the greatest entertainers of all time, Michael Jackson, passed away at the age of fifty. His passing has caused me to reflect deeply on the importance of discovering your inner strength. Jackson's great talents, abilities, and strengths were evident and often on display during his live performances, music videos, and memorable songs, including fourteen number one Billboard hits. From the moment he, along with his four older brothers, auditioned for Berry Gordy, Jr. at Motown Records on July 23, 1968, Jackson was so musically gifted that everyone watching him perform on stage could not take their eyes off him for one moment. Oliver Wendell Holmes has revealed, "Most people go to their graves with their music still inside them." This certainly was not the case with Michael Jackson. Those close to him have stated that he acknowledged he possessed talents, abilities, and greatness, which obligated him to share his inner strength with the entire world. My hope is that people around the world will adopt this same attitude from "The King of Pop." The lyrics to "Man in the Mirror," one of Jackson's number one hits, illustrates this point:

> "I'm starting with the man in the mirror;
> I'm asking him to change his ways.
> And no message could have been any clearer;
> If you wanna make the world a better place,
> Take a look at yourself, and then make that change!"

I encourage people who have not discovered their inner strength to take a look at themselves and then do whatever they can to awaken their sleeping giant within and make that change because one of the biggest tragedies of life is to never wake up and to go to the grave with your greatness untapped. Unfortunately, the wealthiest place on Earth is the graveyard because that is where many of the talents, abilities, and strengths entrusted to people are still buried today. They were never released to the world and because they were not released, they died along with their custodian.

Years ago, John Greenleaf Whittier said, "Of all sad words of tongue or pen, the saddest are these: 'It might have been.' "

To our readers, I say, you might have a gift to discern the good in others, to write, to build, to speak, to mentor others, to sing, to listen, or to make people laugh. You might have an ability to teach others, to play a musical instrument, to repair things, to lead others, to design, to solve problems, to care for others, or to draw. You might have a talent to create, to organize, to encourage others, to paint, to play sports, to market, to investigate, or to recognize the talents of others. What greatness is inside of you? What is the inner strength that you know deep down inside you need to share with the world? What will your legacy be? What is your purpose, your individual assignment while you are here on the planet?

Whatever it is, do something right now to make it happen so that you can be in alignment with your assignment. If you don't know what your purpose is, then find out what it is and then design your life around your inner strength by setting some goals and then map out a plan as to how you will accomplish those goals to awaken your inner strength. Henry David Thoreau, the famous author, has wisely counseled, "I have learned, that if one advances confidently in the direction of his dreams, and endeavors to live the life he has imagined, he will meet with a success unexpected in common hours." Once you have discovered and awakened your inner strength, it is absolutely vital that you maximize that inner strength for your maximum success and to make a lasting impression on the world. Mac Anderson once remarked, 'May it be said when the sun sets on your life, you made a difference.' "

I'd like to close with this poem from Edgar A. Guest, titled "Equipment:"

"Figure it out for yourself my lad,
You've all that the greatest of men have had,
Two arms, two hands, two legs, two eyes;
And a brain to use if you would be wise.
With this equipment they all began.
So start from the top and say, "I can."

Look them over, the wise and the great,
They take their food from a common plate.
And similar knives and forks they use,
With similar laces, they tie their shoes.
The world considers them brave and smart,
But you've all they had when they made this start.

You can triumph and come to skill,
You can be great if you only will.
You're well equipped for what fight you choose,
You have arms and legs and a brain to use.
And the man who has risen great deeds to do,
Began his life with no more than you.

You are the handicap you must face,
You are the one who must choose your place.
You must say where you want to go,
How much you will study, the truth to know.

God has equipped you for life, but He
Lets you decide what you want to be.

Courage must come from the soul within,
The man must furnish the will to win.
So figure it out for yourself my lad,
You were born with all that the great have had.
With your equipment, they all began,
Get a hold of yourself and say, "I can."

WRIGHT

That was great, Dr. B! I really appreciate the time you've taken with me this afternoon to answer all of these questions. You have enlightened me and you've also inspired me.

WILLIAMS

Thank you very much, David. I really appreciate the time that we've invested today! It's been my pleasure to be with you this afternoon.

WRIGHT

Today we've been talking with Dr. Brian Williams, also known as "Dr. B." He is The Head Coach of College Success™ as he speaks to and coaches college students about college success. He is a motivational speaker, author, coach, and seminar leader.

Dr. B, thank you so much for being with us today on *Discover Your Inner Strength*.

About The Author

Dr. Brian Williams, aka "Dr. B," is The Head Coach of College Success™. He is a motivational speaker, author, coach, and seminar leader. Born in inner-city Washington, D.C., Dr. B has overcome many difficult challenges in his life, including a speech impediment and being an underachiever in high school. He also struggled at a local community college, but eventually Dr. B learned how to succeed in college. He has experienced the rare combination of both underachieving in college and attaining the highest level of success in college. Today, Dr. B is sharing his expertise of college success as he speaks to and coaches college students.

His mentor, world-renowned motivational speaker, Les Brown, has called Dr. B "Mr. Charisma." Since 1989, he has delivered hundreds of motivational presentations, including keynote speeches, breakout sessions, seminars, and workshops in many parts of the United States while inspiring thousands of people to tap into their greatness so that they can maximize their potential and achieve all they can achieve. Dr. B is an innovative speaker, masterfully mixing business savvy with inspirational wisdom from his life's experiences. His speaking style includes thoughtful questions, humor, storytelling, voice imitations, and powerful quotations during his high-content messages.

Because of his charismatic personality, Dr. B's electrifying presentations captivate audiences and persuade them to believe that they can reach their potential. His carefully customized keynote speeches and breakout sessions are insightful, funny, dynamic, and full of practical advice as he shares numerous pearls of wisdom to solve problems. Dr. B's audiences leave wanting more and motivated to take action. In 2008, he was called a "world-class speaking talent!" His professional speaking services include:

- Speaker at Colleges and Universities
- Expert on TV, Radio, and Panels
- Keynote Speeches
- Conference Breakout Sessions
- Seminars, Workshops, and Boot Camps

Prior to his professional speaking career, Dr. B worked for George Washington University, the Utah Jazz Basketball Club, the U.S. Senate, and IBM Corporation. His clients include:

- College of Southern Maryland
- Fordham University
- George Washington University
- Marriott International, Inc.
- Microsoft Corporation

He received his doctorate degree in Human and Organizational Learning under the academic advisement of world-renowned Action Learning expert, Dr. Michael Marquardt from George Washington University's Executive Leadership Doctoral Program. His dissertation research about the listening behaviors of hospitality managers at a large Mid-Atlantic Region Marriott hotel was recognized as one "with distinction." Dr. B has an MA in Human Resource Development from George Washington University, and a BA in Communications from Brigham Young University, where he received the "Outstanding Broadcast/Journalism Student Award." He is also a certified coach.

Dr. B is the co-author of *Discover Your Inner Strength* with authors Stephen R. Covey, Ken Blanchard, and Brian Tracy. Dr. B has also compiled and arranged *A Quotation A Day: A unique collection of some of the most powerful thoughts and funny sayings ever spoken for your daily motivation!*

He is a member of the National Speakers Association (NSA), Toastmasters International, Boy Scouts of America (BSA), the BYU Management Society, and Board Member—World Institute for Action Learning (WIAL).

Dr. Brian Williams
Dr. Brian Williams Enterprises, Inc.
P.O. Box 23448
Washington, DC 20026
800-721-1384
www.DrBrianWilliams.com
www.facebook.com/DrBrianWilliams
www.twitter.com/DrBrianWilliams
www.linkedin.com/in/DrBrianWilliams
www.youtube.com/DrBrianWilliams
www.myspace.com/DrBrianWilliams

10

Healed Hands, Healing Hearts a "Survivors" inside perspective from the Australian Outback

An Interview With…
Michael Skupin

DAVID WRIGHT (WRIGHT)

Today we are talking with Michael Skupin. Not many people have a passion for life like Michael, the forty-eight-year-old software entrepreneur, motivational speaker, salesman, author, hunter, athlete, father of seven, and star of the CBS television hit reality show *Survivor: The Australian Outback*. This popular show became the most watched series in the history of television. Michael was the guy who was headed for the winners' circle when he tragically passed out into a fire and was medivaced in a helicopter to two different hospitals for treatment. *TV Guide* voted that incident as the twenty-first most unexpected moment in television history.

Five of the top burn surgeons in Australia were flown in to evaluate Michael's injuries. Michael was told he would have to have a series of three skin graph surgeries to repair his hands. The burns were so severe that skin had to be grafted from another part of Michael's body and stitched or grafted onto the most severely burned areas. He'd burned the nail beds right off and was told his fingernails would never grow back. He was told that the 35 percent of his hands having third degree burns would be left with scar tissue when healed, but they would do the best they could to minimize it. His hands had swelled up to four times their normal size and the surgeons had to wait until the swelling went down to perform the first procedure.

The next ten days in the intensive care unit turned out to be life changing for Michael. After a lot of self-evaluation, deep prayer, and some of the most painful and extensive cutting-edge occupational and physical therapy, something changed. As Michael was being wheeled into the surgery suite to have the first of three surgeries Dr. Pogg, the chief of surgery removed his bandages to evaluate how much grafting he would have to do during the first procedure. Astonished at what he saw, he said, "That's *impossible!* I've been the chief of surgery in the number one burn center in Australia for thirty-five years and what's happened to your hands is medically unexplainable." In a fifteen-minute period, Michael went from being wheeled into surgery to being released from the hospital! Michael went to the hospital daily for the next seven days until Dr. Pogg finally released him saying that he was going to be fine.

After almost an entire year of therapy, Michael's hands ended up completely healed without any surgery whatsoever. His fingernails grew back, he has all the feeling back, and his hands are virtually completely scar free. The only remaining reminders are one small faded circular spot on each wrist and that's a great story, too!

Michael's speaking career began when he returned home and his phone started ringing "off the hook." Michael spoke over three hundred times that first year and more than four hundred times the following year throughout the world and continues to speak frequently to all kinds of audiences.

Michael's story about how his hands were healed and the life lessons he learned in the Australian Outback is incredibly inspirational. He talks about how he was stripped of everything familiar to him including food, shelter, electronics, cell phones, computers, family, and friends. He found that he was able to see much more clearly the life that he was missing out on.

Michael is determined to reach people's souls with a very encouraging and endearing message of family, priorities, life's lessons, and endurance. He uses humor, exciting stories, and dramatic videos from the Outback as he combines them into an adventure story packed with lessons that have his audiences on the edge of their seats.

People come from all over to hear Michael's story of the healing of his hands and they walk away with the story of the healing of his heart.

Michael, welcome to *Discover Your Inner Strength*.

MICHAEL SKUPIN (SKUPIN)

I'm thrilled to be a part of this project, David.

WRIGHT

I understand that *Survivor: The Australian Outback* was the most watched television show in history. You were on the second season. Will you tell us, from the beginning, what interested you about the show in the first place and how you were selected? As I understand it, there were more than sixty thousand applicants for that season.

SKUPIN

It's quite interesting because "reality television" as we know it today was nonexistent at that time. Although I've always been adventurous, my life was ordinary from the standpoint of raising kids and going to work every day. My kids were watching the first season of *Survivor;* I never watched a single episode.

During the first season, after the third or fourth episode, the Network wanted to secure more audition videotapes so they advertised on the screen that they wanted people to apply. My kids begged me for about a month to try out for that show. So, having never watched it, just to placate my children, I went down to a casting call and I filled out an application. This application was approximately twenty pages long. I didn't even know how to fill it out because it asked questions like, "Who are you most like in the current season?" I hadn't watched the current season so I was asking people around me. No one wanted to talk to me because no one wanted to give me a competitive advantage. I still find that very humorous.

Additionally, I remember a question, "If you were president of the United States, what would you change about this world?" I said, "The length of this application." I thought that it was the kiss of death and I turned in the application. Most of my answers were a bit on the sarcastic side, as I wasn't taking the application process seriously at all.

"Where's your video?" they asked.

I said, "What video? I didn't even know that you had to do a video."

They brought a video camera for the one person who didn't know that you also had to submit a video. As I began recording the video I asked, "What do you want me to talk about?" The guy waved his fingers signifying the tape was already rolling. I'm not sure if that's part of what captivated them to even be interested in me in the first place, but after several more interviews, including a ten-day long one in Santa Monica, California, I actually wrote a fifty-plus-page journal while I was there titled, "I Almost Made Survivor: The Final 48," I was chosen for the show.

I had felt for a while that something bigger was in store for me and that I just wanted more. I just wanted to leave a bigger legacy and make a bigger impact. I didn't think a reality television show would be that "something bigger"—certainly my legacy isn't competing in a reality television show.

It's often not the actual adventure but what you do with what happened to you on the adventure that changes lives.

A reality television show catapulted me to do some pretty unbelievable things in life that I would have never had the platform to do had I not been able to get on that show.

I had dinner with the President of the United States, traveled all over the world, went to the movies with Bill Gates, was on so many television and radio shows I can't even remember them all; but the adventure wasn't in the shows—it was in the people. Meeting people of all walks changed my life tremendously.

WRIGHT

You were best known, as I understand it, for falling in a fire. Would you tell our readers about that?

SKUPIN

It's ironic because as a long-time hunter, fisherman, outdoorsman, and camper I'm certainly no stranger to campfires and building fires. In addition to building fires on camping, hunting, and adventure trips, we have a large fire pit in our backyard; we build fires year round as a family. Of anyone there in the Outback, I'd arguably have been the least likely candidate for a fire mishap.

For anybody who has actually seen *Survivor*, or any outdoor reality show, there is no intervention from anybody out there other than the actual contestants. If you wanted to drink, you had to boil the water for twenty minutes to kill any parasites that may be present. If you wanted to eat, you had to go find it or catch it. If you wanted to get warm, you had to build a fire. We did our best to have fire out there

24/7, even when it rained. After a few days, the hot coals were so deep that it was pretty easy to get the fire going again in the event it went out.

On the eighteenth day, I went out in the leaky canoe provided by the producers. On this particular day, I was accompanied by my fishing buddy Roger Bingham. We've stayed great friends to this day. We caught a couple of fish as we often did with a homemade apparatus I'd made from items I'd collected while exploring the Outback. When I returned to camp I noticed the fire had gone out. Knowing how easy it was to reignite the fire, I threw some dry sticks and leaves onto the hot coals in an attempt to restart the fire.

On the eighteenth day we were all in a state of being severely dehydrated; we suffered from malnutrition, and sleep deprivation. We were in a weakened state already. As I was throwing these dry leaves and sticks on the fire and stirring up the hot coals, I bent over the fire and started blowing on the fire. When I blew onto the fire pit, the hot coals started glowing a bright red. The leaves and the sticks started smoldering and the smoke got thicker and thicker until suddenly a gust of wind changed the direction of the smoke. It blew the smoke in my face as I was inhaling to take another breath. I ended up inhaling a big, thick cloud of smoke. I stood up then I passed out, face first, right into the middle of that fire. The last thing I remember was putting my arms out in front of me to break my fall—something anyone would automatically do when falling. As I passed out, on the way down, the weight of my body just buried my hands deep into the hot embers. I laid there for about fifteen seconds face first in the middle of the hot coals. Smoke displaces the oxygen used to keep you conscious. Slowly, as my body began to re-oxygenate, I slowly started to regain consciousness and immediately made a dash across the hot sand. Still a bit groggy, I fell a few times in the sand that was so hot that you couldn't walk across it without shoes on in the heat of the day. I can still recollect how painful it was each time I fell when the exposed flesh of my hands hit the hot sand. I finally reached the river where I thought I could get some relief from the cool river water.

WRIGHT

You are still asked to speak to groups all over the world. As I recall, you were a pretty memorable castaway on that season. Why do you think people still remember you?

SKUPIN

David, I have spoken now more than two thousand times and anything you do that many times, you're likely to get really good at. I have this unique perspective on issues and events. I have discovered a way to tell it that's unlike anyone else has done before. My rule is if anyone has ever said it, I make sure I don't repeat it. I have an unusual zest for living and adventure. It seemed like every time there was something going on out there, I was right in the middle of it, whether it was building shelter, leading or co-leading the competition in a challenge, or hunting/gathering food out there.

In a reward challenge we won four chickens, one rooster, and three egg-laying hens. They also gave us a large sack of chicken feed to keep them nourished. In addition to consuming the actual chickens, I thought that we should start eating the chicken feed. At first, everybody out there was completely grossed out by the chicken feed. I knew how much nutrition played a significant role in the outcome of this game so it wasn't long before I started roasting the chicken feed in the fire. Before we knew it, we were roasting this stuff on the fire several times per day. The corn in the mixture actually popped like popcorn. We were eating the chicken feed all day long.

I remember catching a fish on the third day, David. Cleaning a fish is pretty simple. What you would normally do is slice open the stomach and scoop out the guts so you could cook the fish. I took the gut pile and I threw it to the side. Then you have a choice either to filet it or scale it and cook it whole. In order to maximize the amount of fish we could eat, I scaled it.

The next morning I woke up and noticed the gut pile was gone. I looked around camp and I asked, "What did you guys do with the gut pile?" Everybody said that they hadn't done anything with it. What I realized shortly afterward was that something was eating that gut pile, so why shouldn't we?

The next time I caught fish, I saved the gut pile and we cooked it alongside the fish. We actually started eating the gut piles. We would clean everything out and start roasting everything over the fire. Each day more and more people began to participate as their hunger got the best of them. I can remember, David, carving the meat out of the cheeks of a fish. I can also remember scooping the eyeballs out and everyone had a big philosophical debate as to the nutritional value of the eyeball of the fish. We actually were so hungry, David, that we broke the bones and I remember sucking the marrow out of the bones just for any piece of nutrition I could find. Of course, for the average non-outdoors person watching the show, it was a pretty memorable moment.

We saw several animals out there in the Outback. There were kangaroos, walaroos, wallabees, koala bears, goanna lizards, echidnas, fresh water crocodiles, wild boar, and a variety of birds and reptiles. As a hunter, I manufactured some pretty crude weapons. I made spears, bolases, slingshots, traps, and fishing gear out of anything I could gather. I patterned the animals as best I could and was having very more success as each day passed.

On the fourteenth day I was able to get a wild boar cornered. Armed with only a small hunting knife, I had no idea what to do next. The interesting part of this moment was the primitive need for survival and the instinct for proving food for your tribe of family and how those instincts began to take over. I knew how dangerous these animals were. I'd hunted them with Ted Nugent and seen how they charge using their massive necks and tusks to gore and rip into anything that represented danger to them. The boar suddenly turned around and charged toward me. I had hunted animals for fourteen days and hadn't come this close to catching one until he charged me. As the world saw a wild boar charging me, I saw a giant pork chop! Thankfully, I ended up winning the battle.

We hung the boar between two trees to skin it then filleted it into steaks, ribs, pork chops, and jerky strips. I have a lasting vision of Elizabeth (Filarski) Hasselbeck, a city girl at heart (who is now one of the co-hosts on *The View*), skinning the wild boar and gnawing on pieces of the carcass to make certain there was no waste. She had never done anything remotely like that in her entire life.

Then, of course, falling into the fire was voted by *TV Guide* as the twenty-first most unexpected moment in the history of television. This moment in television history is right up there with 9/11, the space shuttle blowing up, and JFK getting shot. This illustrates how big this moment was and how reality television truly has its place as a significant medium. Reality television had just hit worldwide popularity. It was the only reality show on and tens of millions tuned in each week to see what everyone was talking about. Although no less popular or significant, reality shows have become quite diluted today, as there are so many of them.

WRIGHT

The survival theme is still a number one theme of corporate events, churches' outreach programs, schools themes, fundraisers, charity events, camps, and such. There are so many speakers out there. What makes people ask about you in the first place and keep asking you back year after year?

SKUPIN

When I first got home from the show, my photograph appeared on the covers of dozens of magazines including *TV Guide, People Magazine,* and *US Magazine.* There were billboards, television commercials, radio spots, etc. The show was showcased in a very big way.

I remember my phone ringing and someone said, "May I speak to Michael."

"This is Michael," I said.

"Why are you answering your own phone?" was the surprised caller's question.

It started to hit me. I never thought that I was a celebrity. I was just a regular guy raising my children and living my life. All of a sudden it occurred to me that having been on television, the world starts to view you a little different.

The caller wanted me to come and share my experiences on *Survivor* with his group. I thought it was pretty flattering that they want to hear me speak. Then caller said that the group didn't have a lot of money in the budget. My thought was, "Wow! They are going to pay me to speak!" For my very first phone call, the "low money in the budget" happened to be more money than I had ever made in a half-hour in my entire life.

Another moment was when I when I was dropped off at a supermarket to buy milk. After being recognized in the checkout line because the woman in front of me was perusing magazines and I was on the front cover, she screamed, "It's him!" The cashier made an announcement and every *TV Guide* and *People* magazine in the store sold out. More than an hour later, after signing all of them, I began to realize that this was bigger than I had ever thought it would be.

It turned out to be a very educational experience for me. People have asked me to speak on dozens of different topics and through this process I've created and accumulated twenty-seven different presentation topics that I customize for every group or audience.

I have always been a fan of motivational and inspirational speakers. I think that I have seen most of the more popular speakers on a number of occasions. I have several different tape series. I have just gobbled that stuff up. I've always loved it.

My story is unique because it is an Indiana Jones type of adventure story mixed in with motivational and inspirational lessons mixed in with the adventure. When I am on the platform delivering a presentation, it's not a lecture-driven or a point-driven talk—it's a story. It's an inspiring story the audience is riveted in listening to because they want to hear the ending.

Many people remember that I fell into the fire. They wanted to know how I fell into the fire because it looked like I was headed toward the winner circle. What happened afterward, they all want to know?

Because it is more of an adventure story that I'm incorporating into an inspirational story, it really turns out to be a pretty dynamic talk. I make sure that I don't say anything that any of the other motivational masters have ever said. If anybody else has ever said it, I cut it out right out of my presentation. Nobody wants to come and hear another version of what they have already heard seven or eight times or seventeen or eighteen times. I make sure that what I say comes from my own personal experiences because so many people can say things.

David, here is a great example. My son and I went to see Cal Ripkin speak last year in Detroit, Michigan. As you know, Cal Ripkin is a world record holder. He played in more consecutive Major League baseball games than any other player in history. I told my son that if somebody has a world record, there is no one else who can say, "I am the best ever at that." So, I wanted to go see him. I just wanted to hear what he had to say.

I remember that the very first thing Ripkin said. He said, "Whatever you are going to choose to do as a career, make sure that it is that one thing that you are most passionate about and that you love. Take the thing that you love the most and that you have the most passion for and make that your career." Most of the people in the room applauded in agreement to that statement.

I was at a table of about twelve to fourteen people and I looked over at my seventeen-year-old son. I said, "Michael, that has got to be the worst advice I have ever heard in my life." I must have said it a bit too loud because everybody at the table turned around and looked at me as if to say, "Who are you to disagree with Cal Ripkin? He is a world record holder."

I said, "Michael, whatever you love to do, whatever you are most passionate about, keep it your passion, because if you turn your passion into a j-o-b, you are going to be doing what you love to do even when you don't feel like doing it." After a period of time, if you continue doing the things that you love to do but only because you "have" to do it or when you don't feel like doing it, you are likely to lose your passion and destroy what you were passionate about. My advice is to keep your passion as your passion and do something that is going to make you a lot of money that you might enjoy doing, that you might like doing; but you can do what you're passionate about when you want to do it.

I ask people, "Who is right, Cal Ripkin or Michael Skupin?" The truth of the matter is that we are both right because there isn't anything that fits everybody. There isn't a saying, a quote, a speaker, or a speech that fits everybody in the same way. Sometimes, turning something five or six degrees in a different direction and viewing something in a completely different way, you can achieve unbelievable results. That's how I approach this motivational and inspirational thinking.

David, I'll answer the other question you asked, "What makes people ask about you?" Television has an audience of millions of viewers. I had the opportunity to be on dozens and dozens of television shows from talk shows *and Hollywood Squares* to *Politically Incorrect* with Bill Marr and hosting other programs.

It's funny. They just had the *Golden Globe Awards*. They had a reality award show and you would win "Realies" instead of a Grammy or an Emmy. I won a "Realie" for the most painful moment on a reality television show!

The way it works is that each time you speak, if you inspired or entertained the audience you would get referrals. I'm still getting calls and referrals from events where I spoke seven years ago! The more you speak, the better you get, the more you are liked, and the more referrals you get. Today, almost eight years after the *Survivor* show, I still get dozens of requests every month. In addition to remembering me form eight years ago, it's likely somebody said something at a more recent event that I did.

WRIGHT

You have a big family—seven kids and your wife make nine. That can be a handful for parents. How do you manage?

SKUPIN

We are definitely the nontraditional family in many respects, David. I would love to tell you that I have it all figured out. As of this interview, my kids are twenty-one, eighteen, fourteen, twelve, eleven, eight, and four. Sometimes I sit back and watch them interact and it's magnificent. I see Karen helping Kristy with her projects and Brandon helping Karen with her jump shot in basketball. Jaclyn and Emily may be working on a dance routine together. Michael showing Leo some new football moves and Kalyn is making sure nobody gets hurt. I look at it and think that this is exactly how this is supposed to work—people helping people.

We have a family mantra: "It's not all about me." Sometimes it works, sometimes it doesn't. We've developed a pretty unique system. It was the way that I was raised—the way parents and my parents (the best ever) raised kids back forty and fifty years ago. We don't negotiate with our children, David. I see parents negotiating with their two-year-old kids as they are throwing a temper tantrum on the floor of the grocery store. If you are negotiating with your two-year-old, how do you think you are going to negotiate with that kid when he or she is twelve or in high school?

We make the decisions, even as far back as potty training. My mother told me that at two years old, our diapers came off. So we decided at two years old, those diapers are coming off, too. It's not a choice. It's not when "they are ready." I see five-, six-, and seven-year-old kids still wearing diapers to bed. I see four- and five-year-old kids still walking around in diapers because the parents say, "I am going to wait until they are ready."

We believe kids are smarter than parents usually give them credit for and we believe parents wait too long to start giving kids responsibilities, household chores, and making small (very small) money choices.

When we are going somewhere in the car, all I say is, "Load up." When I walk out the front door and lock it behind me, my children are in the car, buckled up, and ready to go. My older kids all have responsibilities one kid down in age from them and it all gets done. We rarely listen to the radio and refuse to get a DVD player for either of our cars, even when it comes free with the package we select. Oftentimes, the ride to and from school activities and events is the only time we have a chance to talk with our kinds and we use that time very effectively. Often, our radio is never turned on, even on family trips of ten hours or more. Do they bicker at times? Of course they do, but I love to observe how they handle situations of all kinds and use it to parent them later. We praise and use constructive adjustments to raise them the right way.

I think I run it more like a system and we give our kids responsibility at a very young age. I don't believe in allowances. I am not saying anything negative about the people who do give an allowance. My kids get everything they need, but not everything they want—there's a big difference.

The big one today, David, is complaining and whining. I think that is probably a parent's biggest frustration these days. It was mine many years ago and I finally discovered a solution. Instead of getting mad or upset when my kids began whining and complaining, I turn it into being glad. I told my children if they complain about a chore we ask them to do or anything that we ask them to do, every complaint or whine is an additional chore. When they would complain about a chore, I would say, "Great. I am so happy that you decided to complain today because the kitchen floor needs cleaning." If they complained about that additional chore, it was another chore. For the next month or two my house was very clean. Children learn very quickly, as long as you are consistent. People are amazed when I ask my children to do something and they just get up and do it the first time they are asked without complaining. They don't do it because of respect or how much they love me—they just don't want to get another chore. I think my kids are a little smarter than that.

Another subject is meeting people, David. As you can imagine, I meet tens of thousands of people every single year. I try to talk to children and shake their hand. I tell my kids there are four things you need to do every time you meet a person. You need to shake the person's hand firmly, make eye contact, repeat the person's name, and ask a question. When I first instituted that many years ago, I used to give my kids fifty cents for every time they accomplished all four things. They would shake the person's hand firmly, look the person in the eye, and say, "Nice to meet you, Mr. David. How do you know my dad?" Or, "Are you having a good time at the event tonight?" They actually begin a conversation. If my kids wanted an extra treat or something extra, I often made them memorize a Bible verse. They came up to me with a new Bible verse; it actually turned into a positive situation around my house.

I think one of my favorite stories of raising kids is my wife and I are believers regarding the way that you talk and every spoken word. In addition to any kind of swear words or negative words like hate, stupid, shut up we don't allow the word "yeah." You get into a conversation with most people, especially the younger generation, and you will hear them say something like this, "Did you have fun in school today?" "Yeah." It is just not the way that we were raised. We expect them to say "yes."

My oldest son is twenty-one today. When he was in the eighth grade, he came to me and said, "All my friends get to say all the words that you don't let us say. In fact, most of them say it right in front of their parents. Why can't I swear? Why can't I use some of those words?"

"Michael," I said, "that is a great question. Here's the answer. When you are at an age when you decide to leave the nest and go out on your own, it is my job as your parent to make sure that you have been taught and understand all the basic principles of life. One of them is how to communicate effectively.

"I'll give you an example. If you get upset at a police officer after having been pulled over for a traffic violation, would you swear or use slang with him?"

"Absolutely not," he said.

"If you got upset with your teacher at school, would you swear or use slang?"

"No sir."

"What about the pastor of our church? If you disagreed with something that he said from the pulpit, would you go swearing at him to tell him that you disagreed with him?"

"No way."

"So really, what you are telling me is that you have to go up to people and voice your opinion using the English language the way it was created. You need to use words to effectively communicate your feelings without using swear or slang."

"Absolutely," he agreed.

"If, when you leave our home and you decide to revert back to slang and swearing to communicate, it's your option, because you'll be a grown man then; but I'll bet you won't. In fact, I'm pretty certain that you will continue to use the words that were taught here in our home."

"Dad, that makes a lot of sense."

"Michael, I'll bet you will raise your kids the same way."

"I'll bet I will, too."

Even in the early adult years, children respect the fact that you are teaching them to do the right thing. They might not like it, they might fight you on it but they will respect it.

WRIGHT

Kids are very much different today than they were when you and I were kids. I know you speak in schools a lot; what do you say to them?

SKUPIN

It's different depending on what grade level. I go into schools from Kindergarten to college age and even grad schools. I think the first thing is to not use the phrase, "Well, it wasn't like that when we were in school" or "When we were in school we did it." David, it's a different world today. Kids need to be parented somewhat differently. Kids need to be taught somewhat differently. Kids need to be taught spiritual lessons somewhat differently. When we were kids we used to leave the house at sunlight and not come back until sunset. Today I walk to the bus stop at 6:25 AM with my three middle school kids. I do that even though the bus stop is only five houses away because I don't trust the world. We used to be able to go to the bathroom when we were kids at a restaurant. I don't let my fourteen-year-old son go to the restroom by himself. When you and I were young and we kissed a girl, we actually knew it was a girl. It's a very different world.

When I speak to kids I try to make them realize that I do understand that it is a very different world today. As a parent, you really need to understand that. As an educator, you really need to understand that. The most successful parents and educators realize the fact that it is different. The first thing I ask the kids I speak to is for them to pull out their instruction manual on how to have a successful high school career or how to have a successful middle school or elementary life. They all look at me like I'm crazy. I say, "Everybody gets one of those, right?" They look at me and they say, "No, we didn't get one."

Then I say, "When I got on *Survivor* I had never watched a single episode of it. When they dropped us off in a plane in the middle of the Australian Outback I expected there to be instructions of how to play the game because in everything in our lives we are usually given a set of rules. Whether it is driving, playing a sport, how to do your job, there is a set of rules. On *Survivor* there were no rules. They just said Go!

That's pretty much how school is with kids. A vast majority of your "school adventure" you get to create. You need to figure it out on your own, with the assistance of the school administration. I realized quickly on *Survivor* that the reason they don't tell you how to play the game is because you get to play the game anyway you want to. You get to make the choice. You have the opportunity to create your own adventure.

Kids are actually pretty prepared for choices. By the time people graduate from high school they have already made over a million choices. That certainly qualifies them as experts in making decisions. But they still need parents to help them make good ones.

Why is it that people make the same mistakes over and over? Mark Burnett, the creator of Survivor, wrote a book and said what amazed him the most about *Survivor* is that in season nineteen and all the way back to season one, the players are still making the same bad choices. Season after season, episode after episode, player after player, and it absolutely amazes him.

I watch a reality show and say what in the world are you thinking? The problem is that they are not thinking. It surprises me because when you leave for a show like *Survivor*, you know that you are gone for the better part of two months. You have absolutely no outside contact—no e-mails, friends, cell phones, computers, electronics, Internet—you don't have any communication with the outside world. You prepare as much as you can physically and emotionally.

The last thing you say to your family is, "I'm going to do whatever it takes to bring back the million dollars to you." Yet, on the very first episode on the very next season it is almost always unanimous as to who gets voted off. I teach kids today about the power of making choices. It's not in the typical lecture-driven format because science has finally discovered that the part of the brain responsible for making choices is not fully developed until a person is twenty-five years old. This means that the part of the brain responsible for evaluating risk is not fully developed until you are twenty-five years old. I tell kids in school that this is exactly why there appears to be a conflict between what your parents tell you and what you believe to be true and a conflict between what your teachers tell you and what you actually believe to be true. Understanding that principle really helps kids understand.

I carry a note in my wallet from a girl who was going through chemotherapy at the time. She walked up to me after one of my assemblies at a school. She had no hair on her head; she handed me a little note and said, "I'm sixteen years old. I'm going through chemotherapy right now and I have a 50 percent chance of living or dying. I have this note for you." I opened it up and it brought tears to my eyes. Her note said, "I'm paying the price for a choice made by a seven-year-old girl." When she was seven years old, she stole cigarettes out of big sissy's purse because she wanted to be like big sis. She started smoking when she was seven years old. Now, she is enduring the consequences.

You have the power to choose. Parents don't like to admit it; sometimes ministers and teachers don't like to admit it. You have the power to choose, but you don't have the power to choose the consequences of your choices. During my presentations I touch on even the things that you put in your body from a health perspective. I touch on this issue in a survival type adventure way so it's fun for them.

I also talk about the dreaded "I can't" attitude.

I've always been really good at math. It's just one of those subjects I've always worked hard at. I was an accounting major in college because I was so good with numbers. I didn't even like accounting but I was so good with numbers that I gravitated toward something that was I was good at.

My oldest son had me convinced by the eighth grade, which is how old he was when I did *Survivor*, that he was never going to be good in math. He had always struggled to get a C in any math class. At times, he didn't even achieve a C. After many years of battling this, he actually convinced me that he wasn't good at math. It always shocked me. I couldn't understand it because I was always so good at math.

I went onto *Survivor* and I realized that the "I can't" attitude had to go away. People say, "I can't" so often. People on *Survivor*, while they were doing challenges, would say "I can't." and often talk themselves right out of achieving something significant. Or the things that we had to eat, they would say, "I can't do it." Actually, you can do it. So when I got back from *Survivor*, "can't" was added to the words that my kids weren't allowed to say.

When my oldest son would say, "I'm not good at math. I can't do well. I can't get an A." I started saying, "This is what you have to do. If you are having a struggle, a difficulty, or a challenge, you need to try and figure it out on your own. If that doesn't work, you need to seek the advice of one other person—a peer, an educator, or somebody in your school system. If between you trying to figure it out yourself and your peers and educators assisting you and you are still having difficulty, then you come up to your mom and dad and say 'here is the problem I'm having. Here is what I have tried. Here are the people I have talked to. Here's where we tried again and we are still having trouble.'" I communicated this to all my children. I want them to learn how to effectively use the system, knowing I wasn't going to be there for them forever.

Success started appearing almost immediately for my children and they started getting really excited about it. Before long, before the semester ended, my son went from a C/D student in math to an A student in math. He actually told me that he wanted to be a sports statistician when he grew up. That's a desire to do math for a living! What changed? The teacher didn't change, the school didn't change, the educator didn't change, parents didn't change, and house didn't change. The only thing that changed was my refusing to enable him to say, "I can't." He started saying "I can." That's when I started to realize that if an eighth grade boy can overcome something, then certainly as educated, mature adults, how much more can we achieve?

When I speak at a school I leave them with a challenge at the end—in *Survivor* style fashion. I challenge them in some way, depending on the school system. It is a fun thing to do and there is always a reward for the person who achieves the challenge in the best possible manner.

WRIGHT

I understand faith was a very important part of your adventure and you've been asked to speak at hundreds of churches all over the world. It seems a bit nontraditional to have a reality television star speak at a church. When you speak in churches, what is your message—do you choose your presentations quite a bit?

SKUPIN

Faith is one of the most misunderstood subjects out there today. There are hundreds of different denominations all professing different beliefs. Additionally, even a very basic concept such as prayer is rarely if ever even taught. I ask congregations of several thousand how many had taken a class on prayer or how to pray and usually less than ten people raise their hands. I asked an eighty-five-year-old woman if she'd ever been taught how to pray and she said "No." I asked her what she did when she prayed. She stated, "I just make it up." So we have entire congregation making up something they think is right. No wonder it's so confusing to the general populace.

There are so many people committed to sharing their understanding of faith. Although there is nothing inherently spiritual about professional sports, many professional athletes share their understanding of faith and many people come into church who may have never come. The same goes for Hollywood and just about every facet of life. It's not the sport or the movie or the television show, but the adventure God took you on while you were there; finally you opened yourself up enough to understand. You get so passionate about that new understanding that all you want to do is share it, so we do.

The message I share can be so very similar whether I'm speaking to corporate, church, charity, or school audiences. There are so many discoveries that happen inside your inner self when you are stripped of everything that is familiar to you. When you are stripped of what's familiar, somehow it opens spaces in your mind that you had trouble reaching. You don't have to play a sport or go onto a reality show to make your own discoveries.

Fasting is a really good example of something unfamiliar.

I was out in the Australian Outback, exposed to the elements 24/7 and it was a very awakening experience for me. One of the things I discovered on *Survivor* is that you can't trust anybody. Everybody is out there for the exact same reason—to win the million dollars. Even the people you become friends with will eventually, when it comes down to the end, be competing against you for the million dollars.

In the absence of having anybody else to talk to and in the absence of having anybody else to trust, I started talking to God. I was having conversations with God. I was at times wrestling with God. I was strategizing with God. I was sharing my day with God like you would with a friend or a loved one. By accident I stumbled upon this thing that Christians refer to as "a personal relationship." Even though I had been a Christian for years, I never really understood this concept before. People would always say that if you want to get closer to God you've got to pray more. The biggest problem was that I didn't really understand the concept of prayer. After speaking in over five hundred churches, I realized that there are not many people who truly understand the concept of prayer. If you think about it, prayer is the only connection that we have with our Creator. Whatever your belief system is, prayer is the connection point. Possibly the most important part of whatever faith you are a part of is prayer. Yet, I ask congregations if they've ever been taught to pray. More often than not there aren't any hands that go up in a congregation of a thousand people or more?

The problem is that pastors of churches can pray very eloquently because they have been to seminary, they've been doing it for years in front of large audiences, and they often can do it extremely well. When I try to pray like these pastors, I often run out of things to say. If there were a scale of Christianity, Kathy might be a level 9.0 Christian and I may be a level 0.9 Christian and I just couldn't pray like she prayed. I started to realize that the world (corporations, small businesses, schools) does such a phenomenal job at telling us *what* to do and *why* we should do it. They even tell you *how* to do it. Schools are brilliant—they tell you *what* to do, *why* you should do it, and *how* to do it. Churches are excellent at telling you *what* to do. They are phenomenal at telling you *why* you should do it because there is a heaven and there is a hell. But, they often leave out the *how* to do it. So people get really inspired listening to a half-hour message on a Sunday morning, but many might walk away still not knowing how to pray.

Some churches have started to realize this so they have a weeknight class to teach people how to do it but most people don't attend the weeknight class—they come on Sunday mornings. If I hold church on a Sunday morning, as I do often, I always incorporate, "This is what worked for me. Here are some examples of what worked for others." Remembering the Cal Ripkin story, not "one" thing is going to work for everybody.

I did come to realize that when I prayed, I always asked for stuff. In fact that was the only way I knew how to pray. I think that most Christians pray situationally. I ask people, "When do you pray? Do you pray to ask God to bless your food? Do you pray when you are sick or someone else is sick and do you pray for healing? Do you pray when someone is struggling financially—do you pray for better finances? When someone is struggling relationally, do you pray for better relationships?" We are basically saying, "Gimme. Gimme." We pray very situationally and often very selfishly.

I have spoken individually to church members at over five hundred churches. For the thousands of people I talk to, "Gimme" or give them when praying for others is the way that people tend to pray. The Bible is clear about the fact that you can and should ask for things, but maybe this is not the only way to pray.

So people say, "You want to get closer to God?" And I say, "Yes I do." They say, "Well, spend more time praying." Then I would just spend more time asking for stuff. I never really understood that prayer is a time to share. I ask this in the church, "At one point has anybody in here ever had a friendship?" Of course everybody raises his or her hand and chuckles. I say, "Maybe it is just this simple. God gave us the ability to relate, communicate, converse with people, and create relationships and friendships. Maybe this whole personal relationship thing is just creating a friendship. The friendship is sharing good things and sharing bad things, not always agreeing but talking it out."

The Bible says thank God, for "all" the good things come from God. Yet, so often, we take credit for all the good things that happen in our lives. As I travel, I sense there are so many things that people in churches are missing out on spiritually and it breaks my heart because I was once in their shoes.

I walked into a church in Canada. They had an enormous pink neon sign as you walked into the sanctuary that was about eight to nine feet high and twelve to fifteen feet wide. It said, "Expect a Miracle." That really touched my heart. Maybe this group really "gets it." I walked up to the pulpit and I asked the congregation how many of them would consider themselves Christian and 90 percent raised their hands. I said, "Isn't it great to be a Christian? How many people in this room have ever had a miracle happen to them personally?" There were about fifteen hundred people in this congregation and a dozen raised their hands. I asked, "How many people in this congregation actually expect for a miracle to happen to them personally at some point in their life?" An additional thirty to forty people raised their hands. So now I have fifty hands raised in a congregation of fifteen hundred people. Out of the fifteen hundred only fifty expected to have a miracle happen to them in their lifetime.

Then I asked very simple questions, "How many of you were present when your child was born? If you have, you can't tell me that you have never witnessed a miracle."

I ask simple questions like that to help people understand that the whole premise of the church was based on expecting a miracle. Yet, somehow the church has completely overlooked that fact and the people in the congregation of that church in Canada didn't even believe it, in spite of their huge sign. You know what? I am still just nuts enough to believe that God still performs miracles in people's lives today. I believe God does it every day for everyday people. I think that we are so busy looking for the "parting of the Red Sea" type miracles that we miss all the medium and small sized miracles He does in our lives every day.

I think when people pray that most are seeking the presents (gifts) of God because we sometimes pray selfishly. I believe if you turn that five degrees and look at it in a different way, your life can change dramatically. Try seeking the presence (nearness) of God during prayer. When seeking the presence of God becomes our priority and motivation, the Bible promises us that our "nets" will be full every day. The abundance the Bible talks about may come upon us finally. When we are just seeking the presents (gifts), we are going to miss His presence (nearness). Let me share this truth—when we miss His presence, you miss *everything*.

WRIGHT

Michael, I see that you have a heart to help people. Not only have you started a charity of your own called "Victory Over Addiction" but you've helped out dozens of charities with inspirational messages and fundraisers. How did you get involved with that?

SKUPIN

Thank God I have the capacity and the platform to help and make a difference. Whenever anyone achieves any type of celebrity status, your mailbox, e-mail, and voicemail box get stuffed with invitations and requests to help out. There are requests for autographed items to help raise money, and donations and requests to attend events and there are many speaking requests.

There is a perception that when you appear on television your wallet is fat. I often have to remind people that I didn't win *Survivor* ☺. It's funny to me when I show up to work to see people's reactions, "Weren't you on *Survivor?* What are you doing working?" I smile and simply remind them, "I didn't win." Even if I had won the million dollars, after taxes it's about half of that. This is still a significant amount of money, but I start to do the math of seven kids, seven college educations, cars, insurances, seven weddings, and so on, and I realize that the numbers are staggering. I think we all can agree that a half million dollars in today's world, although life-changing to a degree, with seven children doesn't go as far as it used to.

When the invitations came, however, I created ways to help. Here's when it really hit me, David. I walked into Children's Hospital, Detroit. It's one of the largest children's hospitals in the United States. I was asked to inspire the kids in any capacity I could. I brought things. Lynne, from a local charity (LRL) had bought a bunch of Beanie Babies and sports paraphernalia and all kinds of kids' stuff to hand out to the children of all ages there.

I met a little boy named David. David had had thirty-nine brain operations in eighteen months. He lived in a bubble because he was so susceptible to any kind of germ. He couldn't live in any type of environment where there might be contaminates that would further threaten his health. He was probably the happiest kid I had ever met. I had such a good time with him. I gave him a signed Beanie Baby and you would have thought that I had given him the million dollars that I would've won on *Survivor*. That kid jumped and danced around the room. He had more scars on his head than you could even imagine from the many brain operations he'd had.

I was able to talk with his parents. I always thought that if you had a family member who got cancer, then you would get behind the cancer cause. If you had a family member who had Alzheimer's, you would start supporting the Alzheimer's cause because it would be something near and dear to your heart—it was more about something that happened to you personally.

After talking to his mother I said, "How is your life going?"

She said, "It's the toughest thing ever because I have kids that aren't sick at home. Then I have David in here, who is my heart and soul because he can't live a normal life. I am so caught between trying not to deprive my other children of a 'normal life,' in between trying to make sure that David feels loved and edified and to make sure that there is someone who is always here. I'm finding it impossible to do that."

That's when I realized that I've been blessed with seven healthy kids. It's my belief now that the people who are blessed with healthy kids need to be advocates behind these charities and fundraisers because we've got more time than people who don't. If you get one of those injuries, cancers, or diseases that happen to the children in your life, you usually don't have the time to become an advocate or to get behind these causes. I started standing on that platform. I was able to get tens of thousands of people behind causes—people who'd never had any passion for the cause, but started having a passion for causes in general because they realized how lucky and blessed they were.

Survivor didn't and doesn't define my life; it was simply another adventure along the way. I remember one time my wife was reminding me that we had to leave an event because we had another commitment. I had stayed too long after the event talking with the people. One sixteen-year-old kid overheard my wife saying, "Come on. It's time to go honey." He said, "Wait a minute. Why don't you just tell her that you are the *Survivor* guy? The *Survivor* guy doesn't have to go." After I belly laughed, knowing he has absolutely no understanding of marriage and relationships, it struck me in a way that I won't soon forget. Although it's been an incredible journey, sometimes wearing a baseball hat and sunglasses to be anonymous is more peaceful. I've never carried the attitude that "I'm the *Survivor* guy." I don't ever say, "I am the *Survivor* guy, I need to have a better seat." Or, "Can I get a table because I am the *Survivor* guy?" I'd rather be less conspicuous, but if I can raise one more dollar and that one-dollar finds the cure for cancer or finds the cure for Alzheimer's or is able to help a spinal cord injury person walk again, I will use my small amount of fame for as long as I can.

I've learned that you need to give back. Eventually, if you keep taking, something is going to go wrong. You have to take from the world because it is a shared life we live. You have to give back to replenish for the next generation. I've been in children's prisons and adult's prisons. I've been to homes of the mentally and physically challenged and every kind of disease known to man.

A few months ago I was in Saginaw, Michigan, a very economically affected area. Michigan is one of the toughest economies in the country today. Five hundred and thirty came to a fundraiser for a woman who had lost both her arms and she had a tiny little child. They promoted the event by featuring me as the speaker. The interesting thing is the event was for a heightened awareness of postpartum depression. I thought to myself, "Why in the world would they bring me in to talk about postpartum depression? Certainly, I have had seven children and I may know a little bit more about it than most guys, but certainly not even a fingernail-sized worth compared to what women would know about it." They told me, "We've hired the number one authority on postpartum depression from San Francisco and there is no way to talk about postpartum depression without depressing everybody. We need you to pump everybody up afterward because we have a silent auction and a private auction. We need people to spend some money so that we can raise some funds and awareness for this cause." It's interesting the dynamics involved in some of the events I participate in. Being able to make a difference in that event was as fulfilling a mission as I have ever had.

WRIGHT

Speaking of kids, your wife doesn't work outside the house. How on earth do you make ends meet to have money for sports, braces, groceries, automobiles, save money for college educations, weddings, and create a retirement for yourself?

SKUPIN

That possibly could be the biggest challenge I face today. I know that my wife does stay at home and, with seven kids, she has the hardest and most rewarding job of anybody on this planet. When I come home from speaking, I am actually at home. I usually work out of my home to be with my family as much as I can. I know how important it is and it's what I love. In all its chaos, it's a peaceful place for me. When she is home, she is still on the job. I sometimes get up at three o'clock this morning and within a half an hour you could hear the washing machine going. You can imagine, with nine people in this house and everybody involved with sports, how much laundry that poor woman goes through every day. She does the budgeting, pays the bills, and is truly the glue that keeps everyone together and sane. You can't even begin to imagine what our "events calendar" looks like with sports, my travel, doctor and dentist appointments, birthday, and so on.

If you think about it, forty years ago, when you and I were kids, just our dads worked and there was just enough money at the end of every month. Twenty years ago, the trend became having both husbands and wives working because lifestyles changed and families began to require two incomes. Today, often the husbands and the wives both work and yet 95 percent of the people are still drowning in debt. The average American today saves a -1.6 percent of his or her paycheck.

One of my good friends was in Haiti on a mission trip over the summer. He was asked to inspire the Haitian leaders. As you may know, Haiti is likely the poorest country on the planet today. He said, "The average Haitian family makes one dollar a day. The average Haitian family saves zero of it but you are better off than most families in America today because the average American family saves a −1.6 percent per month and are drowning in debt every month."

I made a decision that I am going to win for my family during these turbulent economic times. I am going to make sure that I have a victory over my house and for my family. I told them, "That means that Dad might be working late or you might not see Dad on Saturdays and Sundays because I have to make sure that I am going to win financially, it's not optional."

"What are you going to do?" they asked.

"Whatever is necessary," I answered.

I looked at my wife and I said to my kids, "Our little four-year-old girl obviously needs more care than the rest of you. When that girl needs a bath, when that girl needs to be fed, when that girl needs to be cared for, no matter how sick my wife is or how tired she is or if she feels like doing it or not, taking care of you kids is not an option for her. She needs to do whatever is necessary. Financially I am doing the same thing."

I remember the pastor of our church got up and spoke about a guy who was having a hard time making his house payment. He was a healthy guy and was educated. My pastor asked, "What are you doing to win for your family financially?" The man explained that he had a job but couldn't make ends meet.

"Tell me more about your job," the pastor asked.

"I work full-time."

"How many hours is that?"

"I work thirty-two hours a week."

"I can't help you."

"What are you talking about?" the man asked.

"Are you trying to tell me that you are in danger of losing the shelter you provide for your family and all you are willing to do is work thirty-two hours a week, yet you found time to come into the church here begging for money? I work eighty hours a week and people during these times have to do whatever is necessary. If you came in here saying, you can't find a job, that would be one thing; but you came in here saying you are only willing to work thirty-two hours a week."

Thirty-two divided by seven is a little over four hours a day that the man was willing to work to win for his family. We just see it a much different way. I know that may sound harsh and in this short chapter I don't have the space to tell the full story, but I use this story to illustrate a point. What are you willing to do to win for your family? I had to switch gears because my income had dropped significantly. I created a financial services business where I employ people all over the country to provide an opportunity for people to help others lower their monthly debt without sacrificing savings and their insurance coverage. We negotiated incredible programs with the top companies in the world. These companies' leaders saw that we helped families get out of debt without increasing monthly costs. In these economic times, we hit a home run.

WRIGHT

You've been motivational speaking for a long time—more than two thousand times in eight years. Do you speak about the same thing or does what you speak about change any?

SKUPIN

It changes a lot. It evolves in a manner similar to how life has evolved. Do you know that over thirty years ago, when they talked about the most unattractive aspect of human beings that it was the fact that people quit? Today people quit all the time. I have coached almost fifty seasons of sports so far with my seven children. I coach a lot. I can't remember a season when someone either didn't quit or didn't try to quit. People quit on friendships. Mothers and fathers quit on each other. It's very commonplace today. Life has evolved into a belief that it's okay to quit.

Quitting happened on *Survivor* also. When I competed on the show in 2001, quitting was not an option. I suppose we could have quit but there was nobody to quit to. We were hundreds of miles from civilization in every direction. Today the show, like life, has evolved and they let people quit now. I think one of the most attractive qualities in a person today is endurance. Actually, having the stick-to-itiveness to last, to weather the storm, to commit and stay committed.

I think the reason my talks have evolved is because a huge part of my passion today is about the financial condition of this country and the way it is tearing families apart. Although it's a bit larger than most, I have a pretty typical family. I speak, I inspire, I motivate; then what? Sometimes I would walk out of a motivational speech thinking I know I inspired them. I know I motivated them. Then, after they got all inspired and motivated they said, "Thanks a lot for the message. Where are we going to have lunch?" Then, life just went on. I wasn't sure that I was leaving a lasting impression.

As a speaker, you go to different countries, different states, and different cities to speak but you don't really see the fruits of your labor. I keep asking myself, how do I know that I have made a difference? A solution I found was to ask people to send me e-mails, letters, and messages on Facebook to keep me updated—and they actually did! I asked them to let me know how what I said influenced their lives. After reading comments and letters, I would see what I needed to alter or change. I was determined to make a permanent impression on the audience. That's what's kept my speaking schedule filled.

I've realized that foundational and financial principles aren't taught today. I never knew what the negative influence of a credit card could be until I got one and ran it up to its limit. Financial responsibility is not being taught in homes and it is not being taught in schools. People need to get back to the idea of basic foundational principles. It's biblical, it's vocational, and it's necessary. More than 80 percent of people today are spending more money than they make. I have an extremely effective presentation using the analogy about how people need to get back to the idea of planting seeds. People need to understand the concept of saving and learning how to produce and multiply. The problem is that we keep eating the seeds.

An example is found in the way farmers operate. When they harvest a crop they take the seeds and put them aside for the next season. They tell their families, "Do you see those seeds over there? I don't care how hungry we get or how bad times get or how little money we have this winter or how bad the winter season gets—don't touch the seeds because that is the harvest for the following season."

I look at the illustration of apples and apple trees. Apples represent getting a paycheck. Your paycheck is just a bushel of apples every two weeks. The problem is that we consume *all* the apples. If you get a bigger paycheck, you get a bigger bushel of apples, but at the end of two weeks, that bushel is gone. In the meantime, seeds haven't been planted. Do you know how many apple trees you can get out of one single apple?

We've developed a program where for twenty-five dollars a month, you can invest your money in the same places where Bill Gates and Warren Buffet invest their money. By the time you retire, it can be worth hundreds of thousands of dollars. Less than three out of ten people retire without the need of financial assistance. We are living much longer and the small retirement funds people have run out too soon.

This is preventable with a small amount of education. We employ people and we teach them these principles. We're out there making a difference one family at a time. We need to understand these principles as teenagers and young adults so that we can begin planting seeds.

Compounding interest is one of the most powerful laws in our universe. You can empower your kids, teenagers, and young adults to avoid the financial pitfalls many of us have found ourselves in. These are the things we really need to start doing, today.

One financial principle I will never forget is that money will always find a place where it can settle and grow. For over 80 percent of American households today, it's not with them. We end up spending that entire paycheck or we end up consuming that whole bushel of apples. That money is going somewhere. People use clichés such as "the rich get richer." Well, the rich get richer because money will find a place where it can settle and grow. The vast majority of the rich aren't rich because they got lucky. They are rich because they were smart and they started implementing financial principles early on.

I have a really neat story that I want to share with you about my parents. My parents and my wife's parents are truly my heroes. I know we are what we are and we do what we do because of the way we were raised. I have always marveled at the fact that my dad was a common laborer, yet he always had money. He always had money to bail his kids out when they ran into financial problems. He understood the principles of saving very well. My parents are still very involved in all of our lives. They never come over without toilet paper or groceries or something that they found on sale somewhere.

My dad had shoulder surgery this week. I took him to the hospital and I sat in the hospital while he had the operation. I sat in the recovery room with him and then I took him home. He needed a prescription.

"Mom," I said, "I need to go get dad's prescription." So I grabbed her personal address book and was looking for the local Rite Aid pharmacy.

"It's not under Rite Aid," she said. "It's under the store that it was before it was Rite Aid."

"Oh, it used to be called Perry Drugs."

So, I'm looking under the P's and said, "Mom, it's not in there."

"I meant before Rite Aid," she said. "It used to be a local pharmacy called Arnold's Drugs."

"Mom, Arnold's Drugs has been closed for over thirty years!"

Here's my point. My mother still has her paper phonebook from thirty years ago. My parents don't buy things because they want them. They buy something because they need it. My parents did not make as much money as I have already made in my lifetime and yet they still have significantly more money than I do. They are phenomenal students of basic money principles. The generation that preceded me knew the basic financial foundational principles of money.

I sat down to have a bowl of soup that day at my parents' home and there was a napkin next to me on the table. It was a little bit wrinkled but it didn't have any food on it. I looked at my dad and said, "Don't tell me that you used this napkin already today but you are saving it for your next meal."

"It hasn't been there for more than four days," he replied.

He had used the same napkin for four days! Am I saying that if you save napkins you are going to have enough money to retire on? No. I'm making the point that it's the thought process and the way you think. Your body automatically gravitates toward the way you think. It's just foundational.

WRIGHT

What does it mean to "win for your family"? We are in possibly the worst times ever.

SKUPIN

I have chosen not to participate in this economic recession. My father passed away when I was four years old of cancer. My mother had a five-year-old, a four-year-old, a two-year-old, and a one-year-old. My father never understood the value of life insurance and my mother was in a bad way financially. (I also coach families how to own life insurance without opening their wallets. I've heard it called "your last love letter to your family.") Social security provided my mother with three hundred dollars a month. One hundred and twenty dollars of that was the house payment. She owned her own house and on one hundred and eighty dollars a month, my mother supported herself and raised four children.

Private and Christian education was always very important to my parents and to keep her commitment, my mother worked at the local private school and bartered for our private school education (i.e., she did not work for a salary—her work was in exchange for our tuition at the school). It was her opinion that private education would provide a better life for us.

Supporting five people on one hundred and eighty dollars a month, you can imagine that we never had anything new. I'm not sure I had a new article of clothing until I was well into my teens. Everything was patched together, broken, and used. We made the best from what we had. My tribute to my mother is that I never knew I was poor. I never knew for a minute that I was missing or lacking anything. That's the definition of winning for your family.

There are roller coasters in life. And we are all living the roller coaster of tough times these days. If you are fighting a battle right now, that battle can be overcome and that battle will pass, but there is a new one coming. How do you react in the down times? Michigan might be in its worst economic condition ever. Hundreds of thousands of people have lost their jobs. The Big Three might become The Big Zero at any given date. Yet, I drive by restaurants and the parking lots are full. I drive by movie theatres and the parking lots are full. I'll pass by amusement parks and the parking lots are full. Stadium and sporting events are packed full. Concert halls are full and people. And people are wondering why they are so deep in debt! Times have changed but many people's lifestyles and mindsets haven't changed. Many parents have not made up their minds and they haven't made the decision to win for their family. This recession can actually provide opportunities. Having a desire to win for your family will trump any situation you are going through in your life because everything has come to pass, not come to stay. I tell my kids, we're planting seeds. Even in a time where things are as scarce as they have ever been, we still plant seeds.

WRIGHT

If you could leave our readers with one piece of advice, what would you tell us?

SKUPIN

Every single study, survey, or research ever done to report what people are looking for in a job/career, money never makes the top three and rarely makes the top six. In most studies, it doesn't even make the top six. People focus so much on the money but what these surveys really tell us is that people are searching for purpose or significance. It translates to this: Because I did my job today, why is the world a better place to live? Because I went to work today, why are families more enriched or better off? The problem is that for most people, there is not a good answer for that. It explains why people look like they do during the morning rush hour. If you are in rush hour traffic and you look over to the right and over to the left at the people sitting next to you in traffic, they are not smiling. Many are miserable and struggling because in the grand scheme of things, what they do today doesn't matter. There is no significance. They are replaceable.

I think that the most dangerous and the most frightful place to be is where all of your income depends on your having to get up and show up for work every day. If one day something happens out of our control like being laid off, you would be in trouble financially. Millions of people thought that this kind of situation could never happen to them.

Years ago, when you went to work in corporate America, you were told, "Work hard. Be loyal to this company, and we will take care of you for the rest of your life." That may have been true forty years ago. It may have even been true twenty years ago, but it is not true today. You can get up and work hard and be loyal to a company and you can be without a job in a split second. Companies are going out of business. Stock markets are crashing. Heaven forbid that you get into an accident and you can't work because you are recuperating for a year or two or three.

We teach people business and financial principles based on success. We have a formula that works better in a recession or poor economic times. It can become nauseating to even think about getting up and going to work every day to build somebody else's dreams. Work is a place where people go day in and day out and when that workweek is over, they never get paid for that workweek again. How do you get out of that?

There is a radio personality here in Detroit who has been the morning show host on one of the top radio stations here for decades. This is a guy who made a multiple six-figure income that was a lot closer to seven figures than it was to six figures. A few months ago, this guy lost his job. The radio station changed directions and in a moment his large income went to nothing. I had lunch with him last week and he said to me, "I need to get a job but I am not going to go back to a prison where somebody dictates that I have to show up to work to get a paycheck." This is a guy who made close to seven figures who finally realized, at fifty-six years old, that he had been working his entire life to build somebody else's dream.

We teach people how to actually build their own dreams and how to plant seeds.

I think that I can close with this. I did a presentation at a conference in California where one of the other speakers was Frank Reich. Frank Reich was a back-up quarterback for the Buffalo Bills. During his tenure there, Frank Reich was called the best back-up quarterback in the history of the NFL. They went to four Super Bowls in a row. That is an unprecedented run in the NFL—to go to championship games four years in a row.

Frank Reich got up and talked about a record that he had achieved. In the fourth Super Bowl, their starting quarterback, Jim Kelly, got hurt and Frank had to step up and guide his team to victory. Even though they had had an unbelievable amount of success, they were being seen as the team that had lost three Super Bowls in a row. They didn't want to lose four in a row and become a team of failure. Before the game, Marv Leevy, their coach, gathered all the players together and he stared at them. He had run out of inspirational and motivational things to say. He had said everything for three Super Bowls, three beginnings, three half times, and throughout the season. Now they were at their fourth Super Bowl and they were determined to not have their careers defined by losing four Super Bowls. The silence in the room grew very tense.

Finally, a guy by the name Bruce Smith stood up. He was defensive end for the Buffalo Bills. He is a very large man. He had at one time held the record for the most sacks in NFL history. Because he was such a large man, his presence was felt—everybody looked up at him. He was one of the team leaders about to deliver a word of inspiration. They could hear the crowd just screaming in the background out in the stadium. He looked at his team and he simply said, "Is you coming or is you ain't?" He turned around and he put his helmet on and he started to walk down the tunnel toward the field. The players in that room exploded and jumped up and stormed onto the field with Bruce.

Bruce wasn't talking about physically going out and playing the game. He meant, "What are you going to do individually today to make a difference in this game?"

I ask people, "What are you going to do individually today to win for your family? What are you going to do today in these changing times to adjust?" I think sometimes it is this simple, "Is you coming or is you ain't?" We can complicate it. We can read books. We can watch programs. We can journal. We can spend hours and weeks and days in meetings trying to figure this out, but I think that it really comes down to this: do you have the desire to win for your family, to win for your school, to win for your corporation, to win for your church, to win for your wife, to win for your parents, to win in every aspect of your life? If you are someone who does, I'd love to speak with you and help you create a customized program for success.

And lastly, I'll mention endurance—committing to winning as a way of life. Most people don't stay around long enough to reap the reward of success. This is true in careers, health programs, relationships, churches, etc. My prayer for all of our readers is to find the endurance God has blessed all of us with and make it a part of you every day. I'd love to meet you all one day and swap stories, adventures, and life's lessons.

May God bless you abundantly!

WRIGHT

What a great conversation, Michael. We covered a lot here today and I've learned a lot. This is going to be a great chapter for our readers. I appreciate all this time you've taken to talk with me today and give such useful insights.

SKUPIN

It was a blessing. I always get as much out of it as my audience does.

WRIGHT

Today we have been talking to Michael Skupin, entrepreneur, motivational speaker, salesman, author, hunter, athlete, father of seven, and star of the CBS television hit reality show *Survivor: The Australian Outback*. Michael is determined to reach people's souls with a very encouraging and endearing message of family, priorities, and life lessons. I think that he has done a great job here today. I've listened to him, I hope everyone else will.

Michael, thank you so much for being with us here today on *Discover Your Inner Strength*.

SKUPIN

God bless you, David.

About the Author

Growing up in his formative years in a family of five without a father, Michael Skupin realizes the impact of barely making it. Michael is passionate and committed to helping people all across the country as a consultant, inspirational speaker, coach, and educator. As a father of seven and a coach of more than fifty seasons of sports, Michael loves to teach.

If we just take a step back, have a willingness to learn, incorporate the successes, and eliminate the failures of our past it can give us incredible insight into every area of our life. We can build a healthy "you" spiritually, financially, physically, emotionally, and relationally by employing programs and having the endurance to see them through.

Michael has been incredibly familiar and widely recognized, as Mike has spoken to more than *one billion* people via live appearances, television, and radio.

Michael often states that things happen but it's what you do with "what happened" that shapes the man. For example, had Michael quit after any one of these events, his life and the opportunities he's had would likely have never happened.

Mike was temporarily blinded after being pepper sprayed by an animal rights activist after he returned from Australia where they hunted and consumed a wild boar.

Mike made headlines on the Emmy award-winning episode where he tragically was overcome with smoke and passed out, falling into a fire. He was airlifted to safety via helicopter in front of fifty million people watching worldwide. His recovery took a full year.

"The incident ranks as one of the most dramatic in the history of reality television."
—*Allan Johnson, Chicago Tribune*

Discover Your Inner Strength

Michael Skupin

Speaker, Author, and Consultant

White Lake, Michigan
tammy@mikeskupin.com
mike@mikeskupin.com
www.mikeskupin.com

Using Strategy to Discover Your Inner Strength

An Interview With...
Brian Tracy

DAVID WRIGHT (WRIGHT)

Many years ago, Brian Tracy started off on a lifelong search for the secrets of success in life and business. He studied, researched, traveled, worked, and taught for more than thirty years. In 1981, he began to share his discoveries in talks and seminars, and eventually in books, audios and video-based courses.

The greatest secret of success he learned is this: "There are no secrets of success." There are instead timeless truths and principles that have to be rediscovered, relearned, and practiced by each person. Brian's gift is synthesis—the ability to take large numbers of ideas from many sources and combine them into highly practical, enjoyable, and immediately usable forms that people can take and apply quickly to improve their life and work. Brian has brought together the best ideas, methods, and techniques from thousands of books, hundreds of courses, and experience working with individuals and organizations of every kind in the U.S., Canada, and worldwide.

Today, I have asked Brian to discuss his latest book, Victory!: Applying the Military Principals of Strategy for Success in Business and Personal Life.

Brian Tracy, welcome to Discover Your Inner Strength.

TRACY

Thank you, David. It's a pleasure to be here.

WRIGHT

Let's talk about your new book the *Victory!: Applying* the *Military Principals* of *Strategy* for *Success* in *Business* and *Personal Life.* (By the way it is refreshing to hear someone say something good about the successes of the military.) Why do you think the military is so successful?

TRACY

Well, the military is based on very serious thought. The American military is the most respected institution in America. Unless you're a left liberal limp-wristed pinko most people in America really respect the military because it keeps America free. People who join the military give up most of their lives—twenty to thirty years—in sacrifice to be prepared to guard our freedoms. And if you ask around the world what it is that America stands for, it stands for individual freedom, liberty, democracy, freedom, and opportunity that is only secured in a challenging world—a dangerous world—by your military.

Now the other thing is that the people in our military are not perfect because there is no human institution made up of human beings that is perfect—there are no perfect people. The cost of mistakes in military terms is death; therefore, people in the military are extraordinarily serious about what they do. They are constantly looking for ways to do what they do better and better and better to reduce the likelihood of losing a single person.

We in America place extraordinary value on individual human life. That is why you will see millions of dollars spent to save a life, whether for an accident victim or Siamese twins from South America, because that's part of our culture. The military has that same culture.

I was just reading today about the RQ-1 "Predator" drone planes (Unmanned Aerial Vehicles—UAVs) that have been used in reconnaissance over the no-fly zones in Iraq. These planes fly back and forth constantly gathering information from the ground. They can also carry remote-controlled weapons. According to www.globalsecurity.org, the planes cost $4.5 million each and get shot down on a regular basis. However, the military is willing to invest hundreds of millions of dollars to develop these planes, and lose them to save the life of a pilot, because pilots are so precious—human life is precious. In the military everything is calculated right down to the tinniest detail because it's the smallest details that can cost lives. That is why the military is so successful—they are so meticulous about planning.

A salesperson can go out and make a call; if it doesn't work that's fine—he or she can make another sales call. Professional soldiers can go out on an operation and if it's not successful they're dead and maybe everybody in the squad is dead as well. There is no margin for error in the military; that's why they do it so well. This is also why the military principals of strategy that I talk about in *Victory!* are so incredibly important because a person who really understands those principals and strategies sees how to do things vastly better with far lower probability of failure than the average person.

WRIGHT

In the promotion on *Victory!* you affirm that it is very important to set clear attainable goals and objectives. Does that theme carry out through all of your presentations and all of your books?

TRACY

Yes. Over and over again the theme reiterates that you can't hit a target you can't see—you shouldn't get into your car unless you know where you are going. More people spend more time planning a picnic than they spend planning their careers.

I'll give you an example. A very successful woman who is in her fifties now wrote down a plan when she was attending university. Her plan was for the first ten years she would work for a Fortune 500 corporation, really learn the business, and learn how to function at high levels. For the second ten years of her career she talked about getting married and having children at the same time. For that second ten years she would also work for a medium sized company helping it grow and succeed. For the third ten years (between the ages of forty and fifty), she would start her own company based on her knowledge of both businesses. She would then build that into a successful company. Her last ten years she would be chief executive officer of a major corporation and retire financially independent at the age of sixty. At age fifty-eight she would have hit every single target. People would say, "Boy, you sure are lucky." No, it wouldn't be luck. From the time she was seventeen she was absolutely crystal clear about what she was going to do with her career and what she was going to do with her life, and she hit all of her targets.

WRIGHT

In a time where companies, both large and small, take a look at their competition and basically try to copy everything they do, it was really interesting to read in *Victory!* that you suggest taking vigorous offensive action to get the best results. What do you mean by "vigorous offensive action"?

TRACY

Well, see, that's another thing. When you come back to talking about probabilities—and this is really important—you see successful people try more things. And if you wanted to just end the interview right now and ask, "What piece of advice would you give to our listeners?" I would say, "Try more things." The reason I would say that is because if you try more things, the probability is that you will hit your target

For example, here's an analogy I use. Imagine that you go into a room and there is a dartboard against the far wall. Now imagine that you are drunk and you have never played darts before. The room is not very bright and you can barely see the bull's eye. You are standing a long way from the board, but you have an endless supply of darts. You pick up the darts and you just keep throwing them at the target over there on the other of the room even though you are not a good dart thrower and you're not even well coordinated. If you kept throwing darts over and over again what would you eventually hit?

WRIGHT

Pretty soon you would get a bull's eye.

TRACY

Yes, eventually you would hit a bull's eye. The odds are that as you keep throwing the darts even though you are not that well educated, even if you don't come from a wealthy family or you don't have a Harvard education, if you just keep throwing darts you will get a little better each time you throw. It's known as a "decybernetic self-correction mechanism" in the brain—each time you try something, you get a little bit smarter at it. So over time, if you kept throwing, you must eventually hit a bull's eye. In other words, you must eventually find the right way to do the things you need to do to become a millionaire. That's the secret of success. That's why people come here from a 190 countries with one idea in mind—"If I come here I can try anything I want; I can go anywhere, because there are no limitations. I have so much freedom; and if I keep doing this, then by God, I will eventually hit a bull's eye." And they do and everybody says, "Boy, you sure where lucky."

Now imagine another scenario: You are thoroughly trained at throwing darts—you have practiced, you have developed skills and expertise in your field, you are constantly upgrading your knowledge, and you practice all the time. Second you are completely prepared, you're thoroughly cold sober, fresh, fit, alert, with high energy. Third, all of the room is very bright around the dartboard. This time how long would it take you to hit the bull's eye? The obvious answer is you will hit a bull's eye far faster than if you had all those negative conditions.

What I am I saying is, you can dramatically increase the speed at which you hit your bull's eye. The first person I described—drunk, unprepared, in a darkened room, and so on—may take twenty or twenty-five years. But if you are thoroughly prepared, constantly upgrading your skills; if you are very clear about your targets; if you have everything you need at hand and your target is clear, your chances of hitting a bull's eye you could hit a bull's eye is five years rather than twenty. That's the difference in success in life.

WRIGHT

In reading your books and watching your presentations on video, one of the common threads seen through your presentations is creativity. I was glad that in the promotional material of *Victory!* you state that you need to apply innovative solutions to overcome obstacles. The word "innovative" grabbed me. I guess you are really concerned with *how* people solve problems rather than just solving problems.

TRACY

Vigorous action means you will cover more ground. What I say to people, especially in business, is the more things you do the more experience you get. The more experience you get the smarter you get. The smarter you get the better results you get the better results you get. The better results you get the less time it takes you to get the same results. And it's such a simple thing. In my books *Create Your Own Future* and *Victory!* you will find there is one characteristic of all successful people—they are action oriented. They move fast, they move quickly, and they don't waste time. They're moving ahead, trying more things, but they are always in motion. The faster you move the more energy you have. The faster you move the more in control you feel and the faster you are the more positive and the more motivated you are. We are talking about a direct relationship between vigorous action and success.

WRIGHT

Well, the military certainly is a team "sport" and you talk about building peak performance teams for maximum results. My question is how do individuals in corporations build peak performance teams in this culture?

TRACY

One of the things we teach is the importance of selecting people carefully. Really successful companies spend an enormous amount of time at the front end on selection they look for people who are really, really good in terms of what they are looking for. They interview very carefully; they interview several people and they interview them several times. They do careful background checks. They are as careful in selecting people as a person might be in getting married. Again, in the military, before a person is promoted they go through a rigorous process. In large corporations, before a person is promoted his or her performance is very, very carefully evaluated to be sure they are the right people to be promoted at that time.

WRIGHT

My favorite point in *Victory!* is when you say, "Amaze your competitors with surprise and speed." I have done that several times in business and it does work like a charm.

TRACY

Yes, it does. Again one of the things we teach over and over again that there is a direct relationship between speed and perceived value. When you do things fast for people they consider you to be better. They consider your products to be better and they consider your service to be better—they actually consider them to be of higher value. Therefore, if you do things really, really fast then you overcome an enormous amount of resistance. People wonder, "Is this a good decision? Is it worth the money? Am I going the right direction?" When you do things fast, you blast that out of their minds.

WRIGHT

You talk about moving quickly to seize opportunities. I have found that to be difficult. When I ask people about opportunities, it's difficult to find out what they think an opportunity is. Many think opportunities are high-risk, although I've never found it that way myself. What do you mean by moving quickly to cease opportunity?

TRACY

There are many cases were a person has an idea and they think that's a good idea. They think they should do something about it. They think, "I am going to do something about that but I really can't do it this week, so I will wait until after the month ends," and so on. By the time they do move on the opportunity it's to late—somebody's already seized it.

One of the military examples I use is the battle of Gettysburg. Now the battle of Gettysburg was considered the high-water mark of the Confederacy after the battle of Gettysburg the Confederacy won additional battles at Chattanooga and other places but they eventually lost the war. The high-water mark of Gettysburg was a little hill at one end of the battlefield called Little Round Top. As the battle began Little Round Top was empty. Colonel Joshua Chamberlain of the Union Army saw that this could be the pivotal point of the battlefield. He went up there and looked at it and he immediately rushed troops to fortify the hill. Meanwhile, the Confederates also saw that Little Round Top could be key to the battle as well, so they too immediately rushed the hill. An enormous battle took place. It was really the essence of the battle of Gettysburg. The victor who took that height controlled the battlefield. Eventually the union troops, who were almost lost, controlled Little Round Top and won the battle. The Civil War was over in about a year and a half, but that was the turning point.

So what would have happened if Chamberlain had said, "Wait until after lunch and then I'll move some men up to Little Round Top"? The Confederate troops would have seized Little Round Top, controlled the battlefield, and would have won the battle of Gettysburg. It was just a matter of moving very, very fast. Forty years later it was determined that there were three days at the battle of Gettysburg that cost the battle for the Confederates. The general in charge of the troops on the Confederate right flank was General James Longstreet. Lee told him to move his army forward as quickly as possible the next day, but to use his own judgment. Longstreet didn't agree with Lee's plan so he kept his troop sitting there most of the next day. It is said that it was Longstreet's failure to move forward on the second day and seize Little Round Top that cost the Confederacy the battle and eventually the war. It was just this failure to move forward and forty years later, when Longstreet appeared at a reunion of Confederate veterans in 1901 or 1904, he was booed. The veterans felt his failure to move forward that fateful day cost them the war. If you read every single account of the battle of Gettysburg, Longstreet's failure to move forward and quickly seize the opportunity is always included.

WRIGHT

In your book you tell your readers to get the ideas and information needed to succeed. Where can individuals get these ideas?

TRACY

Well we are living in an ocean of ideas. It's so easy. The very first thing you do is you pick a subject you want to major in and you go to someone who is good at it. You ask what you should read in this field and you go down to the bookstore and you look at the books. Any book that is published in paperback obviously sold well in hardcover. Read the table of contents. Make sure the writer has experience in the area you in which you want to learn about. Buy the book and read it. People ask, "How can I be sure it is the right book?" You can't be sure; stop trying to be sure.

When I go to the bookstore I buy three or four books and bring them home and read them. I may only find one chapter of a book that's helpful, but that chapter may save me a year of hard work.

The fact is that your life is precious. A book costs twenty of thirty dollars. How much is your life worth? How much do you earn per hour? A person who earns fifty thousand dollars a year earns twenty-five dollars an hour. A person who wants to earn a hundred thousand dollars a year earns fifty dollars an hour. Now, if a book cost you ten or twenty dollars but it can save you a year of hard work, then that's the cheapest thing you have bought in your whole life. And what if you bought fifty books and you paid twenty dollars apiece for them—a thousand dollars worth of books—and out of that you only got one idea that saved you a year of hard work? You've got a fifty times payoff. So the rule is you cannot prepare too thoroughly.

WRIGHT

In the last several months I have recommended your book, *Get Paid More and Promoted Faster* to more people. I have had a lot of friends in their fifties and sixties who have lost their jobs to layoffs all kinds of transfers of ownership. When I talked with you last, the current economy had a 65 percent jump in layoffs. In the last few months before I talked with you, every one of them reported that the book really did help them. They saw some things a little bit clearer; it was a great book.

How do you turn setbacks and difficulties to your advantage? I know what it means, but what's the process?

TRACY

You look into it you look into every setback and problem and find the seed of an equal or greater advantage or benefit. It's a basic rule. You find that all successful people look into their problems for lessons they can learn and for things they can turn to their advantage. In fact, one of the best attitudes you can possibly have is to say that you know every problem that is sent to you is sent to help you. So your job is just simply look into to it and ask, "What can help me in this situation?" And surprise, surprise! You will find something that can help you. You will find lessons you can learn; you will find something you can do more of, or less of; you can find something that will give you an insight that will set you in a different direction, and so on.

WRIGHT

I am curious. I know you have written a lot in the past and you are a terrific writer. Your cassette programs are wonderful. What do you have planned for the next few years?

TRACY

Aside from speaking and consulting with non-profits, my goal is to produce four books a year on four different subjects, all of which have practical application to help people become more successful.

WRIGHT

Well, I really want to thank you for your time here today on *Discover Your Inner Strength!* It's always fascinating to hear what you have to say. I know I have been a Brian Tracy fan for many, many years. I really appreciate your being with us today.

TRACY

Thank you. You have a wonderful day and I hope our listeners and readers will go out and get *Focal Point* and/or *Victory!* They are available at any bookstore or at Amazon.com. They are fabulous books, filled with good ideas that will save you years of hard work.

WRIGHT

I have already figured out that those last two books are a better buy with Amazon.com, so you should go to your computer and buy these books as soon as possible.

We have been talking today with Brian Tracy, whose life and career truly makes one of the best rags-to-riches stories. Brian didn't graduate from high school and his first job was washing dishes. He lost job after job—washing cars, pumping gas, stacking lumber, you name it. He was homeless and living in his car. Finally, he got into sales, then sales management. Later, he sold investments, developed real estate, imported and distributed Japanese automobiles, and got a master's degree in business administration. Ultimately, he became the COO of a $265 million dollar development company.

Brian, you are quite a person. Thank you so much for being with us today.

TRACY

You are very welcome, David. You have a great day!

About the Author

One of the world's top success motivational speakers, Brian Tracy is the author of many books and audio tape seminars, including *The Psychology of Achievement*, *The Luck Factor*, *Breaking the Success Barrier*, *Thinking Big* and *Success Is a Journey*.

Brian Tracy
www.BrianTracy.com

Strength Lessons from the Living Room to the Board Room

An Interview With…
Dr. Lynn Workman Nodland

DAVID WRIGHT (WRIGHT)

We are talking with Dr. Lynn Workman Nodland, psychologist, marriage and family therapist, and Master Certified Coach.

Dr. Nodland, welcome to *Discover Your Inner Strength*.

You work with individuals and organizations to develop their strengths, but what would you like to share with us about discovering your own inner strength?

NODLAND

I enjoy sharing about inner strengths because I believe inner strengths are what make the "world go 'round," from personal to business to world relationships (i.e., from living room to board room and beyond). How we use our strengths and relate to each other is vitally important.

There are a couple of things that stand out for me. One of them is what Dr. Martin Seligman and Dr. Christopher Peterson, the authors of *Character Strengths and Virtues*, said about strengths. They said that core strengths are "inherent" and that "everyone can readily identify a handful of strengths as very much their own." These thoughts intrigued me so I started thinking about when I first recognized some of my inherent strengths and I found that it was pretty early in life.

WRIGHT

What was the first experience you had that led you to recognize your inherent inner strengths?

NODLAND

One of my first recollections about what inner strength really meant came at the tender age of about five years old. My family rented a farmhouse near the small airport where my father taught flying. Living there was a delightful experience. I have many wonderful memories of being there such as winters when my mother and I made crêpe paper flowers of bright colors and tied them on the bushes outside the old farmhouse porch. We thought that would make it seem like spring was coming sooner. Summer days were glorious with all the wildflowers and smell of new-mowed hay.

Lucky for me the farmhouse came complete with a farm dog named Tippy. He was one of those shepherd-type black and white furry sheep dogs. One day I was in the orchard, sitting under an apple tree arranging the fallen apples into as big a "mountain" as I could imagine. My constant companion, Tippy, played nearby. All of a sudden I heard a snort and when I looked up a huge bull was charging toward me. I ran for the fence, screaming all the way. My mother came running to help but she couldn't fight the bull and I knew it. I am sure she was afraid that I would be gored and trampled to death by the angry bull, and, unfortunately, I had that very thought, also. Ta-da! Tippy to the rescue. Tippy ran at that bull barking and nipping at the bull's heels. The bull didn't like that too much and he forgot about chasing me and bolted around to chase Tippy, who luckily was able to run under the wooden fence to safety while the bull was stopped in his tracks by the fence.

My hero, Tippy, saved me! He was my buddy, he never left my side and I even let him sleep next to me. You probably wonder why I bring up Tippy when I think of inner strength. Maybe animals have inner strengths, too—that inner strength to reach inside and do courageous acts when needed. I sure felt Tippy had strengths! But the reason I brought up Tippy is that this little furry friend brought me to my first encounter with discovering my own inner strengths.

WRIGHT

How did it happen? How were your own inner strengths triggered by your relationship with a dog?

NODLAND

Well, I must say that to a little girl, Tippy was not just "a dog" and anyone who has ever loved a pet will understand what I mean. The wonderful times at the farm had to, unfortunately, come to an end. My father had decided to move from Hartland, Wisconsin, to Minneapolis to go to grad school for aeronautical engineering at the University of Minnesota. That meant we would live in a small apartment in the city. I realized this was not the best place for an active farm dog and I knew what that meant, too.

As the time to leave drew near, I cherished my time with Tippy more and more, knowing that he was the "farm dog" and would have to stay with the farm.

Finally the day came. We packed as much as we could into the car, including me—but not Tippy. I gave Tippy the biggest hug a little girl could give a dog, knowing it was our last hug. I told Tippy that I loved him and I always would. Then I quickly turned away.

As we drove away we passed the chestnut trees where Tippy and I had sat and played together—wonderful memories. I didn't want to look back as we drove away from the house and down the dusty road. I didn't want to see Tippy sitting there watching as we drove away. But I couldn't help it, I just had to take a peek and look back—and as I did I saw something terrible—in the dust I could see Tippy was running as fast as he could, trying to catch up to the car. I sobbed until I could hardly breathe. I kept hoping that he would just stop running and return to the farmhouse but he didn't—he just kept running, running, running, until I could no longer see him in the distance as we sped away. I had to tell myself that he was, and would be, okay.

At that moment I had to reach deep down inside of my little girl heart to find my inner strengths—those core strengths. I didn't really understand "strengths" then but now I realize that I used those inner strengths to help me understand that the best thing for Tippy was to remain with the farm. I knew that the owners of the farm would take good care of him. So my inner strengths helped to ease the grief of leaving him by focusing on the warm memories I had with Tippy and the joy of thinking of my furry friend finishing out his life with the freedom of running and playing in the open fields. Fortunately, we did call back to the farm later and found out Tippy was just fine because he was loved by the farm owners, too. But upon leaving Tippy behind, I had to rely on inherent strengths to make it through that time. The inner strengths that I used there can be identified (as categorized in the book *Character Strengths and Virtues*) as To Love and Be Loved, Optimism, and Courage. I loved Tippy enough to want the best for him and I knew a tiny apartment in the city definitely was not it. I used Courage to face the reality of a very tough situation and I also used Optimism to look forward and know that

Tippy would be fine (hopefully, he had happy memories, too) and that I was going on a new adventure.

Leaving Tippy was difficult but, fortunately, I have had three other wonderful dogs in my lifetime. But with the passing of each one, it is a reminder to reach again for those inner strengths that apparently were inherent and carried me through that challenging time when I was a little girl.

WRIGHT

Thanks for sharing your story. Now tell me how you do success coaching with individuals and organizations. What is important about how they discover their inner strengths?

NODLAND

What I realize is that discovering and developing inner strengths is so very important for success. All strengths are valuable. To emphasize these points I'd like to share an old Chinese proverb: "The person who says it cannot be done should not interrupt the person doing it." Now that I have shared this proverb I will tell you that while strengths are exhibited in this proverb, the strengths can be viewed from different perspectives.

This proverb highlights at least two different kinds of "strengths." The person doing the action might be very Industrious and a hard worker or possibly too Optimistic and that person could be wasting time by trying to complete an impossible task. The person interrupting might be right to interrupt if the task is impossible or the person might be too cautious (Prudence is also a strength) and might be missing an opportunity to finish a project. I often see this type of dynamic playing out with people who are good visionaries (the optimistic doers) and the people with good analytic skills (the more prudent types who want to protect by pointing out the challenges and protecting from disasters).

I coach a wonderful woman CEO who is a great visionary. She learned to help prepare her people who have the analytic, prudent strengths by giving them her agenda and her vision before meeting with them. This gives them time to think about what the real concerns are and also to rule out ones that really are not valid concerns.

Another person I work with is a restaurant owner who uses the strengths of Humor and Spontaneity to engage his employees and create a good culture. However, he also has to watch that he keeps the respect of his employees by being able to set boundaries and make hard decisions. An executive I know uses Leadership, Integrity, and Self-regulation to provide a model for others. By using each strength for the right purpose it is easier to reach the best outcomes. How we identify and use strengths appropriately is important.

I see people as having more than one inner strength, so I will often be referring to *strengths* rather than just one strength. Because people have several inner strengths, they can use the ones that fit the situation best. Some strengths are inherent and will appear naturally but others can also be learned and developed as we stretch, change, and grow.

WRIGHT

When did you first become interested in peoples' strengths?

NODLAND

I became interested in discovering inner strengths many years ago because it seemed to be an effective strategy to use to help people. Also, there was a movement starting to use inner strengths to reach success. This growing interest has been in both the areas of psychology and coaching. I received my PhD from the University of Minnesota over twenty years ago and at that time the prevailing thought was to encourage people to work on their weaknesses to help them do better. People wanted to know "why" they did something that didn't work and they felt that this knowledge would help them move forward and not make the same mistake again. While finding out "why" and what *not* to do can be helpful knowledge so people will not repeat the same mistake twice, it still means that they have to develop strengths and learn how to make better choices. Some research also shows that it can even be counterproductive for people to revisit their mistakes because, if they have a negative focus, it can reinforce them feeling like a failure. It is usually much more productive to *not* focus on the failure but instead to focus on their inner strengths. This is the fastest way for them to learn new ways of thinking, feeling, and acting. By focusing on strengths, they delight in discovering their strengths and learning to use them more. When they use their strengths more, they feel more positive, perform better, make better choices, and get better results.

WRIGHT

We have been talking about inner strengths, but how do you define a strength?

NODLAND

In the book I mentioned earlier, *Character Strengths and Virtues*, Martin Seligman, PhD and Christopher Peterson, PhD describe the fact that a strength is different from a talent. As mentioned previously, a strength is inherent and a talent is the result of using a strength. They talk about "Signature Strengths" as strengths that when used, people feel authentic, and that they are "the real me." They are energized and they learn more easily. They feel invigorated when using the strength and there is a propensity to use the strength to create and pursue projects that use those strengths. This often results in people feeling happy and competent.

WRIGHT

Using strengths sounds like the thing to do to make life easier and more pleasant. You mentioned that there was a movement happening that focused on recognizing strengths. Would you elaborate on this movement?

NODLAND

Yes. New strategies that worked well by focusing on peoples' strengths were emerging years ago. In fact, in 1966 Peter Drucker wrote *The Effective Executive* in which he stressed that effective executives "build on strengths—their own strengths, the strengths of superiors, colleagues, subordinates, and the strength of the situation." Then there was *The Strengths Model*, written by Charles Rapp in 1997 that also signaled a movement to "amplify the well part" of people. This writing was a positive advancement in the area of mental health.

The business world also began to follow in the path of developing strengths rather than spending intense time on overcoming peoples' weaknesses. Many leaders in psychology and coaching, such as Donald O. Clifton, PhD, Marcus Buckingham, and Martin Seligman, PhD, promoted discovering and using inner strengths. In his writings, Marcus Buckingham states that "the radical idea at the core of the strengths movement is that excellence is not the opposite of failure, and that, as such, you will learn little about excellence from studying failure." Dr. Seligman agrees with this theory and in his book, *Authentic Happiness*, he has many exercises designed to help people discover their strengths and build on them to reach success.

WRIGHT

Would you explain how one of these exercises works?

NODLAND

There were many good exercises but here is one of them that is extremely meaningful. It is writing a Gratitude Letter. This exercise is just as it sounds—you write a letter to someone you care about to express your gratitude. Whenever possible, it is good to deliver this letter in person and read it to the person. If that is not possible, then sometimes it is read over the phone and then sent. People who have done the Gratitude Letter say that the people receiving the letter were extremely moved and they themselves found it a very rewarding experience. Some people do it for their spouses, teachers, children, and/or parents. People even sometimes write this letter to someone who has passed away. They feel good about doing it, especially if they feel they never expressed gratitude while the person was living. They report that it brings forth happy memories of the person and is comforting to them. In doing this exercise, people bring forth several different strengths including Gratitude, To Love and Be Loved, and Creativity.

WRIGHT

What interests you most about inner strengths?

NODLAND

I must say that one of the things that seems most interesting to me is something that Carl Jung pointed out. A strength can also be a weakness if it is misused or overused. For example, Leadership is a wonderful strength to have unless the person overuses it and never helps people to grow and achieve. Leadership can then become controlling behavior, stifling the motivation of employees. Humor is also a nice strength to have if it is used appropriately and not used to put people down through sarcasm. There are several ways to learn about inner strengths. Some of these ways are through taking assessments, observing others, and self-observation.

WRIGHT

If someone wanted to get to know their strengths through taking an assessment, what should they do?

NODLAND

There are many types of strengths assessments. A few of them are Insights, DISC, and StrengthFinder. These assessments work best when a trained professional can "debrief" and do coaching about the results. This is where the real learning takes place and people discover not only what strengths they possess, but how to use these strengths most effectively. Another alternative that does not have a "debrief" with it but it can be quite informative, is to take the free assessment of strengths on www.authentichappiness.org or on www.viastrengths.org. These assessments outline a person's twenty-four strengths and rank orders them. When people are aware of their strengths, they can look at how and where they can use their strengths. Then, as a coach, I hold them accountable to using and developing these strengths in the best way.

WRIGHT

When you have people take these assessments, what are some of the things they learn in the "debrief" and coaching?

NODLAND

In my business, we have people take assessments to help them identify their strengths and their "natural energy." "Natural energy" is about identifying, in particular, which strengths come easiest and most naturally to people. When using these natural inner strengths people don't have to put in as much effort to bring out and use those strengths.

One thing surprising to people is the assessments show how they appear on a "good day" when they are using their strengths in the best ways. It also shows what they can look like on a "bad day" when they are misusing or overusing their strengths. Many of the assessments will show personality traits as reflected in their actions.

In the Insights assessment there is also a section on "blind spots" to help people see what they might not recognize but what others might see about them. If they don't think the blind spots are accurate, we have them check with someone who knows them well. Often these other people will support the validity of the assessment, so this is why they are called "blind spots."

By being mindful of the ways they use their strengths, people can communicate more effectively and enhance the positive use of their strengths. They can also try to avoid the negative misuse or overuse, which could result in inappropriate actions with sometimes serious ramifications for themselves, their relationships, and their organizations.

WRIGHT

You say that assessments are a good way for people to identify their strengths. What are some other ways that people discover their strengths? I think you mentioned observation; tell me more.

NODLAND

Yes, observation is a good way to learn about inner strengths—observation of others and self-observation. There are a couple of stories that I like to tell to show how people learn about strengths. This first story is about strengths you see when observing others.

This story is about something that happened to me some years ago. I had to grab a quick lunch at a fast-food restaurant. The place was packed with long lines and impatient people all trying to get their food as fast as possible. There was a woman behind the counter who seemed to be about seventy-some years of age. She was rushing, jumping back and forth between the customers at the front counter and the food at the back. It seemed that burgers and fries were flying everywhere. She was swift and efficient, but some people were still extremely rude to her.

When I got up to the front counter so she could take my order, I thought I'd say something to her that might let her know I recognized how hard she was working to help people who were still not being very nice to her. By doing that I thought I could bring a bright spot to her day. I said, "Wow, it sure is busy in here and people are not always very understanding of that fact." That is about all that I got out of my mouth before she quickly said to me, "Honey, don't feel sorry for me. I love it and I love the people. They can get upset when they are hungry and rushed. They are not feeling good because they need food and they need it fast. I can help them get fed and get going. That makes them happy and it makes me happy, too. I'm having a ball!"

That little woman taught me a lot that day. She wasn't just flipping burgers—she was helping people to get fed, feel better, and get back to their business. In her way she was contributing to the success of their day, which meant success for her. She used inner strengths of Optimism and Perseverance (and probably several other strengths) to keep going and to not let a rushed crowd get her down. Her life had meaning.

I have never forgotten her as she served others graciously and efficiently and felt satisfaction for what she was doing to help others. I wonder how many people, besides me, went in to get a quick lunch and went out with much more—not only were they satisfied and happy, but they also had a wonderful memory of this elderly woman's joyous spirit and the lesson she showed of caring about people, loving her work, and feeling she was contributing to others' lives. Her life is an example of using inner strengths to have a successful life.

If people are in a career they don't like, they can either find a way out or use their inner strengths to create a new perception of their job. If they are staying in the job, how can they find a way to love what they do and see the larger meaning of their job? It is like the story of the two bricklayers: one said he was laying bricks while the other one said that he was building a cathedral. We will never know what strengths the second bricklayer used, maybe Appreciation of Beauty and Excellence or possibly Future Mindedness. Whichever strengths he used, he made his job meaningful for him.

As a coach, I help people to "think big," to find their inner strengths, and define their own success. For the woman in the fast-food place, her job was her "big" and it was her success. It worked well for her and she was happy. It is important that we don't judge others' choices for a successful life. Sometimes our society today seems to reward achievement by looking at how busy people are, how high they advance in their career, or how much money they make. I often coach people to achieve these very things—if they want them—and yet the most important thing is for them to have balance in their lives, feel their strengths, and live their values so they have happy and meaningful lives. It seems that CEOs and professionals can easily get lost in the world of achievement and not realize other important strengths and values. But, the measures of strengths, values, and success are individually determined. To some people success means ramping up and to others it can mean slowing down.

WRIGHT

Once people know what their strengths are, how can they put them to use in their lives in the best way?

NODLAND

That is a good question. At times, busy professionals and executives feel like they are rats on a treadmill and they can't hop off and stop long enough to think about what they would really like to see happen. These are cases where people have to use their inner strengths, especially the strengths of Courage and Bravery, to stop long enough to see what needs to change and take steps to make those changes. This is not easy to do because there is often a high monetary reward for staying "on the treadmill."

As coaches, one of the things we do is to actually have them look at how their values and priorities are aligned with their actions and how using strengths can help them achieve what they really want for themselves and their businesses. We have them put time in their schedules to vision and work on these important aspects. Positive results happen when they do this for themselves and for their organizations. They learn how to use their inner strengths to meet the demands of the outer world in a rewarding and personally fulfilling way.

It is important to note that strengths can be used in many ways. It is not only about what you "do," it is also about "who you are" as a person and how you use your strengths. Not only can a strength be misused or overused slightly, as I mentioned before, it can be misused or overused to actually create great deception and in some cases, commit crimes. A creative person could be a stealthy burglar living a life of crime or a talented artist bringing joy to many people through his or her artistic works. The strength is still Creativity but the ways it is used varies greatly. In other words, it is again back to values and how strengths are used to live out values. Strengths can be used for evil or they can be used for good. We have seen how this can happen in individual relationships, in families, in business organizations, and in the world. That is why it is so important for us to learn how to use strengths to honor each other and have integrity in our lives and in our dealings with others so our actions can help to make the world a better place.

Sometimes one of the hardest things for people to do is to actually discover what strengths they have themselves. Assessments and observations of others are important but another way to discover strengths is to just take some time to reflect and realize strengths by listening to your mind, body, and spirit.

We live in a busy world and I often ask people to take some time away from the "doing" to spend some time just "being." The body, mind, and spirit are very wise and they know us intimately. The body, mind, and spirit are trying to get messages to us about our life and our strengths but in our busy state we ignore those messages. Often people will get physical symptoms. Their physiology tries to give them some strong signals. They need to take time to listen to what their physiology is saying and also take time to listen to self-talk—things like "my gut is tied in knots." That gut is talking to you. Dr. Paul Pearsall has another view about the body's messages. In his book, *The Heart's Code,* Pearsall says, "I have no doubt that the heart is the major energy center of my body and a conveyor of a code that represents my soul." He believes that we have been too focused on the brain and that the heart can tell you a lot if you listen to it. What is your physiology telling you about your values and your inner strengths? What is right in your life and in alignment, and what is wrong and needs to change? Often, if people can get in touch with their values, these values will lead to the discovery of inner strengths that are required to make the needed changes. When your values are challenged, your strengths can be called upon to "make it right." When you are using your strengths and things in your life are right, then physiology calms down because the body, mind, and spirit are aligned and at peace.

I consider the people I work with to be "creative, resourceful, and whole" but sometimes they need an objective observer, the coach, to help them realize their strengths and what is really going on in their lives. They have the strengths and answers within them but, as their coach, my role is to ask powerful questions to help them access the answers. If they get stuck, I help them find the information they need. It is not my job as a coach to decide what success means for them and what strengths they should use to get there—my job is to be a guide on their journey.

Here is another story that I share with people to help them recognize strengths in others and in themselves:

The following story, called "But Senor," illustrates how the two people have different strengths. It also shows how they have different values and success means different things to each of them. I am sharing this story with you because it is a story that I share with people to help them realize their strengths, their values, and to identify what success is for them.

The "But Senor" story goes like this:

An American businessman was at the pier of a small coastal Mexican village when a small boat with just one fisherman docked. Inside the small boat were several large yellow fin tuna. The American complimented the Mexican on the quality of his fish and asked how long it took to catch them. The Mexican replied, "Only a little while, senor." The American then asked why he didn't stay out longer and catch more fish. The Mexican fisherman said, "I sleep late, fish a little, play with my children, take siesta with my wife, Maria, stroll into the village each evening where I sip wine, and play guitar with my amigos. I have a full and busy life, senor."

The American scoffed. "I am a Harvard MBA and could help you. You should spend more time fishing and with the proceeds buy a bigger boat. With the proceeds from the bigger boat you could buy several boats; eventually you would have a fleet of fishing boats. Instead of selling your catch to a middleman you would sell directly to the processor, eventually opening your own cannery. You would control the product, processing and distribution. You would need to leave this small coastal fishing village and move to Mexico City, then Los Angeles, and eventually to New York City where you will run your expanding enterprise."

"But senor, how long will this all take?"

To which the American replied, "Fifteen to twenty years."

"But what then, senor?"

The American laughed and said, "That's the best part. When the time is right you would announce an IPO and sell your company stock to the public and become very rich; you would make millions."

"Millions, senor? Then what?"

The American said, "Then you would retire; move to a small coastal fishing village where you could sleep late, fish a little, play with your kids, take siesta with your wife, stroll to the village in the evenings where you could sip wine and play guitar with your amigos."

Although the author of this story is unknown, the story illustrates some very interesting things.

WRIGHT

That is an interesting story but where does this story fit in with helping people and organizations find their inner strengths? How do you use it?

NODLAND

I have people reflect on the story and then answer some questions for themselves. These are some of the questions I ask to get them thinking:

What thoughts does the story bring out for you?
What strengths do you think it took for each of them on their journey?
What values are exemplified by each of the men in the story?
What did each man consider was a successful life?
What influences and contributions do you see each of them contributing to the world?
What do you see about your life in this story?
What are your strengths?
How are you living your values?
How is the balance in your life?
How do you really want your life to be?

Those are just some of the questions that can be raised with this story.

With organizations, the language changes somewhat and a different story might be used but it still gets down to these basics—what are the goals and how do people find the inner strengths to live their values to reach those goals? If a company wants to "go big" and grow, that can be a wonderful thing as long as it doesn't eat up the people and spit them out on the way. If an organization has the strengths of good strong values and a healthy culture, it can accomplish the best growth by also honoring and serving its employees. When an organization recognizes and develops its employees' strengths, the company benefits in many ways. Some of these ways include less sick days taken, less work comp claims, less turnover and better retention, happier and more productive employees—and guess what—that generally positively affects the bottom line.

WRIGHT

The story you told does provide a way to look at the results of different strengths being used. I can see where in today's world people can get caught up in "achievement" and not really recognize what they have sacrificed for achievement's sake.

NODLAND

You are so right. Sometimes they are so caught up in the work world that they are surprised when their spouse decides to leave because there is no relationship left between them. Some people who are very dedicated and persistent at work put many hours in to their careers only to find that their children grew up and they never had a chance to really know them. An important question I ask is, "What do you need to say 'no' to in order to say 'yes' to something else?" It is important to identify and say "yes" to the real priorities. People need balance in their lives so they don't get so far off track that they lose sight of their priorities and hit rock bottom, or close to it. The strengths of Creativity and Spirituality often get lost in a frantic world. Balance in life allows people to reach for the strengths that get shoved aside or ignored. When these types of strengths are used, people often feel peace and happiness. Brian Tracy reminds people in his book, *Maximum Achievement*, to "make peace of mind as your highest goal." He goes on to say that "you will enjoy better health and you will accomplish much more than you ever could otherwise."

WRIGHT

Are there times when people have a tendency to develop more of their strengths?

NODLAND

Yes, as I mentioned, it is in the midst of their biggest challenges or darkest hour, that people often discover their inner strength. Have you ever had a time when you wondered if you were going to make it? Maybe it was a time when you or a family member faced a serious illness. Or maybe it was when you lost a job and as you faced rejection after rejection, you didn't know how long it would be before you found another one. Maybe it was a business venture that went bad or having to file bankruptcy. Or maybe it was when you lost a loved one and felt you couldn't go on. You felt empty, lonely, exhausted.

WRIGHT

When the going gets tough, where do people go for that strength?

NODLAND

It is in the toughest times when people reach deeply into their soul to try to find their inner strengths. This revelation of inner strengths often comes when people feel they don't have the answers and they have to reach for strength they don't feel themselves—a strength beyond their own strength. This is when they feel broken and they get down on their knees.

This is when their inner strength comes from their Higher Power. For me my Higher Power is God. God provides that strength beyond my own strength and gives guidance to me on my journey. It is easy to take that help for granted when life is running along just great. Then when faced with challenges we are reminded of our need. I do ask for that guidance daily. When people look to their Higher Power they find strength, peace, and calm assurance that everything will somehow work out. However, people still need to take action and use many of their inner strengths—their gifts—to see opportunities and take action; but they are not alone and they receive help along the way.

Ken Blanchard, Stephen Covey, and many great leaders have strong beliefs and find comfort, strength, and guidance from their spiritual beliefs. Ken Blanchard wrote a leadership book, *Lead Like Jesus*. Wayne Dyer states his beliefs in his book, *There is a Spiritual Solution to Every Problem*. He writes that "you must be willing to ask for divine guidance." They credit their Maker in their writings.

Intention and belief are important to persevering to overcome challenges. People need to focus on what they want to see happen—the good intention—and not on all the bad that they are facing. In psychology and coaching, we call that "reframing" and taking different perspectives; it works to help people move forward when they are feeling stuck. It is having "faith." Looking to your Higher Power is the strength of Spirituality and looking at things positively is the strength of Optimism.

Even in the book, *The Secret,* by Rhonda Byrne, she talks about how life is abundant and how you can attract good things to happen by having positive expectations. I was on a telecall with her one time and she pointed out that people do need to act. Even if people ask and believe, they still need to open doors and act to be able to receive results. So it is about trusting your Higher Power, using your inner strengths, and taking action using your strengths to reach success.

WRIGHT

I can see that is the way. You have talked about how important it is for people and organizations to use strengths. You also mentioned how you first found inner strengths as a child. What have you observed about your strengths journey and how you got started helping others with their strengths journey?

NODLAND

My journey is definitely still a "work in progress" as I try to learn and grow each day. However, my life took some detours that actually ended up with my being on the right road for me. See, it is God, that Higher Power thing again, with guidance along the way.

First, I started out by building a large successful psychology practice in one city, moving and building another successful practice and then moving again—from Minnesota to Arizona and back to Minnesota again. These geographical moves were prompted by caring for ailing parents who were in different states. It was rewarding to care for them but it meant that I built three successful practices and each time I had to start over. I lived in a suitcase for a couple of years and flew back and forth between states as I made the transitions. These moves took the strengths of Optimism, Perseverance, and Loving people to keep going and rebuild.

During this time, I soon realized I needed to change or add to the method I was using to help people in my profession as a psychologist. It took Courage—another strength—to add coaching as my profession, but it also felt like a positive change for my practice. I decided to start coaching over fifteen years ago and it was not always an easy transition. Finally, however, coaching gave me a business that I could do anywhere and not have to leave it to start over again. I coach locally, nationally, and internationally. Through coaching, assessments, and workshops I enjoy helping individuals and organizations identify ways to use their strengths, communicate more effectively, increase efficiency, improve culture, and to also increase the bottom line. Basically, it is about using strengths and building relationships. When people and systems understand and respect each others' strengths, they relate well to each other and organizations run well.

When people are visioning what success is for them or their organizations, I ask them to try to go beyond the generalities and actually "see" the complete picture of what their successful life or success for their company would look like. I ask them to just imagine, "If you used all of your inner strengths in the best way, what would your personal and professional life look like"?

WRIGHT

For you, what does using your inner strengths in the best way mean? What does that look like?

NODLAND

To use my inner strengths in the best way means honoring others by serving them well. But it also means keeping balance in my life to promote good health and good relationships. This has resulted in having a home in Minnesota on a lake, an office only six blocks away, and another home in Florida where I can coach by phone from the beach, spending the rest of the time with family and relaxing activities. Watching the dolphins is an occasional distraction that I can live with! Walking on the beach nourishes my soul, helps me appreciate all of God's natural creations, thus allowing me to renew so I can use my inner strengths in the best ways to continue to help others.

Using strengths helps people reach success. I have just shared what is important for me, but what is important for others may be entirely different. Finding your own vision and values are the keys to using your strengths to move forward to achieve it. The vision will be fueled by your values and it will drive you to discover your inner strengths to achieve your goals. Jack Canfield states that "It is like a car driving through the night . . . if we just trust that the next two hundred feet will unfold . . . it will eventually get you to the destination of what you truly want, because you want it." Covey shares some helpful guidance when he says, "Start with the end in mind." This is so true. The "end" goal might change somewhat as you refine your vision but knowing the direction you are headed makes for a clearer path. When they are used appropriately, your inherent strengths will help you get there.

WRIGHT

Tell me more about the process of how people can use their inner strengths to make and maintain changes?

NODLAND

The question people most want to know is how to develop good habits and maintain them and how to get back to good habits if they have fallen back into bad habits. I use James Prochaska's book, *Changing for Good,* as a guide. Prochaska delineates six stages of change as Pre-contemplation, Contemplation, Preparation,

Action, Maintenance, and Relapse. I help people see how to use their inner strengths in these stages of change so they can make and stay with positive changes. Let's take a look at this process.

In Prochaska's Pre-contemplation stage he says, "It isn't that they can't see the solution. It is that they can't see the problem." They are not even thinking about strengths at this point. Others around them often recognize a change would be helpful, but they are still unaware.

Next, in the Contemplation stage, people become aware of a problem and also recognize what will happen if they continue down the same path, but they are still not ready to commit to change. At first, they do not recognize their strengths and they feel they will fail if they attempt the change. However, the problem usually becomes more critical and they start to think—"maybe I can do it. I think I will try." Now they might start to wonder how they will do it and what strengths are needed to make the change.

Then, in the Preparation stage they finally start making preparations to change even though they might still be ambivalent. This is where making a public statement can help a person be committed to going forward and changing. The public statement takes Courage, definitely an important strength. Coaches often become frustrated if people come to them and do not make progress in the way the coach feels they should. Actually, if the coach recognizes the stages of change that people are facing, the coach can help them recognize their strengths and use these strengths to help them get through these stages and get into action.

By the time people are in Preparation, they are already starting to use the strengths that are needed to make a change. Their decision to change pushes them to reach for their strengths. Sometimes the strength needed is not one of their top strengths. Then it can be more difficult for them to change. Let's take the example of quitting smoking. If Diligence and Persistence are not a person's top strengths she or he might use other strengths. For example, a person might use To Love and Be Loved in caring enough for family to stop smoking. The person might carry a picture of a family member and look at it as a reminder of "why" to quit and to discourage use of cigarettes. The person might also use the strength of Creativity in finding unusual ways to "beat the habit."

Finally, people move into Prochaska's fourth step, Action. They are using their strengths fully now and, hopefully, they see that they are making progress toward their goal.

As the period of correct action increases, they move into Prochaska's fifth step, Maintenance. This is where they hope that the progress they have made becomes a positive habit and this is self-reinforcing. They might not be quite as aware of the actual use of their strengths because the action they are doing seems right for them, but if they used their identified core strengths in this process they are more likely to reach and maintain success in their goals. Eventually, what took an effort becomes an automatic habit.

The sixth and last step that Prochaska outlines is Relapse. If they have a Relapse, hopefully they will use the strengths of Forgiveness and Compassion for themselves and just start over again to reach their desired goal. They will recognize what needs to change for them to maintain their goal and not relapse again. Revisiting their true values and purpose can help people to continue to use their strengths to define a path to make and maintain changes and be able to again reach their goal.

WRIGHT

You mentioned recognizing purpose can help people use their inner strengths for making and maintaining changes. Are you willing to share how you recognized your purpose and inner strengths and what changes you made in your life when you recognized your strengths?

NODLAND

Yes, here again, I'll tell you a little story I wrote called *Feeding the Heart*. I shared my story when I was on the trainer team working with Martin Seligman, PhD and

Ben Dean, PhD and the Authentic Happiness Coaching Program. In that program we helped more than 350 people worldwide with exercises to identify their strengths, find their purpose, and to become more authentically happy. Here is my story, written in response to one of Dr. Seligman's exercises to identify one's strengths. This exercise also helped me to identify my purpose. Here's the story:

For many years I worked in the fashion world modeling, and doing television commercials and industrial films. I joked that I had to go into that field because I was skinny and couldn't type. I ran myself ragged and ended up sick, exhausted, and hospitalized. At mealtime the elderly man across the hall from me had difficulty getting the milky mush he was eating from his bowl to his mouth. The nurses and aides were understaffed, stressed, and didn't have the time to sit down with him. When I offered to help feed him, the nurses agreed.

He ate quite slowly so the old man and I had plenty of time to talk. I told him of my "exciting" career in the world of fashion and media. He told me of his life rich with purpose. I was transfixed by this man who seemed so weak and vulnerable and yet so strong. He told of a life filled with helping others, a life rich with meaning. He was happy and fulfilled. He shared of his life—a life "well-lived."

A part of that man stayed with me. When I got out of the hospital I volunteered there. It felt good. Maybe I could go back to grad school, get my doctorate in psychology, and help lots of other people to have lives "well-lived."

"You'll never make it," I was told by the grad school secretary and also by the academic counselor. I was competing with the top students and I must admit that my social life had definitely affected my grades—not positively. I didn't let these realities stop me. My reality was that I had found my "heartpath" and I was going to find a way to help others find their "heartpaths," too.

Many wonderful people rallied around me to help me on the way and I successfully completed my PhD in grad school at the University of Minnesota. The sign on my refrigerator that said, "You can do it" finally got turned over to say, "You did it." When I was a child and my mother read *The Little Engine That Could* to me, I never realized that it would be one of the most important books to help me complete grad school.

Now I've had a psychology practice since 1983 and a coaching practice since 1991. I have the joy of helping others to identify their dreams and goals—their "heartpaths"—to help them create an action plan to get there, and to celebrate their successes. It's an honor to be on those journeys and to share the love and joy of so many terrific people.

I believe that we are all connected in this universe. We all have gifts to share and the world is abundant. When you get on the right path for you, others will help you and nothing can stop you. Little do we know how far-reaching our words and actions may go.

Through sharing his wisdom with me, that elderly man in the hospital changed my life and the lives of many, many others. How ironic, all the time I thought I was feeding him—but in actuality, he was feeding me.

So that's my story.

WRIGHT

That is an interesting story. How else did meeting with that elderly man affect your life?

NODLAND

It helped me to find my strengths. Notice that it happened at a time when I was very challenged—being exhausted, ill, and in the hospital. That meeting caused me to look at my life, to reach to the depths of my soul, and to ask God for the courage and strength to use my gifts and strengths to help others. I found my purpose that day with that elderly man and, at the time, I did not realize how that moment with him dramatically affected my life.

If people will write their story of strength that was captured in one moment in time, it may help them identify their strengths and their purpose. In my story, I thought that my strength was Perseverance and that I got it from my parents.

There was a lot of Perseverance showing up all around me. My mom was definitely very caring and she did not give up. I remember that one time she washed a polka dot dress and all the polka dots washed off. That didn't stop her, she just painted every last one of them back on—with permanent paint, of course. My father, Dr. Kenneth O. Thompson, came from humble beginnings in the Upper Peninsula of Michigan to eventually get his doctorate. He worked and taught in the aeronautical and space industry. His Perseverance also set an example for me. Henry Ford said, "If you think you can or if you think you can't, you're right," and my parents were good examples for me. My mother passed away and I have a stepmother now who also has Perseverance; she does not give up no matter what obstacles she faces. I observe Perseverance in my husband, Doug, and children, Matt and Nicole. Even my sister, Mary, didn't give up when she decided to choose her own path as a journalist. My ninety-seven-year-old mother-in-law lives alone, drives, and plays drums and ragtime piano. She has come through many challenges to have a full life and that's real Perseverance. So, I have many good examples of Perseverance all around me in my life; people do learn strengths through observing others. I was surrounded by people with Perseverance.

But although Perseverance is one of my strengths and that was definitely there, too, it was actually To Love and Be Loved—another Signature Strength—that is my highest strength. It is this strength that gives me the sense of purpose and contributes to the Perseverance to do what it takes to help people. I love all my clients and I try to honor them with good service.

WRIGHT

Are there any strengths that are "better to have" than other strengths?

NODLAND

All of the twenty-four strengths Drs. Seligman and Peterson identified are good strengths but some strengths have important implications for health. In his book, *Authentic Happiness,* Dr. Seligman indicates how important Optimism is as a strength. Research shows that people who are more optimistic, grateful, and happy tend to live an average of eight to ten years longer. There are several studies that show the positive advantages of happiness and Optimism. One study found that the best way of predicting whether men would suffer a second heart attack and die was whether they were a pessimist or an optimist. Lifestyle, family history, and cholesterol levels were much less reliable predictors. The study reported that optimistic men were much less likely to suffer a second heart attack. So identifying and using strengths, especially Optimism, can also have a positive effect on health.

Other authors also talk about the importance of strengths but they use a little different language. Stephen Covey in his book, *The 8th Habit,* says that "when you engage in work [professional, community, family] that taps your talent and fuels your passion—that rises out of a great need in the world that you feel drawn by consciousness to meet, therein lies your calling—your soul's code." I love the term "soul's code" because when someone is that engaged in their calling they are usually very happy and using their strengths to the highest level. Notice also that he talks about several facets of a person's life. It is not just about work life, it is about personal life also. I feel that the "soul's code" is an embodiment of values and strengths that also leads to the purpose and passion that Covey talks about. Using their strengths helps people to bring the purpose they are passionate about into reality.

WRIGHT

In coaching people, how do you help them to form a plan to discover and use their strengths? What does that entail?

NODLAND

Actually, what I do as a coach is to help people create their plan by first doing an assessment of their strengths and values. I have learned that my plan to get there is not always the way someone else would get there. Coaching is a "designed alliance," which means that we are working together but it is always the client's agenda. Clients come to me with all the information about themselves; I just help them with the steps by asking powerful questions to stimulate their thinking. I also ask them to look at things from different perspectives. Sometimes I slip into consultant role if they feel stuck. I find that people are tremendously creative. As a coach, I am an objective observer with only their best interest in mind. When people are clear in their intention or an organization is clear about its goals, then what they are trying to do becomes easier and the roadway becomes visible. I help them find the best route for them. Then I hold them accountable to taking steps forward, using their strengths to reach their goals.

A famous quote by Antoine de Saint-Exupery is "A goal without a plan is just a wish." Life is so busy that it can get in the way of moving toward goals. It amazes me how innovative people can be when they make a determined effort to use their strengths in the best way possible for them. The key is to find a way to balance the reality of life's demands with working toward success in goals. I own The Balance Center where we help people with stress management and finding life-fulfillment. If you work too hard and fast, there is a tendency to burn out before reaching the goal. It surprises me how many times organizations miss the mark by trying to stuff people into positions that do not take advantage of their natural strengths. This will result in unhappy employees, less productivity, and more turnover. You know what that means to profits—they go down. When people are placed in positions where they can use their strengths, they shine and the organization shines, too.

WRIGHT

It is great to have people in positions where their strengths are used best, but what happens when that is not possible?

NODLAND

That is a good point to consider. It sometimes seems difficult to get people in positions that use their strengths. This goes back to the hiring process. If organizations would spend more time selecting candidates who fit the positions the best by assessing their strengths, then there would be fewer poor matches. Firing and rehiring can be expensive, so taking time to get the right person in the beginning saves in the end.

Another thing that can happen in an organization is that there will be challenges from what might be called a "strengths clash." A "strengths clash" occurs when the strengths of one person are not understood and valued by another person. Values will differ, personality styles differ, and communication styles differ. In organizations (and in families), having respect for all the different strengths people possess will result in the best use of these different strengths for the common good.

Some challenges are difficult but they still can be learning experiences to help produce better strategies for working together. As a coach, I encourage people to look at situations from different perspectives, which can include looking at them from the perspective of someone who possesses the opposite inner strengths. For example, a person who has the inner strength and natural energy of someone who likes to analyze can be very frustrating to a person who has the inner strength and natural energy of a spontaneous person. The spontaneous person's strengths encourage him or her to be able to make quick judgments and jump ahead while the analyzer's strengths often cause him or her to be thoughtful, careful, and take time to make decisions. Spontaneous people can often bring liveliness and fun to an organization and they can be good team-builders; but if they overuse and misuse this strength they can also "put people off." If someone is more reflective and studies a project in more detail before responding about it, the person's input can sometimes be missed at a meeting when he or she doesn't speak up at all or doesn't say something fast enough. Helping people with different strengths to all contribute generally makes for the best outcome. Everyone wins in this type of interaction.

WRIGHT

How can people be encouraged to develop their strengths further?

NODLAND

Noticing and positively reinforcing people when they are doing a good job is important. In his book, *Whale Done*, and in other writings, Ken Blanchard shares the importance of catching people doing something right and then praising their progress. Often people are praised when they are using their natural inner strengths because that is what they do best. Also, this type of management is often a motivator for people to bring out their inner strengths even more and it encourages them to keep improving on their jobs.

WRIGHT

You talked about Perseverance as one of your strengths and an important inner strength for people in general. Tell me more.

NODLAND

Yes, to reach success, Perseverance is needed. There will be tests of your resolve to keep going and days when you feel like quitting. Vince Lombardi said, "Winners never quit and quitters never win," and, "It's not whether you get knocked down, it's whether you get back up." These are examples of the strengths of Optimism, Perseverance/Persistence, Courage, and Resilience in action when someone chooses to "get back up."

If you persevere and don't give up, you will find a way. You will learn, grow, and be better for the adversity. You will use your strengths to gain knowledge and rise to overcome the challenge. I work with a lot of executives, professionals, and entrepreneurs. These people are smart, creative, and hard-working. They are also risk-takers. Because they take risks, sometimes there are things beyond their control that affect the outcomes of their goals. However, what I have learned is that these people are tremendously Resilient (another important strength) and have Persistence; they find ways to be triumphant over challenges. Using their strengths, they tend to end up better at their professions and happier with life. They reach more successes because they continue to use their strengths and they delegate and resource out the areas that are not their strengths.

WRIGHT

What happens when people actually feel they have discovered their inner strengths and they are using them well?

NODLAND

That is an interesting question. You would think that they would relax and enjoy the moment. Some of them do relax, but a majority of them are strong leaders and strong visionaries. Their ability to create the vision, their sense of purpose, and their passion usually call them to the next goal. They are happiest when they are creating and they usually want to challenge themselves to move to the next level in applying their inner strengths to reach an even bigger goal. We take time to celebrate their journey and their success but often for them the joy is in creating the next vision with the next set of goals. The further people get on a goal, the more future goals they see and this fuels their motivation to achieve more. There are always more visions, more challenges, more goals and more successes if you want to reach for them. There are also a limitless number of ways to use your strengths to help you get there.

I have shared with you some of my ideas on how to discover and use inner strengths. As we close this interview, I'd like to share one more quote that is meaningful to me and I hope it will be helpful to others. This was written by Marianne Williamson and is from her book *A Return to Love: Reflections on the Principles of A Course in Miracles*. It is called "Our Deepest Fear."

"Our deepest fear is not that we are inadequate, our deepest fear is that we are powerful beyond measure. It is our light, not our darkness that most frightens us. We ask ourselves, 'Who am I to be brilliant, gorgeous, talented and fabulous?' Actually, who are you not to be? You are a Child of God. Your playing small does not serve the world. There is nothing enlightened about shrinking so that other people won't feel insecure around you. We were born to manifest the glory that is within us. And as we let our light shine we unconsciously give other people permission to do the same. As we are liberated from our own fear, our presence automatically liberates others."

I hope that this quote will help people to find and use their strengths to confront their fears, meet their challenges, and stretch to reach happy, meaningful, and successful lives.

It has been a pleasure to share my thoughts with you. Thank you.

WRIGHT

It has also been my pleasure to interview you, to get to know you, and have you share your thoughts on how to discover and use inner strengths.

About the Author

Dr. Lynn Workman Nodland has helped many people and organizations to change, grow, and reach success. She is an influential motivational coach, psychologist, marriage and family therapist, facilitator, trainer, and speaker. She received her master's and doctorate degrees from the University of Minnesota and has advanced training from The Coaches Training Institute and MentorCoach. She was a trainer for both MentorCoach and the Authentic Happiness Coaching Program and she is also a Certified Executive Coach.

She is a member of Minnesota Facilitators, Minnesota Coaches Association, and International Coach Federation, where she holds the highest certification of Master Certified Coach. In addition, she is a member of Toastmasters International. She coaches locally, nationally, and internationally. As owner of The Balance Center and Lynn Workman Nodland and Associates, Inc., she understands and works well with entrepreneurs, organizations, and anyone wanting to reach success.

Her clients refer to her as "The Velvet Hammer" for her ability to foster powerful, positive change through coaching that is incisive and direct, yet caring and respectful.

Lynn Workman Nodland, PhD

684 Excelsior Blvd., Ste. 120
Excelsior, MN 55331
952.452.2664 / 888.260.0390
Lynn@LynnNodland.com
www.LynnNodland.com

Quantum Communications & Learning: Reaching Your Subconscious Mind

An Interview With...
Dr. William Kenner

DAVID WRIGHT (WRIGHT)

Today we're talking with Dr. William Kenner, Doctor of Medical Hypnotherapy, Divinity, and Metaphysics. He is a lecturer of Communications for the University of Michigan and a professional trainer specialist for Quantum Communications: Reaching Your Subconscious Mind.

William, Welcome to *Discover Your Inner Strength*.

So many people are looking for ways to focus their minds, regain their physical abilities, or simply apply better communication skills to their jobs. These are issues in almost every facet of human communications and science seems to play the game of tug of war. Your work has been one that has inspired work, engaged the minds of others, and challenged individual creativity to comprehend the enormous real potential for applying new information about life, learning, and discovering one's inner strengths.

DR. WILLIAM W. KENNER (KENNER)
Thank you, I am honored.

WRIGHT
What is "quantum communications"?

KENNER
Cutting edge research has evolved into a new scientific paradigm indicating that the mind and body are not two separate entities but are, in fact, one of the same. It is a single indivisible organism that we call the self. For those with an inquiring mind, there is a host of scientific research to support an individual understanding of the mind, body, and spirit as one. The mind has a physical and biological connection.

WRIGHT
Why the shift into quantum mechanics for the study of developing human communications and inner strength?

KENNER
If you want to watch the evolutionary emergence of a new science in human cognition, look in the mirror. Zukav (1999) said that the entire human species is in the midst of a great evolutionary transformation. Zukav states that humans have the potential to become a more highly intuitive species. Humans are emerging as multi-sensory information gatherers from the old system of power-driven receivers. Freire (2000) refers to this as "banking education," a one-way depositing of information by the controlling supplier into the passive recipient. At the heart of Zukav's perspective is his belief that human evolution is creating a connection between the conscious and subconscious minds. "We are co-creators in our own evolution."

WRIGHT

Is there an example of this that could help to explain what you are saying?

KENNER

In the evolution of quantum science, there is this evolving form of higher order thinking that appears to be part of the shifting of humans who are becoming more information gathers rather than information processors. At the heart of this research is the simple system of the human communication process. It all begins with perceptions. It is the idea that all information can simply be defined as energy in a system that flows in multiple directions simultaneously in human communication. In the Newtonian physics world of law and order, communication looks like a simple flow for one information context to the other. It flows in one direction from start to finish. It would look like Figure 1:

Information Flow

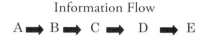

Newtonian Linear Flow of Information

Figure 1

The change in quantum communications allows for more energy to flow in multiple directions simultaneously. The flow in communication looks like Figure 2:

Information Flow

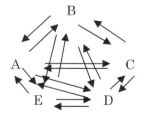

Quantum Holistic Flow of Information

Figure 2

WRIGHT

What kind of research is there that can help to provide evidence of this cutting edge new science?

KENNER

There are many thoughts on this and the subject of metacommunication and learning. Every thought, every feeling, every attitude, every emotion, every action is information and is energy. Research from scientists include Dr. Amit Goswami (2009), a leader in Quantum physics and the consciousness of human interaction with the unknown; Dr. Bruce Lipton (2005), a bioengineer and professor who has researched a biological connection of human perceptions, thought, and behavior with cellular movement and creation; and Dr. Lee Paulos (2004), a psychologist who research the subconscious firing of neurons in cognition and subconscious thought. These are only a few of the possible foundations to this paradigm which includes a shift in a biological and psychological connection of the subconscious mind to human behavior, learning, and memory. This exciting quantum based science will inspire the human spirit, engage the mind, and challenge the old paradigm of cognitive higher order thinking and creativity. This is the path by which all humans can begin to discover then own inner strength.

WRIGHT

This is ground breaking information. Where did you begin your understanding of this connection to human communication and learning?

KENNER

As the study in human communication and hypnosis become more and more applied to changing human behaviors and discovering one's own strength, the research had to visit the space where subconscious communication takes place.

WRIGHT

These are some strong words and an ambitious assertion! We try to explore through research towards better understanding, but to actually "prove" something would be quite a feat in the context of a post-positivist conventional science paradigm.

KENNER

It is in reviewing the power behind human perception that affects the receptors of the communicator. It is communication at a cellular level. Every thought and action a person has contributes to communication and learning. Affirmations (positive or negative) actually do affect us biologically. We qualify our energy with our own thoughts. The self-talk matters; think good, positive things not destructive, defeating thoughts change the energy of information in communication.

WRIGHT

Western science has long ignored descriptions of energetic components of physiology because their existence could never be documented by dissection or viewed under a microscope. How has this changed?

KENNER

It is only through the acceptance of this multidimensional framework of the human energy field of quantum physics that scientists and educators have begun to comprehend the true nature of human physiology in communication, learning and cellular memory.

Figure 3 demonstrates that all information must go through the part of the mind called the critical faculties. It is then stored in the subconscious mind only if the information is in agreement with what is previously stored or if it is the first time the information has been received. If either of these is true, then the information goes into the subconscious automatically. Using the psychological theory of the law of compounding, if the information is supported three times with matching information, the information is then moved into permanent memory. The dilemma, "the subconscious cannot judge" (Parkhill, 1996, p. 121).

Human learning has evolved into something that has several connective layers within the conscious, subconscious and unconscious minds. Figure 3 helps to explain this concept:

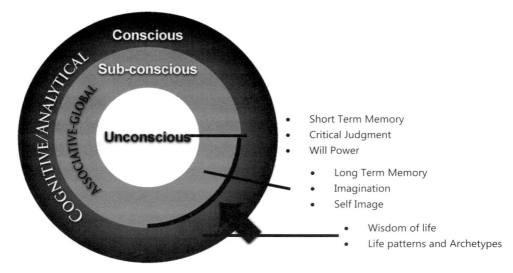

Figure 3 Source: Parkhill (1995) The mind Model
Original Graphic:: Dr. William Kenner

CRITICAL FACULTIES

All information must pass through this "gate" called the critical faculties. If prior information is stored, it is compared and is either accepted or rejected based on currently stored "truths." If nothing is stored on this topic, then the gate remains open to take in new data. If compounded three times, it is then "accepted" and stored into long-term memory.

As long as our rational mind can come up with reasons for our actions, our "critical judgment" will keep us at peace. Willpower (cognitive judgment) cannot affect internal (associative) change.

The subconscious mind works to achieve the perceived self-image. If there is nothing to judge against, there can be no critical faculty

Here, I touch upon the limits of empiricism, which translates to issues of epistemology (how we think we know what we think we know), which basically refers to genotypic and phenotypic realities. Historically, the limits of empiricism is now widely accepted (that's why the scientific endeavor is still largely *theoretical* work). Even the connotation of "facts" ought to be tempered when it comes to our assertions based on mere empirical research. The philosophical and practical study of epistemology continues to rage, especially given an ongoing debate in academia on postmodernism and relativistic paradigms. All of this bears weight on what we can rightly assert through research. It again goes back to what we mean by "prove" or "proof"—all interesting discussions with contestable platforms.

WRIGHT

These thoughts are a revolutionary perspective! As we begin to see that as humans evolve into energy understanding machines, we are also able to take in the perception that infinite unknown information can be something that must be acknowledged outside of what you can merely see, hear, feel, taste, or touch.

KENNER

Discovering your inner strength is not a mathematical equation. We are dealing with organic evolving humans in a constant state of change and chaos. Positive/negative thought (perceptions) affect the body and mind as a whole. You are what you think. Stored subconscious perceptions may create a diluted perception of reality. Perception is the process of attaining awareness or understanding of multi-sensory information that creates the reality of human strength.

WRIGHT

What do we need to do to become better human communicators to discover our inner strengths?

KENNER

We need to not worship the evaluation process of communication. It does not take into account the internal change that is required for external change. Just like anything in the study of psychology, philosophy, or communications, the process of implementation and evaluation needs to be a living, breathing process. Think of evaluation as a tool rather than the final word. "The survival and thriving of our species will depend on our nurturing of potentials that are distinctly human" (Gardner, 2006, p. 167). This is where discoveries of inner strengths begin.

Coaches, trainers, teachers must develop programs to educate the individual on all levels of the body, mind, and spirit connection. The subconscious is where these informational energies will meet to discuss or discover strengths and weaknesses.

Subconscious communication is an energy science affecting the subconscious perceptions for physical change. The cells of the body require active subconscious involvement of the person requesting discover or change. "Cells generally respond to an assortment of very basic perceptions of what's going on in their world . . . the simultaneous interactions of tens of thousands of reflective perceptions switches in the membrane, each directly reading an individual environment signal, collectively create the behavior of a living cell." (Lipton 2005, p. 129)

WRIGHT

As old models that no longer work give way to the new ones, we are left to weave the old patterns of higher order thinking and learning into forms that fit our new understanding of multisensory learning and change. Are there any thoughts or ideas that can help with this process?

KENNER

"You want to reach a critical mass of advocates so that the change reaches a tipping point and people flow naturally into the advocate pool" (Shapiro 2004, p. 93). It is time for everyone to jump into the pool of the space in between conscious and subconscious communication and discover their own inner strengths.

WRIGHT

What a great conversation this has been. Thank you for such an in-depth subject. You were able to help with how discovering an inner strength really happens.

KENNER

Thank you. It has been my pleasure and I look forward to more information to come in the future.

WRIGHT

Today we have been talking with Dr. William Kenner, a professional trainer, educator, and researcher on human communication and the power of the subconscious mind and human communications.

William, thank you for your help in discovering our inner strengths and how we are evolving human beings.

KENNER

Thank you.

References:

Gardner, H. (2006). *Five minds for the future.* Boston: Harvard Business School Press.

Freire, P. (2000). *Pedagogy of the oppressed.* New York: Continuum.

Goswami, A. (2009) *Consciousness does matter.* Center for Quantum Activism. Eugene, OR: Center for Quantum Activism. Retrieved: September 2009. http://www.amitgoswami.org

Lipton, B. (2005). *The biology of belief: Unleashing the power of consciousness, matter and miracles.* Sana Rosa, CA: Mountain of Love.

Myss, C. (1997). *Anatomy of the spirit: The seven stages of power and healing.* Kalamazoo, MI: Three Rivers Press.

Parkhill, Stephen C. (1995). *Answer cancer.* Fort Lauderdale: Omni Hypnosis Publishing.

Pulus, L. (2004). *The biology of empowerment.* Niles, IL: Nightingale Conant. Audio Program.

Zukav, G. (1999). *The seat of the soul.* New York: Simon & Schuster.

About the Author

Dr. William W. Kenner has been working in education, psychology, business, and performing arts for more than twenty-two years. A doctor of Medical Hypnotherapy, Divinity and Metaphysics, with a Masters of Arts in Education, he teaches and consults as a Medical Hypnotherapist, Education and Business Professional, and Development Trainer. He is currently completing his dissertation for a PhD in Education. William's professional accomplishments and abilities are as eclectic as his education. He is a lecturer for the University of Michigan–Flint, and adjunct faculty member for St. Clair County Community College, Michigan. With a very busy schedule of keynote and workshop presentations in education, business, and industry, psychology, health, healing, and the performing arts, William has traveled the world with his lectures on Quantum Communication and Learning: Reaching the Subconscious Mind. He has been honored by several national educational, community, business, and arts organizations for helping gifted and at risk populations.

Dr. William W. Kenner

Medical Hypnotherapist and Professional Development Trainer
2809 Peavey Street
Port Huron, MI 48060
(810) 388-0539 (Office)
(586) 256-5822 (Cellular)
wwkenner@comcast.net (Office e-mail)
wwkenner@umflint.edu (University Email)
www.ThisIsASquare.com